The Old Enchanter

George Johnston

Barker Fairley, *George Johnston* c. 1955, oil on masonite (40.7 x 50.8 cm). Private collection. Courtesy of the Barker Fairley estate.

The Old Enchanter

A Portrait of George Johnston

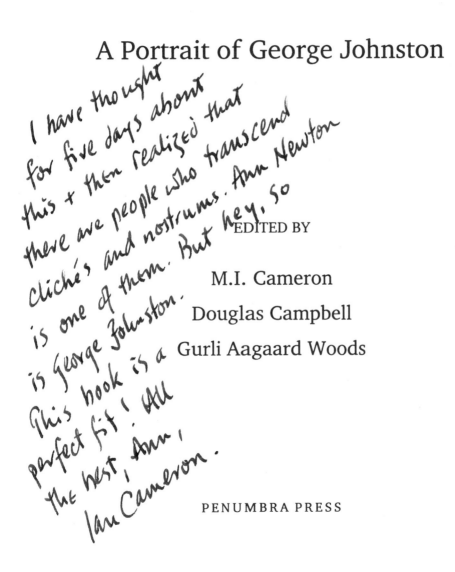

I have thought for five days about this + then realized that there are people who transcend clichés and nostrums. Ann Newton is one of them. But hey, so is George Johnston. This book is a perfect fit! All the best, Ann, Ian Cameron.

EDITED BY

M.I. Cameron

Douglas Campbell

Gurli Aagaard Woods

PENUMBRA PRESS

CANADIAN CATALOGUING IN PUBLICATION DATA

The old enchanter: a portrait of George Johnston

Includes bibliographical references.
ISBN 0-921254-85-7

1. Johnston, George, 1913 Oct. 7– 2. Canadian poetry (English)—20th century. 3. Canadian essays (English)—20th century. I. Cameron, M.I. (Maxwell Ian) II. Campbell, Douglas (John Douglas) III. Woods, Gurli A. (Gurli Aagaard) IV. Johnston, George, 1913, Oct. 7–

PS8519.)437Z64 1998   C811'54   C98-901382-0
PR9199.2.J65Z64 1998

Published by Penumbra Press. Design and Editing by M.I. Cameron, Douglas Campbell, John Flood, and Gurli Woods. Cover design by Edith Pahlke and John Flood, with thanks to Christopher Lea Dunning. Printed in Canada.

Contents

Publisher's Foreword

THIS TRIBUTE TOOK shape four years ago when Gurli Woods and I met to discuss the future of Penumbra's Scandinavian series. Among the works she recommended was one previously suggested to her by colleague Ian Cameron, a festschrift in honour of George Johnston, who had been a significant presence in the Department of English at Carleton University since its heyday in the Glebe area of Ottawa. I was enthusiastic about the idea because I had already published a number of books by George, including a biography of Carl Schaefer, a volume of poems, and a handful of translations by contemporary Scandinavian authors such as Knut Ødegård, Olafur Johan Sigurdsson, and Christian Matras. On discussing the idea with others, I received nothing but positive feedback, especially from George's long-time friend and colleague at Carleton, Naomi Jackson Groves, who is also a major Penumbra Press author and supporter.

In fact, it was with her generous support that we assembled the editorial team of Gurli Woods, Ian Cameron, Douglas Campbell and myself, and we set out to realize the publication date of October 7, 1998, George's 85th birthday. Although several events beyond our control prevented us from publishing in time, I am nonetheless proud of the contribution our editors and authors have made to the project. What I find most appealing is the eclectic range of *The Old Enchanter*'s content and forms — from memoirs and critical writing to poetry and artwork, as well as a previously unpublished prose piece by George himself. The title of the book is a testament to the quiet charisma and quick charm of the man — poet, translator, teacher, colleague, and friend.

My special thanks to Gurli Woods for helping to envision the book, to Ian Cameron for designing and typesetting it, to Douglas Campbell for his exacting copy-editing, and to the ever-constant Naomi Jackson Groves.

John Flood

Preface

IF WE HAD ever thought that poetry in our time was a dying art, those thoughts were shattered on the fourth of June, 1979, when, sitting on the stage of the Opera of Ottawa's National Arts Centre, we saw two thousand people rise to their feet in front of us — some of them shouting, many crying — to acclaim a poem that George Johnston had written for them and had just recited in his clean, almost radically personal way. The poem was his Convocation address to the graduating class of Carleton University, and no one who was there to hear it has ever forgotten it. You will encounter it again in the book that follows.

The book is a tribute to George Johnston at the age of 85, produced by his friends, students, and colleagues, mostly from his 29 years in Ottawa and Carleton University. Its keystone is a piece written by George himself, an account of a promising university friend of his and the bicycle trip they took as young men through Hitler's new Germany. The book as a whole is a miscellany, a collection of essays (both personal and academic), recollections, poems, some art work, part of a new translation of an Icelandic saga, and even a talk and a little play. Miscellany may be the natural form for George Johnston. His interests and accomplishments have always been wide and varied, and the people who have been drawn to him have been a heterogeneous group, working in different métiers and animated by a variety of enthusiasms. There are certain things they share, however, things that come from the man himself, and these run through the miscellany to give it its own coherence: a fascination with poetry, with our language and its structures and textures, with its roots in the language and culture of early medieval England and Scandinavia, and with the experience of ordinary people, then and now, who drew and draw a human existence out of a hard environment, making something permanent there, even if it is only the respect and the wonder with which they stood before life and its mysteries.

We are pleased to acknowledge the willing and generous help of Bryan Gillingham and R.L. Jeffreys in producing the book, the assistance of Sylvie Hill, Jennifer Lee, and Mark Molnar in preparing the manuscript, and the enthusiastic initiative of William Blissett in getting the project under way in the first place.

M.I. Cameron
Douglas Campbell
Gurli Woods

George Johnston

JC, A MEMOIR

HIGHWAY TWO, THE oldest paved road in Canada, and we are on it, two newly-fledged philosophers on our first flight into the world, heading for Montreal and the cattle boat *Norwegian*.

We are being driven there by JC's parents, Mr. and Mrs. James Taylor. Mr. Taylor's theory of overtaking is unlike any I have known. He comes up behind another vehicle and maintains a reasonable distance so long as the road ahead is clear. Then an approaching vehicle, still far off, stirs him to action. Mrs. Taylor, also in the front seat, has been offering a running commentary for his benefit in a sweet, high voice, on the state of the road, the behaviour of the car, other vehicles, and his driving. Now, in an altered tone, she advises him not to pass.

I think you should wait, James, she says.

He edges back in. Then he changes his mind, puts his head down and edges back out again. Mrs. Taylor gasps and stiffens. I imagine her feet pushing against the floor. My feet are pushing against the floor behind her. I am sure that floors are being pushed in the cars beside and approaching us, and I observe the look of incredulity on the face of the driver we are overtaking. There is a moment or two in limbo, honking of horns and squealing of brakes — not ours — and then somehow we are past and driving on, leaving stopped vehicles at the sides of the road behind.

This, or something like it, happened again. Mrs. Taylor conducted a patient post-mortem each time, though I wondered if her good man's hearing aid was turned on.

JC scowled beside me, and said nothing.

I began to see something fateful in these escapes. We were meant to reach Montreal without damaging ourselves or perhaps anyone else. I knew that JC's parents were good church-goers and, sceptic though I was, I could not resist pondering our near misses. In any case, we got there and stayed the night with Mrs. Taylor's sister and her family.

Next morning we were signed on at the docks and put to work loading the cattle. These were steers from the wide prairies, all but unacquainted with mankind till they had been rounded up and transported the long way east, to encounter us. Now they were bawling constantly as we herded them from the cattle cars and down temporary gangways into the ship. Cowhands, who had come from the West with them, straddled the gangway fences and urged them forward with blows and shouts. Hoofs thundered on the boards and skidded on the metal decks of the ship.

Three of the cowhands from the West stayed aboard for the voyage. During the first two or three days, till the cattle were penned, they were like corporals, a rank above us greenhorns, on hand where they saw that they were needed and telling us what to do. Aside from them and JC and me, the crew of cattlemen comprised a fifty-year-old family man from Vancouver, and five professional wrestlers with their manager. The man from Vancouver had left his family there on relief, and hitchhiked across the continent to Montreal. He hoped to find work in England, where his brother-in-law had an insurance agency. The wrestlers had been invited to do a tour in England if they could pay their way across, and while they were pondering the invitation in a restaurant they heard talk about cattle boats, pounced on the information and took it up, in the spirit of a dare. Their manager argued that it would be good for them, better than the soft life of a passenger ship, and they would have the money they saved to spend over there.

All right, they said; if it was good for them it should be good for him too, and he agreed.

Leather was what they called their manager, because he looked like leather, an old leather strap. His wrestlers look not at all like leather, capital or lower case. They were amiable-looking bulks with flat faces, cauliflower ears and no necks. One had tusks for upper front teeth, and his professional name was Tiger.

Leather had sharp eyes, a long nose and a lipless mouth. He was a talker, as his charges were not, except among themselves. They were friendly however, and seemed not to mind being overheard when they were on to mat gossip and the technicalities of their art, and they would answer questions, but they did not initiate conversation except once or twice when they opened up on the subject of good eating. About that they took on the airs of connoisseurs.

JC and I were surprised that there were no other students. It was a cheap crossing, twenty dollars to a Montreal lawyer who normally arranged it, and no obligation to make the return voyage. The work was heavy, but not unduly so, and the quarters and food were adequate. Many a future scholar or professional began his youthful European tour as a cattleman, but there were no other scholars aboard with us. And we had dodged the twenty dollars, for my father had a friend in the Anchor-Donaldson office in Montreal with whom he arranged our passages.

We were soon identified as an odd pair. I need hardly say that I did not consider myself odd. I knew that JC was, yet it had not occurred to me before now that his oddness might prove awkward. I had given little thought to our friendship. At the beginning of our first year in university he had brought his name to everyone's attention by running away from home. The papers gave notice of his disappearance, the radio broadcast his description, and groups of volunteers from the university hunted for him on Scarborough Bluffs, where he had been known to go wandering and climbing by himself. After two days of concern and conjecture he was found by a relative on the Montreal docks, seeking a working passage to Europe.

At his first lecture, a fortnight late, he bore himself as an impenitent solitary. I spoke to him, and his response was not encouraging, but I persisted and we became friendly enough. We were in the same small honours course and together for most of our lectures. I invited him home to supper. My mother complained afterwards about his low voice.

He mutters, she said, impatiently. I can hardly hear him.

She might have been more emphatic, but did not wish to discourage my bringing friends home.

He came again, and by and by there was a return invitation to supper at his home. His sweet-voiced mother and I did most of the talking. He and his father had virtually nothing to say.

JC was not what we called him to his face. McRae may have been the first among ourselves to refer to him by his initials. They soon became dignified to Mr. JC. Then McRae proposed Giacomo as better suiting his intellectual loftiness, and to go with this he proposed that the C must represent Chizzebaldo on account, he continued, of the baldness of his chizzy. I am sure that he was loftily unaware of any such names.

In my third year I began to publish light verse anonymously in *The Varsity*'s humour column. JC commented on the verses and was surprised and generously pleased to learn that I was their author. I had been shy about my versifying, and these comic squibs were my first appearance in a university publication. He showed a new interest in me after this, and our friendship entered a somewhat brighter phase. He longed to write poetry, but could never keep his personal demons out of it. He could tell me how to exorcise mine, however, and he became my earliest and most helpful critic.

During the summer before our last year as undergraduates I persuaded him to do a four-day canoe trip with me. Canoeing was new to him, and though he was awkward and absentminded, he was also strong, hard-working and keen, and he made serious efforts to be easy company, little notion though he had of how to go about it. I enjoyed the trip, and he seemed to.

The European expedition was on a different scale. How had we undertaken to be together for a whole summer? I looked at him on our first evening downriver from Montreal. He was a medium tall man, slight of build, awkward and yet with a touch of the feminine in his movements. There was also a grimness about his attack on the world. McRae said that he hurled himself across the campus with the aid of his heavy brief-case. He was very strong, conscious of his endurance and vain of his appearance, though his features, all fine except for his wide nostrils, did not make up a conventionally handsome face. His eyes were soft brown, and their normal expression was of deep concentration.

We leaned together against the stern rail as the *Norwegian* steamed by Quebec in the late twilight. The city was an exotic vision, with its garlands of incandescent light gleaming above the river in the dusk. For both of us it was the first departure from Canada. I had not been as far east as Montreal before. The undergraduate world, in which we had become self-important figures, was dropping behind us too. I told myself that I was glad to be leaving it, to be venturing into the big world, of which Canada then seemed a not very significant part. Yet I now began to wonder about the weeks of interdependent comradeship that lay before us both.

When JC proposed biking around Germany, and my parents told me that I had a small inheritance to pay for it, I simply said yes. Roy Daniells, then a friendly young lecturer at Victoria College, encouraged us. He thought it a good project, especially now, when the Nazi government, in an effort to build up reserves of foreign currency, was selling cheap travellers' marks outside their borders. Hitler's Third Reich had been in existence for three years. To many of us it seemed a menace that had loomed up in our lives. One of our undergraduate circle came back after a year in Munich, in love with the people, but mistrustful of what their Führer was transforming them into. A different response came from a young German intellectual who had acquired some prominence as a student at Toronto. He returned to his home and declared himself a convinced Nazi.

JC's interest derived from his study of German in High School and University. He had read Spengler's *Decline of the West* and Hitler's *Mein Kampf*, and though he was unconvinced by Hitler and what he stood for, Germany was nevertheless the country he wanted to see, and German was the language he wanted to converse in. Soon after Christmas he had proposed our expedition and now, aboard the *Norwegian*, we were each other's company in a way we had not been before.

Neither of us could have foreseen our separate, yet mutually dependent predicaments on the cattle boat. Had our fellows been students, no doubt he would have seemed less odd, but in this company we were both strange birds. I was soon on familiar terms with the other cattlemen and sailors, but he never became so. He seemed to enjoy the work and was cooperative, but in off hours he kept to himself, and at meals had little to say. Such aloofness was not new to me, but after a few days on board I began to feel responsible for him. I sought him out from time to time, and we stood against the rail at the stern, a place we invariably had to ourselves, and talked and watched the icebergs and the birds.

We were both glad to be working our passages, and enjoyed the routine of ordinary labour. Our day began at four a.m., with the feeding and watering of the cattle. Feeding is easy enough, but water has to be fetched in pails from erstwhile molasses barrels, and as the level in these descends they have to be bodily bent down into. The sweetness of that hollow space, with its mingled aroma of oak and tar, is punishment to empty stomachs. The steers add their bit of trouble by reaching into each other's pails instead of their own, and knocking them over. For the second half of the voyage the cattle decks were awash. Between these labours and breakfast there was an hour or so of free time. Then, after breakfast, came the raising of hay, straw and feed from the holds, distributing it among the cattle decks and filling the water barrels. Feeding and watering before supper again, and after supper nothing till four a.m.

Our quarters were cramped: two rows of narrow triple bunks with a long table down between on which we ate our meals or attempted a bit of reading, all in a windowless deckhouse aft. The food was plentiful, characterless but nourishing, and we ate it hungrily.

After icebergs and fog have been left behind, the *Norwegian* enters the warmth of the Gulf Stream. There is fair weather and a comparatively calm sea. The wrestlers, to keep in shape, displayed their art on the canvas cover of the hatch astern of the deck house, with cattlemen and sailors for audience. A free show. JC watched briefly from time to time, saying nothing but gazing with seeming concentration. Twilights are fine and long, and the motion of the ship easy. The combatants roared and grunted and banged each other, and there were whiles that they seemed to be knotted together and inert; one hardly knew how they got so entangled or how they broke loose again. Much of their loud groaning and complaining was said to be sham, but their strainings and thumps would have raised a noise from me. Flattened noses and cauliflower ears must have hurt when they got them. On the other hand, their sufferings seemed to be over soon, what we observed at any rate, and back they came for more.

There were talk sessions in the bunkhouse from which JC absented himself, and I was given to understand that his doing so was noted and resented.

What's the matter with your pal? asks Leather. We don't like the way he avoids us.

I don't think he's avoiding anyone, I say.

What does he go away by himself all the time for? Stares over the rail all the time, as though he likes the fishes better than us. What's the idea of that? He better look out, we'll send him to join his fishes if he likes them so much.

I had seen him in the dusk, staring at the wake of the ship, his intellect ranging, no doubt, where no-one else's in that bunkhouse, not mine either, could, or for the matter of that would, follow.

Don't pay attention to his manner, I say. He is a lonely bird. He stays away from me too, he's different, that's all.

What are you friends with him for, if he stays away from you?

I don't mind it, I've got used to him, and he knows a lot, I learn from him.

What can you learn that's any good from a guy that's always off by himself?

He used to be a boxer, I tell them. He looks lean, but he's very strong.

I watched Leather and his wrestlers after this. They eyed JC in a new way, or so I thought, and made no offer to be unpleasant.

What does he think about? Leather asks.

Oh, I say, he's deep. Some people consider him a genius.

We dock at Cardiff thirteen days after sailing from Montreal, and JC and I go to a huge luxury cinema on our first evening ashore to see an Astaire-Rogers film. His willingness to enjoy such entertainment surprises me a little. I report back to Canada that he had come out of the theatre whistling "I'm putting all my eggs in one basket" as nearly as his tone deafness will approximate it. Very soon I leave off my facetiousness about him in my letters.

The sailors had warned us against pickpockets in London, and on the train journey up, amid the novelty and rush of my impressions, I keep feeling for my money and documents. JC looked at the countryside with his soft brown eyes and maintained a self-possessed manner. Then out of the blue he confessed that he had written a twelve-page letter to a student we had known as undergraduates, a literate lass with an accent and worldly-wise air. He asked me if I thought there was something out of line in his writing such a letter. I was amazed, but also amused. What a thing to report back to Canada! I resolve, however, against it, somewhat ruefully. Who might have guessed that the Ravishing Finn had been in his thoughts? Had he been mooning at her image in the *Norwegian's* wake? Was he in her thoughts as she was in his?

He had little to say about London, but as for me, from the moment we stepped down to the platform of Paddington Station I felt as though I had come home. It was my city, and the fortnight it took us to prepare for Europe — get Youth Hostel memberships, Cyclist Touring Club member-ships, bicycles, kit bags and so forth — was full of wonders. It was also full of Canadians, not just at Canada House, but in any street, pub or cafe.

JC bought a single-speed bicycle second hand. Roy Daniells had already offered to loan me his three-speed Raleigh on which he had toured Germany in 34. Earle Birney had done the same on the same Raleigh in 35. I picked it up from Roy's cousin in Catford, and was given a convivial supper on the occasion. The bicycle was a good one, but for all its three speeds JC easily kept ahead of me with his single speed by dint of mere wiriness and will power.

An injury from our crossing came back on me now. On our second day down the St. Lawrence I damaged the nail of my right index finger helping to pen the one bull in our cargo. It began to fester when we were half way across the Atlantic, and the steward put iodine on it. The festering did not let up; the nail had to be removed after we got to London, and a bandage that looked like a club was imposed on the whole finger. I was instructed to soak the finger in hot salt water every day, anoint it with a yellow liquid they gave me, and put the bandage back on. I bought a china cup for the treatment and attached it to the outside of my bicycle pack behind.

The first day, which took us through Kent to Canterbury, straightway asserted JC's energy and stamina, and also his notion of what kind our excursion was to be. He was what would now be called a competer with himself, and he expected me to keep up with him. There were sarcastic exchanges on the subject, and he was grudging when I once or twice called for a rest.

Late in the afternoon we came to Canterbury and made for the Youth Hostel. It was a good place, an old weavers' cottage, now managed by a married couple who enjoyed having guests talk with them. I obliged them

while JC went and looked at the Cathedral. My indolent self still argues, Do
I or do I not, at the end of a fatiguing day, exert myself to look at Canterbury Cathedral? The Cathedral does not always lose, but that day I wanted
something else too: a brief respite from JC's company. I had enjoyed such
a thing before we left London, when one of JC's school friends, Charley
Armstrong, turned up. He and I were both quick to laugh, and especially in
contemplation of the absurd. I was sorry to leave him behind, for his wit
had been a relief from JC's silences and sardonic humour.

Next morning the road looks inviting again. On to Dover and a swift
Channel crossing to Calais in fine weather. The rail yards we landed into
confused us briefly, but we enjoyed both the excitement and the pleasure
of feeling underfoot for the first time a continent that had hitherto been
territory of our imaginations.

A man comes up and offers to help us, wagging an Old Bill moustache
and speaking what might have been town English, though he was probably
a French local, on his way home perhaps.

We tell him that we do not need help, but he attaches himself to us and
we abandon our attempts to pretend he is not there. His help is helpful,
moreover; he tells us where to go and what to do, and passes us through
officialdom into France with hardly a muttered interview. Now he is standing
by, looking away, and not offering to move. Spoken thanks seem not to be in
order. Generous though we are with them, his look is unchanging.

How much?

We have no experience of tipping, and had not intended any of our
small store of sterling for such assistance. He is still looking away; nothing
is holding us. I put sixpence in his hand, a respectable coin in our exche-
quer.

He looks at us now, then at the sixpence, then at us again.

Wot's this ere? he asks. Ere, you tike this back, put it on the clection plite.
He strolls off.

We offer more, but in vain, so up we get on our bikes, and our wheels
take their first bite of Europe.

After soup in a small cafe we strike out for Germany, having decided to
ride as it were day and night, and avoid spending more of our exchangeable
cash than we have to. Our money is all in travellers' marks except for a little
sterling to take us from Calais to Aachen and then back from the German
Frontier to London again.

The road along the coast was a pleasure, flat and smoothly paved, till
we entered the first village and encountered cobbles, a transition we could

hardly believe. Our spare clothing and other gear for six weeks was carefully tied and strapped in over and around the black bicycle packs behind our saddles. Somehow the cobbles shook none of these off or loosened the nuts and bolts of the bicycles. On we pumped through village after village and the returns to pavement at the other end were blissful.

The evening wore on. We stopped at a little street fair a few yards from the highway and ate fried potatoes. The fair, if this was the proper name for it, was no more than three or four pushcarts lit by oil flares, and a scatterment of light-hearted folk. The mood of the countryside had not yet disclosed itself to us, and we were cheered by this interlude, with its carefree humanity.

It grew dark. Airport searchlights wagged back and forth across the sky. There were many of them and somehow they seemed ominous. With the moon as well we needed no other light. The sleeping villages we rattled through were lit by gas lamps. They made a roar, and dogs hailed our progress, one after the other, cumulatively. There must have been a law against so much noise at such an hour, but no-one was about to enforce anything.

Before midnight we arrived at Ostend and found a cafe where we had coffee and bought a roll and piece of cheese each to take with us. Then off into the flat country again, with its wagging beacons. A cool breeze comes up. Then some of the beacons ahead change character and tempo: they are not beacons but lightning. We bike into a few low hills, pull up on the side of a slope that overlooks Bruges and fetch out the rolls and cheese. The town below, as the uncertain moonlight and the flashes of the approaching storm reveal it to us, is beautiful, a medieval scene. The storm is not far away, we begin to hear its thunder.

Skunk!

How can there be skunk?

But the odour seems unmistakable.

Mistaken just the same. No skunk — cheese. The cheese we had bought in Ostend, tasty for all its bouquet of skunk.

The storm is almost on us. We coast down the slope and into the huge market square of Bruges, where we take refuge on a cafe verandah, already wet beyond its awnings from the first drops. The time is four o'clock. The verandah faced on the square, and its tables had chairs upside-down on them. After the wind had blown itself out and the rain was over, we found clear spaces on the floor and slept. It is gray daylight when we begin to stir. A single noise seems to come from the other side of the square, a more or less regular clop, clop, that stops, takes up again, stops and takes up again.

Then it comes to a full halt very near, and its attention is no doubt on us. Now the only noise is a drip still falling from the awning. We sit up and look. An old man in a sweater coat, cloth cap, shapeless trousers and sabots, is staring at us.

Bon matin! we say.

He seems amazed by our greeting. After giving it a moment to sink in he turns and clops off. It is our first acquaintance with sabots.

When our cafe comes to life we order rolls and coffee, our breakfast, having eaten which we set out for Germany again. We are beginning to regret the concentration of our funds in travellers' marks. It seems too bad to be biking through Ghent and Antwerp with scarcely a glance to either side, and we would gladly have seen more of Bruges.

The Spanish Civil War broke out. JC made what he could of its significance from a Flemish newspaper. With the help of his German and his knowledge of current events, he could read and interpret them well enough. He did not take it to be the beginning of something widespread, not yet at any rate.

We came to Brussels late in the afternoon and stayed the night in the Auberge de la Jeunesse there. It is a huge place, full of down-to-earth travellers like ourselves, cyclists, motorcyclists and hitch-hikers, a very few motorists. More of them were middle-aged than I would have expected, from England and the Continent especially. Many of the young were from the United States. All, by the rules of the Association, were transient, and vacated the hostel for the day after an early breakfast. Supper was to be had at the Brussels hostel as well. The din at both these meals made me feel good. Somewhat to my surprise JC appeared to enjoy it. There were times when his mood was all but gregarious. Then he would speak enviously of my friendlier ways.

There was much talk of the Civil War in Spain. The English and Europeans were most concerned and thoughtful, the Americans less so. I was dependent on JC's knowledge of current events, and learned much from him that summer. In the Brussels hostel he found a German lady of middle age glad to talk with him, and he had a long conversation with her, blissful, as I had not seen him before, that he was using her language. She was the wife of an English small business man. It was her opinion that the war we were all expecting had begun in Spain, but might not involve the rest of Europe for another six months. She hated the Nazis, and was sure that they would involve Germany in this civil war. JC wondered if they had not done some good things. Had they not strengthened the German economy and brought peace and order to the streets? "Ruhe und Ord-nung" was their slogan.

They have brought Germany back into the Middle Ages, she said. Their peace and order is all a sham.

I could follow none of this and had to hear about it later.

We took off promptly after breakfast and came, at the end of the day, to the frontier with The Netherlands, opposite Maastricht. The inspection point being in open country the question presents itself: Do we go on to Maastricht for the night? JC would have biked right on to Germany through Limburg in the dark, but I plead fatigue, and though he did not confess to the same, neither did he raise an objection. The Border Official, perceiving our dilemma, suggests that we sleep in one of the hay stooks in the field across the road. He offers shelter for our bikes in a room behind his office.

The stooks were comfortable, at any rate our fatigue made them seem so. Some time after midnight a noisy wind rouses us. I have a vivid recollection of JC standing up and the hay swirling around him. Hay is swirling everywhere, and lightning and thunder are almost incessant. We waste no time hurrying back to the customs house, but the night shift, two men, have already thrown the barrier into the building, locked the door and are wheeling off into the storm, which is beginning to rain. The only shelter for us is the small roof over the senior official's front door, and we are pressed in close under that and laughing and talking when the door opens behind us and we all but fall in.

It is the official himself, come with his moustaches to investigate.

He invites us in and leads us down the narrow hallway to a room at the back. An oil lamp is lighted on the table and candles are burning before a shrine to the Virgin in the corner. The official's wife and teenage daughter are kneeling and praying to the shrine in low tones, and with every rumble of thunder their voices rise. The storm is passing, and thunder is less frequent. JC and I sit on chairs against the wall, and the official looks at us, a bit sheepish for his wife and daughter till a late bolt shakes the house and brings him, briefly, to his knees. I expect JC to scorn all this piety, but his look is far away.

Soon the storm was quite over. Papa told his daughter to fetch us a pillow each, and we put our heads on them and slept till, at six o'clock, the daughter brought bread and jam and coffee for our breakfast. She was a sturdy lass with two fat, fair braids, blue eyes and a friendly manner. When we had finished our breakfast she brought us each a big ham sandwich wrapped in paper to take with us, and would accept no money for it or the breakfast. Papa agreed, the breakfast and sandwiches were on account of our coming from Canada, a faraway and half legendary country. JC felt that his independence of spirit was threatened by all this, but he gave in.

The sun shone brightly, a post-storm sort of morning, and the wet pavements and cobbles of Maastricht sparkled as we biked in. Some of the shopkeepers were giving their pavement out front its matutinal scrub. To us, the Dutch seemed as neat as the Belgians had seemed untidy, but both folk were friendly with us. We changed our few big Belgian coins for a few small Dutch ones and, having eaten the sandwiches the lass had given us, we bought a banana and a bit of chocolate and a beer each, and then pushed on to Aachen, where we came in the early afternoon.

Our entry into the Third Reich was suitably impressive and disciplined. Big red, black and white flags were flying outside of the official building. Indoors the same flags were draped on the walls around huge photographic portraits of Hitler, Hess, Goering and Goebbels. Whereas in France, Belgium and The Netherlands the officials were informal or friendly, here they are in aggressive uniforms, and their manner is gruff. They scrutinize our travellers' marks and other currency and give us a record of them which we are to present when we come back out of the country again. Then, with a brief glare, they dismiss us. They have granted us entry into a country very conscious of its newly-regained power.

Great Karl's city was bright and steeply up hill and down. A teenager on a bike offered to guide us to the Jugendherberge when we ask him for directions. JC followed him close behind, but for me the up and downhill became hair-raising. I cussed myself for having neglected my brakes through the easy flat country we had traversed before now. Yet, for all that I was honked at several times, and only just missed being hit more than once, I somehow kept the other two in sight, and arrived not far behind them.

The universality of Nazism in Germany impressed itself on us in this our first Jugendherberge. We had expected these equivalents to Youth Hostels to be unofficial, as the English and Belgian had been, but the Third Reich had taken them over along with the Boy Scouts and other such movements. The latter had been given a military uniform and organization. Boys were now Hitler Jungen and girls Hitler Mädels. The boys wore black knee-length trousers and black jackboots, and for hunting knives they carried small bayonets at their belts, with the motto "Blut und Ehre" etched on their blades. The girls wore modest skirts and blouses and marching boots, and many of them, younger and older alike, did their hair in long braids. They used no make-up, and their scrubbed faces shone.

A small troop of Hitler Jungen were already established in the Aachen Herberge, twelve or thirteen-year-olds, and a brisk leader in his early thirties with them. They marched smartly and came to attention the same. At table they were courteous and passed the condiments duly, but elsewhere they were aloof.

We went on to Cologne for our second and third nights. There on our first afternoon we had some talk with a Hitler Youth named Werner. He was keen to practise his English and kept telling us how he made out with the girls. We were seated on a slope, watching the barge and steamer traffic on the Rhine. JC was bored by his chatter, though he would no doubt have put up with it more cheerfully if it had been in German. Werner was keen to practise his English, however. By and by he switched his attention to the Jews. We must not take the anti-Semitism too seriously, he told us. It was a necessary means to uniting the sentiments of the country and was not directed at individual Jews, only at Jews in general. We must remember that Jews in general had done a great deal of harm to Germany. But as concerning the caricatures and propaganda and all that, it had to look worse than it really was, like a dog with a noisy bark.

We soon became familiar with this line. Werner asserted it with an agreeable assurance of manner and persisted with it, as though to convince us. Then he lost interest and went to join some friends. He was a handsome fifteen-year-old with a confident manner.

We had a good look at Cologne Cathedral, which was still having some work done on one of its towers. JC, having seen Canterbury, was not as impressed as I was, though he conceded that its hugeness was awesome. He felt that Canterbury more faithfully expressed the mood of the Gothic.

The German army had moved into the Rhineland that spring, and reoccupied it. Throughout the year before the actual reoccupation there had been considerable intimidation by single men or small groups, in uniform or not. We heard stories of men having been shot in bars for expressing anti-Nazi sentiments, and we were conscious sometimes of tension yet among the people. A Catholic saint's day procession along one of Cologne's streets drew our attention. It had a crucifer bearing a medieval Crucifix, clerics, altar boys with candles and an urn with relics, followed by a small body of parishioners. All had an air of wary defiance. We were to encounter such a mood again, not just in the Rhineland but also in other parts of the country. We knew that Earle Birney had been knocked down the year before on a street in Bonn for jeering at a Brownshirt parade he and a friend were watching.

Bonn was serene, on the surface at any rate, while we were there. We stayed in a little alkoholfreies Gasthaus near Beethoven's birthplace, kept by a pleasant young housewife. A journalist friend of Roy Daniells had recommended it. Next day we visited the friend, who gave me two hundred and fifty marks that Roy had left with him two years before. They were marks Roy had failed to declare. Another two hundred and fifty had perished when he attempted to smuggle them out in his bicycle tires. Dünnwald, the journalist, and his wife, were most friendly, but said little till they had led us to a room in the middle of the house. He then made a final tour to assure himself that the maid had gone out. We spoke in low tones for all that, and what we said was mostly non-committal. They seemed to trust us, but how could they be sure of our discretion? For our part, we felt that it would be discourteous to press their friendliness and candour, though there were questions that I knew JC much wished to ask. Our talk soon moved to Roy, Canada and, on their side, to the beauties of the lower Rhine. They gave us coffee and cakes, and made a small ceremony of handing over the two hundred and fifty marks. The visit was amiable but its tone was guarded, our first encounter with the hand of dictatorship as it bore down on the spirits of fellow intellectuals.

I bought a camera with most of the marks, a second-hand Voigtländer, which recorded that trip and many other personally historical matters that have come since.

In the town center of the beautiful city of Bonn we first saw the public display, in a handsome, glazed, standing frame, of the sort of anti-Semitic posters and texts that we were to find in many other villages and towns we biked through. Obscenities that revealed what lay beneath all the "quiet and order", and the marching.

The route we follow is JC's, he proposes it and we discuss it as we go along, he fetching out his Baedeker and reading bits to me in a somewhat self-mocking tone because it seems a touristy thing to be doing. And why not? What do we think we are if not tourists? Our motives are mixed however, or crossed. He is more than half competing with himself, and I am reining him in and dawdling whenever I can. Yet by and large we are both enjoying it all, besides looking at a castle or two and some churches. I have asked myself since if there could have been a better way of taking in the country and its folk as well as the tourist items, unless it would be on foot.

A side benefit of the bicycle, for us certainly, is its way of attracting people. All ages and sorts feel free to collect around us when we are at a halt, and talk to us. During the early part of our tour, before I had learned much German, JC would leave me with the bikes while he scouted for food or directions or some other desideratum, and come back to find me at the center of a small crowd, all of us trying to achieve mutual intelligence.

Where did we come from?

Canada.

The next question seldom varied: All the way by bike?

They were incredulous.

Under JC's tutoring, as we rode side by side along the quieter roads repeating paradigms, rules of grammar and idioms, I acquired some fluency in German. His voice was not easy to hear at any time, but his teaching manner was compelling — persistent and patient — and I learned. What German grammar I have retained is almost wholly what remains from his teaching on those roads.

While we were yet in the Rhineland a burly peasant answers our request for directions to the Jugendherberge by taking us a hundred yards or so to his own house, a plain white structure which contained a few pieces of scrubbed furniture and a general ambient of humanity. He demands an immediate yes or no, and we say yes, and stay.

We sit at his scrubbed table, having leaned our bikes against the wall at the bottom of some outside stairs.

Geblick! Geblick! says he, and goes away to another part of the house.

In a moment he is back with a platter of bread, butter and ham, which he sets before us, gesturing with both hands as though to push it all at us. Then, sitting opposite, he watches us eat, and talks at us in a series of barks. His yellow hair is cut short except for a slightly longer curl that falls over his ruddy forehead. His shirt and trousers hardly pretend to cover his bright body hair and muscle, or to contain his energy.

JC followed most of what he was saying, though it was not like any German I had yet heard, and it seemed to be full of geblicks. We slept well in his feather beds, and breakfasted well, again waited on by him, in his energetic and talkative way. A soft-eyed woman appeared in the background during breakfast. She had nothing to do with us, except that she smiled now and again as she emerged briefly from somewhere in the house and merged back into it again. After breakfast she brought us a bowl of hot water each to shave in. No mirror. I also needed hot water in my china cup for the bathing of my finger. This called for much explanation, and when the shy housewife at last brought it I had to thank her for it as I best might, and be content, but it was not hot.

By now the farmer has gone to work out back, and we do not see him again except once behind the house, carrying a pail and waving his farewell to us. His wife collects the payment for our bed, supper and breakfast, and it is very little, less than at a Jugendherberge. There has been no talk of the Third Reich during our stay, nor any Heil Hitler salute, for all that the signs on the streets and roads everlastingly proclaim it as the German greeting.

Speaking of which, we observed a solitary, well-dressed old man one day as he came to attention while a parade of Brown Shirts marched by. He was like a saluting machine, beginning with his right arm horizontal across his breast, hand flat and palm down, then swinging it out like a semaphore and snapping it back again smartly, and so again and again till the parade had passed.

The Heil Hitler, with its salute personally given, was a challenge that we often met, and sometimes we would be looked at sharply to see if we would answer in kind, but we could not bring ourselves to say the words, much less raise our right arms. We would say Guten Abend or Guten Tag, and in Catholic country, when we were greeted with Grüss Gott, which we most often were by farm folk, we would answer the same. Our failure to give the Nazi greeting may have been tolerated more readily that summer on account of the Olympic Games, and the many visitors expected for them, with their money.

We did meet a very few who pointedly omitted the salute and then we knew that we were in the presence of a heroism that hardly bears contemplating. An impulsive young blue-eyed blond German, dressed in working clothes, came up as we were standing in a street one morning, greeted us without saluting and spoke to us briefly. We would have been glad of a talk but JC, who followed his German, hesitated to encourage him. We were awed even so, by the grimness with which this young workman rejected Hitler and all he stood for.

Everyone seemed to assume that we had come for the Olympic Games. It often happened that I was wearing my white pullover, which had red and black stripes in its collar. Children and young folk shouted after us that we were wearing the German colours. Deutsche Farben! They shouted gleefully, and their tone became more and more gleeful as the summer went on, and the games proceeded. An American black, Jesse Owens, was one of the more spectacular competitors; he carried off one running and jumping trophy after another, and the ordinary Germans were delighted. That an officially despised "non-Aryan" should triumph over their own champions seemed to give many of them, even Nazis, a naughty pleasure.

With the Baedeker's guidance we had a look at Bad Godesberg, the sunny Rhineland village that was to spring into prominence, not to say notoriety, two years later, when Hitler and Chamberlain held the second of their three fateful meetings there. We paid attention to its spa, its expensive villas and hotels, and its castle ruins. Then up the Drachenfels because it seemed not right to pass it by, but though its view was splendid we did not stay long among its crowds and tourist shops. On we biked upstream to Coblenz.

It is a hot afternoon, we have eaten little for lunch and I suggest we have a glass of Mosel wine, glimpsed over the hedge of a shady weingarten, its knobby glasses irresistibly beaded with condensation. JC agrees. On occasion he did seem to make peace with his Spenglerian fatalism, perhaps as an indulgence to me. It was not often called for in this way, for I knew as well as he that a glass of anything at such an hour was a luxury out of proportion to our limited funds. Perhaps for that very reason the Mosel in the arboreal quiet of that weingarten seemed especially delicious.

It went to my knees, so that I could hardly push the pedals. JC was ready to drive on, to Mainz perhaps. I say nothing about my knees, I just hang back, and after a few mutterings we do not drive on but stay, instead, in Coblenz. I wonder if he may not have been weak in the knees too, and yet I know that he was a truthful man, painfully so.

Next day, Mainz and Frankfort, a long day's push to make up for the time lost in Coblenz. Then south to Heidelberg through Mannheim.

Our mealtime routine was seldom altered: breakfast where we had spent the night, a Jugendherberge almost always, and supper at the next, if it was available. Lunch was what we could pick up for as little as possible at market stalls or shops on the way: cheese, bread, milk, fruit, one or sometimes two of these. One day in Bavaria we came upon yogurt, a discovery. We had heard of it, but not encountered it before.

JC shopped for our lunches during the first three weeks. After that I had enough German to do some of it. To his chagrin, my accent was sometimes more intelligible than his, mimicking as it did what I heard here and there on the way. It was usually at my instigation that we pulled up in a village or town, when odours from cafes or shops or market carts became too much for me, and if I was in the lead and stopped suddenly I might bring on a brief drama behind me: — a squeal of brakes, then a rattle and clatter as JC's bike fell to the road, and last of all a hoot from his hooter, a derisive note. Somehow he would come out of this scramble upright.

We are in Mannheim, he is off to buy something for lunch and I am left with the bikes. Two gentlemen in cloth caps and mackintoshes eye me across the way. After a moment's consultation between them they cross and stand by me, the taller of the two, who seems to be in charge, points his finger right into his mouth, takes it out again and says, syllable by syllable: Wo kann ich mittag essen? Mittag essen?

I hesitate, not wanting to say a wrong thing, but he is getting his finger ready for his mouth again so I ask: What do you speak?

O ma gawd! says he. You're English! I might have known by your flannel shorts. Where can we get some roast beef and potatoes?

The two gentlemen, who were somewhat elderly, came from Leeds, and it was their second day in Germany. The shorter gentleman had a glum look and said nothing, but the taller was game for much yet. He was delighted to be released into English, and greeted JC as an old friend when he came back on the scene. The other cheered up too, as much as was in him to do so, when we found a hotel for them with a restaurant in which English was spoken. They invited us to lunch with them and to have a look around Mannheim afterwards, but push on was our motto, especially JC's; he gave a grunt and mounted. I felt that we had made friends who deserved courtesy, at least a brief oration and benediction, so I spoke a few words before I too pushed off. I wondered if they had had the notion of making us their guests. Perhaps they wondered too.

Our German lessons on the road were against the law. Twice we had been shouted at by police, and as often by responsible citizens, for cycling two abreast. The law was wise. In England, where it seemed to be inadequately enforced, week-end cyclists were being killed or maimed in shocking numbers because they would not move in single file. The law could not be everywhere, not even in Germany, though it did seem to be virtually omnipresent there, and we tried to keep a watch, but sometimes we became preoccupied, on a quiet road from Frankfort, for example, going over some irregular verbs. A policeman appears in front and stops us; we might have collided with him. He is sternfaced and armed. He glares at us for seconds, then his arm shoots up and he barks the Nazi greeting. We had worked out a response to this but not yet mustered the nerve to try it. Now seems to be a time.

God save the King! we say.

The policeman glares. Then his look breaks and he grins. He barks at us just the same, about breaking the law.

Doppelt ist streng verboten! Streng verboten, meine Herren!

JC has begun a snicker, but now he scowls, and for a while he drops behind me, an indulgence to my slower pace.

Our obedience to the law was short-lived, however. We cycled several miles two and sometimes three abreast, on the way to Heidelberg, for example, when we had a young intellectual with us. JC had struck up one of his more absorbing conversations with him after supper the evening before. He was a third-year undergraduate in science, well informed and literate. JC was enjoying the exercise in his High German, and the two of them rode side by side, talking back and forth steadily. The student was a handsome Nordic type, an ideal youth on the Nazi pattern, but he was not one of them. He could see no need to join the Party or any of its organizations and preferred to be on his own. This sort of talk raised JC's hopes that there might be some exchange of political criticism with him, for he did seem genuine and independent, and what he had to say about the violation of the Locarno treaties was fair enough, it had given their self-respect back to the German people. But his routine about the Jews and militarism had become all too familiar. He was not anti-Semitic and neither were his friends, he said. The propaganda was unpleasant, but it served a purpose, and in any case the Jews had a lot to answer for. As to Hitler's warlike preparations, war was the last thing he wanted.

It seemed obvious to us that Hitler was indeed preparing for war and arming Germany swiftly while the rest of Europe looked on in a daze. Marching men in uniform were everywhere, women too. One morning, as we are up and doing in a charming village Jugendherberge, we hear what might be an army squad in hobnail boots march into the courtyard beneath and come to a halt with a crack. We look out: it is a troop of teenage girls in white blouses, black skirts and boots, their hair, with few exceptions, in braids. They are standing to attention, and their leader, a woman, is walking smartly between their ranks, inspecting their outfits and the shine of their faces.

We encountered few younger German men in the Jugendherbergen; most were in adult uniform — brown, black or the field gray of the army. Others, in the Arbeitsdienst, marched singing through the streets to or from their labours, picks and shovels at the slope on their shoulders, like rifles. The young civilians we did meet were good company, ready to talk and sing and become friends for an hour. JC's reserve often gave way to their mood. Few of them felt, as we did, that events were moving swiftly towards making us enemies.

We were now cutting across towards Rothenburg-ob-der-Tauber, biking through beautiful hilly country. Even with my three speeds I found some of the hills too much and walked the last bit, while JC pumped on doggedly every inch and waited for me at the top. The down slopes were long and sweet, but of course they were always followed by another climb. At last we come to Rothenburg, late in the sunny afternoon, and find space for ourselves in the most spacious herberge we have encountered. It comprises a farm house and buildings below the walls of the town, and it is overflowing with guests, every square foot in every building put to use, no segregation of sexes, all bedding down where they may. We picked up a supper in the town and walked around it till dark. There were very few streets, and no vehicular traffic. It was all set on a hill, and said to be unchanged since the seventeenth century.

Next noon the clock on the square goes through its daily performance. First, a procession of knights rides jerkily round the tower. Then a door opens on either side of the clock face and in one a figure raises a boot to his lips and appears to drink it. He represents a burgomaster who saved the citizens a siege by drinking a heroic draught of wine. In the door on the other side of the clock face the commander of the besieging force shakes his head in disbelief. Then the doors close and the clock's performance is over. A small detachment of the Wehrmacht, who were part of the crowd of spectators, then form up and do a march past in the goose step, a smart operation, their boots noisy and in exact unison on the cobbles.

Our money was beginning to run out. I had bought another tire for my rear wheel and repaired it twice. We left Rothenburg early in the lovely clear morning, making for Munich — where we intended to wire home for more funds — via Ansbach and Ingolstadt. The air was fresh and the scent of earth strong after a pre-dawn shower. By and by comes another shower and then another, brief, but long enough to cool us and wet the road. We were still in the hilly country, exhilarating downhill coasting followed by endless climbs. The hills were paved with small granite blocks laid fanwise. We are coasting down one hill in high spirits, enjoying the beauty and peace of the hour, JC, as usual, ahead. All at once I observe that his angle, as he banks around a corner, is becoming acute. It seems to be happening in slow motion. Caution informs me that the same will happen to me unless I take care, too late, for as it does I too lie down, bike and all, on the rough surface, and skid along it for a stretch. JC was lying ahead of me around a gentle curve, making no effort to get up. Nor did I feel moved to rise from the granite and learn the nature of my injuries. It would not do to stay there, however; the few cars that had passed us had been speeding. JC began to stir and I too stirred. Becoming vertical was painful, and so was progress. Stiffly we moved to one side of the road and stiffly walked our bicycles a half mile downhill to where a small group of houses stood in the sun, and the road levelled out for a bit. There we sat on a low wall and let the heat work on our offended flesh and bones. JC fought his trembling, but I could not, it was many minutes before I was in charge of my lower jaw again and could propose that we stay on a while and rest — a long while perhaps, perhaps overnight. He pondered my words, as though taking them seriously, but it was clear that rest was not what we would do, we would carry on, we were not damaged, merely shaken up. He was right; after a few miles we had lost much of our discomfort.

In Munich we wire for more money and then await its arrival in the big Jugendherberge. A group of young Americans, men and women, had more or less settled in there, though this was counter to the spirit of hostelling, and they spent many of their daytime hours in what they called the Hoffbrow House. They were pleasantly easygoing, and I gossiped with them somewhat. JC scorned their company. He and I did some sightseeing in Munich, in consultation with his Baedeker, and we too visited what we more conscientiously called the Hofbrauhaus and the Löwenbrauhaus, though our visits were limited by shortage of funds. We were also glad enough to spend time apart from each other, the occasion having presented itself. In due course our money comes, we declare it and take off again.

We make first for Kelheim on the Danube to visit the Kloster Welten-burg, whose chapel had been designed, built and decorated in the Baroque style. On the way we stop to study a village war memorial, a stone pillar with names engraved on it of men from the neighbourhood who had died in what was then known as The Great War. Every face of the monument was covered with names, closely spaced and in small letters. How could this district have spared so many men of working age, and how had their places been filled again? The column stood for what then seemed an unimaginable mass of death.

We found lodging in a tiny village near Kelheim, having decided to stay at the inn and luxuriate in our renewed supply of marks. The landlord, who was also a farmer, had Kaiser Bill moustaches, though with no glower on his lean face to go with them. His wife was a small, thin woman with dark hair parted in the middle and pulled into a small bun high on the back of her head. Both looked shrunk and aged, though they may not have been very old, for their son, who ran the farm, seemed hardly over thirty. He was a burly bachelor, a hearty beer drinker, muscular and paunchy. They were all ardent Nazis, flew the swastika flag in front of the inn and had three different big photographs of Hitler hanging on their walls. They fairly gathered us in, and made their hospitality irresistible. That we had come from Canada amazed them, all that way, from a remote place they had heard of but never expected to see anyone who lived there. They regaled us with beer, wurst and sauerkraut, and watched every bite as it was cut, left the plate and made its way into our mouths. Then comes the familiar question: What do Canadians think of the Third Reich? We tell them that we do not like anti-Semitism, and this opens the floodgates. Unlike many we talked to, they were not either real or pretended apologists for an unfortunate necessity, but deep-down haters. They had been born into and brought up with their convictions, though what they argued did not suggest that they had known much, if anything, of Jews at first hand. There was no real arguing, they were good-naturedly stubborn and considered us ignorant on this subject.

They had greeted us with the Nazi salute and we had answered with Guten Abend, which they received with a look that as much as said: When you know better you will do better. At bed time they showed us to our room and bid us a cordial good night, followed by a salvo of Heil Hitlers. Then they stared at us. We broke down, for the first and last time. Our salutes were feeble, but they were accepted.

JC was up before me in the morning, reading a newspaper that had been brought to the room. After breakfast, which we ate in the garden, we ask for our bill. Nothing. Postcards from Canada, they say. Canadians are a novelty, and they will accept no money.

At Weltenburg Monastery we were taken across the current of the Danube, along with four others, in a boat rowed by a sturdy woman. The boat had to be towed upstream again after each crossing either way. The chapel of the Monastery, dedicated to St. George, said to have been decorated by the Assam Brothers, was what we had come to see. It was a single vaulted chamber dramatically lighted here and there by a few shafts of sunlight. Its pillars and ceiling were crowded with energetic baroque modelling in gold and silver on a dark green ground, and it gave an impression of brooding splendour. Before the altar a small, gold, bored-looking St. George on a gold horse thrust his lance into a gold dragon.

We are now on our way north to Berlin through Regensburg, Plauen, Leipzig and Halle, driving hard, so many kilometers a day, often eighty or more. I no longer feel that I am slowing our progress, except for my rear tire. I never did find a replacement in Germany that was the right size. JC damned and blasted about it now, not so much at me or the tires as at the anti-JCness of things. His swearing was noteworthy, for its content and even more so for its tone. It was like a brief black mass.

Neither of us had a watch, and he missed keeping track of the time of day. The hostel mother at Halle gave him an address in town where she thought he might find one that would suit him. The street was central and short, off by itself, its windows displaying used cameras, musical instruments, jewelry and such, a street of pawnbrokers, the three balls hanging over many of its doors. We chose one that displayed watches in its window. Its proprietor was a tall, well-built man, perhaps fifty years old, with a gray look about his eyes. His manner was not forthcoming, he seemed reluctant to give us much attention. JC ignored his manner and asks to see some watches. The man brings out two, then a third. I point to the third. It is like the railroaders' watches that my great uncles had carried. JC was indecisive, he knew nothing about watches, he said. Then all at once he decides on the railroaders' watch. How much? The shopkeeper names a price and JC begins to count out the money.

Such a prompt response, and so positive, startled the shopkeeper and then dismayed him. He mutters a lower price but JC goes on counting out the money. I remonstrate in a low tone of voice and he pays no attention to me either, puts his money on the counter and out we go with the watch.

The shopkeeper's look had seemed uneasy to me, and now I note the emptiness of the street. It dawns on me that it is Jewish.

He expected you to haggle.

I do not haggle, says he. If I am asked a reasonable price I pay it.

You frightened him.

It took him a moment to grasp my meaning.

The price was low enough anyhow, and the watch kept good time.

Berlin is crowded when we arrive, and the Jugendherberge full. They find us a place in Potsdam, an ordinary house kept by a pleasant, rather timid widow, in her fifties perhaps. We were comfortable there for eight nights, and given good breakfasts. We spent the days in Berlin, walking the streets, talking with anyone who would talk with us, and exploring parks and museums. The city was full of life, and its mood was easier than any we had encountered, sophisticated, less under restraint, less reverent and awestruck by its Nazism. A Berliner, about forty years old, attached himself to us one morning, and again another day. He typifies the city and our sojourn there in my memory, his smooth, round face, natty suit and beret, and his amusing, unintellectual, uncritical friendliness, enjoying the life of the streets as we did, watching it and drifting along with it. He told us not to take Nazism too seriously.

It's a phase, he said. And it is not true that one cannot say what one likes. I say all sorts of things. I say them to Brown Shirts, Black Shirts, anyone I talk to. Nothing happens to me.

We did not hear him say anything that would have got anyone into trouble, his views were as bland as his look. He showed us a little photographic booklet, big as an oversize postage stamp, in which Hitler might be seen making a speech with gestures, when its pages were flipped. This seemed comical and slightly subversive to him, and he insisted on taking us to a kiosk that sold them. I bought one, but JC did not.

These are such enjoyable days that I suggest we stay another week, ship the bicycles back to England and hitch-hike. An American in Munich had told me that hitch-hiking was easy, everyone picks you up, he said. His views were beginning to seem attractive, but not to JC. He had hitch-hiked in Canada twice, when he had run away from home, and had not liked it, it offended his soul. Moreover, it was not according to our agreement.

Once on the road I was glad to be cycling again. I too was grateful for the independence, though I was nervous of the traffic in this part of the country. It was heavier than elsewhere, impatient and unfriendly. Cars slowed down to cuss at us. But the days were good and our spirits high, we were heading west and our separation from London, to which I had taken such a liking, was growing shorter. JC felt the same, except that it was Cambridge and his books that he was looking forward to.

Before Hanover the most successful of all the tires I had bought ruptured twice, the second time irreparably. JC cursed it black. We took a local train into town and walked the bike to a repair shop.

Come on, I say. Let's give up the bloody tire and hitch-hike.

He was not convinced.

We keep giving the rear wheel another try, I say. We shall run out of money for new tires. They told us this one would take us to England.

He shook his head and scowled.

The Hanover repair shop did not commend itself to me, it was too big and its mechanics talked too much. The tube they sold me looked too big.

Inflate it hard, they tell me, arguing that a hard tire is less likely to blow.

Twenty miles beyond Hanover they were proved wrong. The tube had a great rent and several worn places. I assume that we shall take it back to where we bought it, but this time JC says no, and by two in the afternoon the bikes are in the hands of a shipping agency and the tram is taking us to the outskirts of town. From its last stop we walk to a spot near an intersection where we think that cars will have to slow down, and begin to thumb.

After half an hour's patience we persuade ourselves that our luck may improve if we are seen to be active, so we walk up a hill and then down, and then up another. At last we come to a likely-looking place again where it is level and the traffic, such as it is, does not hurry by. Many vehicles had ignored our raised thumbs while we were walking uphill or down, but now — what had become of them?

We had picked a desolate location, a wasteland of corrugated iron warehouses and junkyards with steel fences, an industrial fringe. Now and again a cyclist wheeled by and waved, otherwise nobody paid attention to us. JC looked miserable. The decision had weighed on his spirits since we had made it, and though he had resolved to give it a fair trial, his struggle with revulsion had now become obvious. The sun was casting longer shadows. For an hour we exchanged hardly a word. A pair of cyclists coming the other way slowed down and looked at us as they passed.

Allo tramp! shouts one. Gute sport!

His tone was friendly, but his words struck JC to the heart.

Come on! Let's go back!

First thing in the morning we persuade the shipping company to return our bikes. Surprisingly, the repair shop accepted our complaint and were embarrassed. They found a more suitable tire from a source they had not investigated the day before and did not charge us for it. Nor did they charge for their labour putting it on. Nobody raised an arm and said Heil Hitler! We set out westwards again with renewed faith in ourselves and humanity.

Our last Jugendherberge was in Mönchen-Gladbach. We and a band of young Hitler Youth shared the only male dormitory, and about filled it. We walk into town for supper, and on our way ask a pretty brunette for directions to a good place, inviting her to sup with us. We have a few travellers' marks to use up. She takes us to an inexpensive cafe and will hardly be persuaded to let us pay for the little she eats. We observe that she is wearing lipstick.

Some girls have their faces washed for them, she says. In the street. But I glare and walk straight on, and the Brown Shirts leave me alone.

I understand much of what is being said, and enough of the rest is explained to me as the talk goes on.

JC is shy, only half audible, and his mood is very intellectual. If he is asked to repeat something he fairly roars the first two or three words, an old foible he had almost left behind. The girl is another intellectual, and is not put off by his manner.

Her name was Hannelore. I have wondered what happened to her, for she may have been Jewish, but if so she had not lost her confidence.

We had exchanged a few words with the leader of the young Hitler Youth before we went out for supper. When we got back he and his troop were in bed, but not yet asleep. After a few moments, when the lights have been turned down, the young voices begin to pipe up. They wonder if Canada is joined to England. Their leader thinks it is, in some way.

Will England oppose Hitler when he asserts Germany's just claims again? How about England and the United States? Were they not run by Jews?

I understood only part of this, but felt its unfriendliness. The leader tells them to stop, go to sleep.

The Canadians speak very good German, he tells them.

This sweetens it.

Next morning, near the Dutch frontier at Roermond, we ask directions of a farm labourer. He is curious about us. Where do we come from? Why all the way to Germany?

His questions are friendly, and they multiply. Then he insists we have a taste of his lunch, bread and hot milk in a wide-mouth thermos jar. We have a mouthful each, and then he wants me to have it all.

Take it! he says, trying to hand it to both of us at once.

At this we make off across the open and flat countryside. We could still see him for a while, shaking his head and trying to call us back. We are beginning to think he had given us wrong directions till all at once we find ourselves at the Border.

The building was small, but it was flying the big swastika flags and displaying the same outsize flag-draped photographs indoors that had faced us when we entered the country. Two humourless officials attended to us. We must have been their first of the day. We present our documents confidently and declare the money that had been wired to us in Munich.

They search our kit and find nothing out of line, but one of them is not satisfied, he keeps looking through our documents as though he thinks something is missing. He asks about my camera. I had bought a leather case for it, and a tripod as well. His manner is bullying: How had we fed ourselves for six weeks and bought a camera on what we had declared? At this I remember Roy Daniells' money that I had picked up in Bonn. I had actually forgotten about it.

We describe the meals we had eaten, pieces of cheese for lunch, suppers in the Hostels. A beautiful roadside apple tree came into my head, half its pink and yellow fruit on the ground, sweet apples we had gorged ourselves on, and somehow not made ourselves ill. The official's glare made it seem inappropriate. Even so, he could see that we had not feasted, there was no fat on either of us. What if he had known about the tires and tubes I had bought?

He hands us back our documents and turns his attention to writing something. We stand there a moment or two, wondering what next, and all at once he looks up, surprised.

Dismiss! he barks, and scowls at our departure.

We crossed the tiny bit of The Netherlands and were soon in Belgium. The first person we saw there was a thin body in dirty, threadbare clothing and cocky hat, riding a bicycle. He gives us a mock Nazi salute and grins and we grin back. The air we breathe feels fresh again.

On we bike all day, with hardly a stop, and at ten-thirty in the evening we came into Ostend, where we had bought cheese and rolls nearly six weeks before. JC thinks we should go farther, so we step into a small cafe near the harbour for a bite to eat and coffee. The owner, an older woman, was alone. She was mildly curious about us, and concerned that we look so fatigued, and we relax and give in, both at the same time, and ask about somewhere to stay the night.

Like the French porter at Calais, who had rejected our proffered sixpence with scorn, she spoke English with a distinct London accent.

Booked solid, she says. Ole plice. Asnt been a bed for weeks.

We had come to a standstill, and did not pursue the subject.

Wy not stop ere? She asks. Ere, you bed down ere, ere's a blanket for you.

She puts me on a lumpy sofa behind the counter and takes JC into the kitchen and puts him on a day bed there, and our next awareness was of the morning. She would take no money for our beds, but she let us pay for coffee the night before, and coffee and rolls and the usual unidentifiable jam for breakfast.

A young English couple we talked to on the ferry were distressed by our seeming ambiguity about Nazi Germany. How should we answer? We had found no fault in many of the young Germans we had met, older ones too, whatever we may have thought of their politics. We detested what we knew of the Nazi regime, but that surely went without saying. The young couple, no doubt, had a firmer grasp of political realities than I, at any rate, had, but how much did most of us know?

Back in London we found a flat at 9, Lamb's Conduit Street, which JC soon left for Cambridge, and after a fortnight by myself I was joined by fellow graduates from Toronto, McRae, Mackay and Harris. JC visited from Cambridge a few times, and I went there twice to see him, up and back on the same day. He was living a gentlemanly life in residence at Trinity

College. Ludwig Wittgenstein, under whom he was studying, was all his talk, and he made some effort to explain Logical Positivism to me, but I found it hard to understand.

I returned to Canada and did not see him again till the summer of 39. We had kept up some correspondence meanwhile, and he had gone to California, where he took his PhD at Berkeley. There he had read *The Grapes of Wrath* and been so moved by it that he rode the freights back to Toronto in an epic eight-day journey, having spent one night in a hobo jungle. McRae and I were tenting in Haliburton, and he hitch-hiked straightway to see us and tell us his story before returning to his parents in Toronto.

No-one had made that ride before in less than a fortnight, he tells us. He is dirty and tanned almost black, elated by his achievement, and wants to tell us at first hand, in his understated, softspoken way, that he had proved himself. The German bicycle tour had had compensations, but his patience with me, and my rear bicycle tire, had made it no proper test. Now he is satisfied.

At Cambridge his political views had taken a decisive swing to the left, politically, hence his reading of *The Grapes of Wrath*. Moreover, he had now resolved to take no part in the war, which was clearly imminent. The working man stood to gain nothing by it.

I did not see him again till late in the War, when I was in Ottawa, briefly, as second pilot of a Liberator that was undergoing special test flights. Friends had told me that he was in Naval Intelligence, so I located their offices in a mare's nest of temporary buildings on Elgin Street, and hunted him out. Our reunion was somewhat strained, and it was cut short then by a meeting he was to attend. I tell him that we are doing airborne tests after supper. Would he like to come?

He would, if he could clear it with his commanding officer. Anti-submarine intelligence had been the subject of his department, but he had not flown in an anti-submarine aircraft, and he would be glad of the opportunity. I tell him to come to the mess for supper, six o'clock.

Supper was rushed, we did little visiting then. The captain of the aircraft had been in Ferry Command. He was fond of awkward hours, and he was stiff on the subject of punctuality. He liked to keep his crew on their toes, as he put it.

JC was a lieutenant and looked well in his uniform. He had become a gentleman again, as he had been at Cambridge; no trace now of the dirty suntanned hobo McRae and I had talked to so long ago, as it seemed, in Haliburton.

For crew we had only a flight engineer and wireless operator, aside from the captain and me. Two engineer officers from HQ and an American civilian aviation engineer were also on board to direct the tests. I was not needed in the cockpit except for takeoff and landing, and after we had climbed to our test altitude, eight thousand feet, I showed JC around the aircraft, instrument panels and offices forward of the wing first, dodging the experts, and then through the bomb bay to the rear of the fuselage.

The openness of this part of the aircraft was a noteworthy and, in my view, attractive feature of the Liberator. Each side wall had a three-foot by four-foot panel that opened inwards and upwards. These were positions for side gunners, and had fixed stools for them to sit on. Deflectors turned the slipstream away. Sitting on the gunner's stool one might lean out and enjoy an unimpeded view of the country below. I opened the two panels and JC was delighted. He had clearly not been so free in an airborne aircraft before. Back and forth he went, from one opening to the other, and I had to restrain him somewhat for fear that he might fall out. We shout at each other over the roar of the engines and the slipstream.

Back to the mess for a drink afterwards, at about ten o'clock. The usual party was under way, someone at the piano and much singing. JC was not used to mess life. He lived in a room in town and ate most meals in restaurants. One of his colleagues in Naval Intelligence, who had made an effort to befriend him, said that he would sit in Mme. Berger's fine restaurant in Hull with a gourmet meal and a bottle of expensive wine before him, and eat alone.

Our time in the mess is awkward, for he has no desire to sing or join in the general gossip. I, on the other hand, am reluctant to stand aloof from my fellows. I had spent four years away from his sort of intellectuality, and he had not let down at all. In his way he had liked my undergraduate self and the biking comrade I was in Germany, impatient though he must often have been, but the distance had widened between us since. We lean against the bar, and he asks me questions about anti-submarine flying, but I can tell him little of value, my experience is more than a year out of date and moreover it had been in the tropics. His concern is with a new kind of anti-submarine warfare, and in the North Atlantic. By and by he calls a taxi and departs.

A year later, in September, after the War was over and we were civilians again, our paths crossed on the campus of the University of Toronto. He was bitter about his fate. He had wanted and was sure he deserved an appointment in Toronto, but he was offered nothing there, or anywhere else in Canada or the United States, that he would consider. He accepted an offer in Australia, but that seemed banishment to him. He was convinced that the Department in Toronto simply disliked him, and that may well have been so.

We had a long talk together by one of the paths in front of Hart House, a bit stiff-legged, not unfriendly but non-committal. He was to leave for Canberra in a week. He wondered why I had not answered a letter he had sent to me in Africa. I said I had received no letter, and he found this hard to believe, though I assured him that letters did go astray, and mentioned a cable from Canada that had taken ten months to reach me. I would have answered his letter if I had received it, I told him, and then he seemed to believe me. A few days later a message came in the post, telling me that our meeting in Ottawa had jarred him, in the teeth he said. He was sorry that our differences seemed so irreconcilable, and wondered if he had ever known me properly, or perhaps we had not been clear about each other. He was glad that I was married, and he wished us both well. I felt a pang over this letter, yet I knew that there was nothing I would do about it.

Three weeks passed and then shocking news appeared in the papers and on the air. He had been murdered in a waterfront cafe on his first evening in Australia. We who had known him searched our memories in vain for a clue that might help account for this event. The Principal of Victoria College, whom JC had not much liked, though he was an old friend of his parents, made the first conjecture when he was interviewed on the radio. James, he suggested, was probably still working for Naval Intelligence on an important mission and carrying secret documents. An enemy agent would have been his murderer.

What comfort there might have been in this improbable theory lasted for part of a day; then Naval HQ in Ottawa simply denied that he had been carrying documents of any sort for them. He had had no connection with the Navy since the end of the War.

His body, returned from Australia in a lead-lined casket, was buried in his birth-place, Hanover, Ontario. Principal Brown, as yet uncontradicted by facts, preached a handsome funeral sermon twice, once in Toronto and once in Hanover, though there were already hints that the circumstances of his death might be unedifying. They were not referred to in the sermon except as "Death" with whom "James Taylor held his rendez-vous" in Australia.

Naval intelligence did not accept Mrs. Taylor's suggestions that they send a pallbearer, so she asked me if I might find two others besides myself among his friends of undergraduate days, and I asked McRae and

Harris. We all three felt sorry for his parents, knowing how inadequate any sympathy would be. They were proud of him, whatever the circumstances of his death may have been. He was their only child, and during his last weeks with them he had been both dutiful and affectionate. He had always been fond of them, though he had also been rebellious and impatient, and stingy when it came to displays of feeling. At his funeral they bore themselves with dignity, were gracious in accepting expressions of sympathy, and showed that they had lost none of their pride in their son.

A young Australian, whom I had known on the squadron and with whom I was exchanging an occasional letter, sent me a newspaper clipping that reported the trial over his death. This revealed the circumstance that he had got drunk within hours of coming ashore on "plonk", a drink made from the lees of wine. It went on to say that he had quarreled over a waitress and been beaten senseless. His advances had been coarse and brutal, his opponent had interfered and was acquitted on a plea of self-defence.

We, in our different ways, tried to fit the man we had known into this story. I had not been present when two of us had once seen him rebuffed, with surprised laughter, over an attempted no-nonsense seduction. Nothing at all of the sort had occurred in my time with him. I had hardly seen him drunk. He was probably beside himself with bitterness and loneliness that first evening in Australia, and the "plonk" had been too much for him. Of his few friends I had known of one in Cambridge and another in California, and I had known of two attachments to women. An older professor's wife had befriended him when he was an undergraduate, and then there had been the Ravishing Finn, to whom the long letter got written while we were on the cattle boat. Did it ever get posted? The circumstances of his death slowly took on a coloration of plausibility in my mind, though the proportion of malicious chance in it was hard for me to accept. It seemed fateful, a classical tragedy perhaps.

An uncle had flown to Australia to identify his body and have it sent home. It came all the way in a lead-lined casket. His mother and father said they would have had him cremated there, if the decision had been theirs to make. Slight man that he had been, his casket with him in it weighed six hundred pounds, and we six pallbearers had all we could do to carry it up a short rise to his grave.

* * *

COMPANY OF THE DEAD

In lead and gumwood
  you came
  a long way home
your bitterness
abruptly
thugged out

  and we laid you
  under the bright
  October turf
  of your birthplace
awed that the Brute
had felled you.

  For your disdain?
  your innocence?

We spoke our words
of comfort
hoping to be excused
  — not by you
  whose pride
  was truth, truth pride.

  A little sun
  scud-broken
warmed us a little.
though not your undertaker:
  Hats on, said he,
  outdoors.
  One funeral at a time.

Survivors
do not choose
among their dead
  whose sidelong eye
  will haunt them.

Among more beloved
your presence
lingers,
   your elegance
   and lurch.

   No staying power
   you said once,
   not for my ears, but I heard.
Outstayed you, though,
half a life
at cost
of knowing my dark.

I feel yet
the wrath
of your death,
   may envy its youth
   one day
but not now,
least now,
grown vulnerable
in my loves.

Nor shall I lay your ghost
   which I know
   as I did not you.

White butterflies are flying
outside my window — there comes
a little boat sailing by.

Edith Pahlke
Icelandic Poem
linocut 12 x 12 inches

Lore Jonas

NEW WORLD, OPEN SPACES

GEORGE JOHNSTON WAS our first Canadian friend.

In our second year in Canada, my husband, Hans Jonas, joined the Philosophy Department at Carleton College, as it was then called. Among the colleagues we found there, George and his wife, Jeanne, were those who appealed to us the most. His poetic sensibility and her forthrightness were the attraction.

We also sensed in him a largesse of spirit, which we connected with the land that had produced him. If the word "original" had not been misused, he was that. He was always himself, immutable. He lived through his own resources, unspoiled — as this new land, of which he seemed a wonderful representative, was in our European eyes. Tall and gangly, he had somehow a charm not unlike that of Gary Cooper in *High Noon*.

George told us that his father, or perhaps his grandfather, had been an engineer for one of the Canadian railways, and, driving from Montreal to Vancouver, he entertained himself over the noise of the engine by reciting Milton's *Paradise Lost*. Open spaces and English literature seemed to us a proper heritage for George.

We also heard a more comic story from him. As an undergraduate, he wanted to visit England, the "mother country" as it was called then. He hired himself out on a cattle ship, which brought live cattle to the slaughterhouses of England. This was before the time of refrigeration. The cattle got seasick and it was the job of the hired hands, who were perhaps seasick themselves, to clean up the vomit. We took this trip as a sign of his devotion to England and, by implication, to English literature — to undergo these hardships in order to see the land where the great poets had lived and had been buried. Were we right?

Our children were the same ages as Jeanne and George's, although we had only two at this point in our lives. They had three and four already, and we admired the trust in the future this indicated. Eventually they ended up with six. This optimism we also thought belonged to this country.

A lot of kindnesses we experienced in Canada came through them. George, for instance, tried to teach me to drive a car, a necessary skill on this continent.

Although this is being written to honour George's eighty-fifth birthday, let us not forget Jeanne, his wife, the daughter of missionaries. Born in China and speaking Chinese as her first language (if I remember rightly), she provided a lovely counterweight to him with her good sense, her practicality, and her firmness of purpose. She was and is a truly remarkable woman.

Wanting to further my education, I took a poetry class with George. He taught us Chaucer and read the old English in his lovely baritone voice, persuading all of us that Chaucer had to be read just that way. He also made the point, which stuck in my mind, that Shakespearean comedy is more interesting and important than tragedy (again, if I remember rightly), because implicitly comedy has already overcome the human tragedy.

George's first book, *The Cruising Auk*, enchanted us. Who or what is an auk? An extinct bird! Was he perhaps himself something of an extinct specimen? Well, his verse did rhyme — and his sly humour contrasted with the furious earnestness of much of modern poetry. Later, George's work also included the translations of the old Icelandic sagas, adding to our knowledge of the unique heritage of this part of the world.

There was a summer theatre somewhere out of Ottawa. We went with the Johnstons. The play was by Bertolt Brecht, *The Good Woman of Setzuan*. Brecht was not well known on this continent in the early fifties. It was the first time that George, now a professor of English, saw or heard of Brecht. He was flabbergasted, enthralled. "A real poet," he said. The poet in George immediately recognized Brecht, the poet, by his work, without further introduction. This made us very happy, because throughout our emigration we had carried a poem by Brecht with us. It had been smuggled out of Germany and had arrived in Jerusalem handwritten and was circulated and copied among friends as a token, a promise, and a personal talisman. The poem was "The Legend of the Creation of the Book Taotekin on the Way into the Emigration by Laotse." Our love and attraction for the same poet confirmed to our mind the rightness of our friendship, if it ever needed confirmation.

We loved George's poetry. I still possess a typed copy of his first poems, collected before his first book appeared, dedicated to Hans and Lore J., January, 1955. A wonderful line in "Us Together" reads,

> Nothing makes me feel so nearly at home on Earth
> As just to be with you and say nothing.

We left Canada in 1955 and continued to correspond but have not seen each other since. George and Jeanne Johnston have remained very much a presence in our lives.

Jay Macpherson

SMOOTHING THE WAY

IT MUST HAVE been in my last year at Carleton, 1950–51, that George Johnston came to the English Department. As I wasn't at the time an English student, I got to know him by sight but made no particular connection till "War on the Periphery" came out in the *New Yorker*. Others around me must have felt as I did — that it was a pretty riveting poem, and much more so from someone who looked so mild and unworldly.

I can't remember how we became acquainted — and I'm writing from outside Canada, away from old letters and diaries. Hans Jonas came to Carleton the same year, and he and Lore very much liked George and Jeanne. I started working for Hans during the summers, and in the academic year 1952–53, when I was at McGill Library School, also at the weekends, and that may have improved my acquaintance with George and family, as by spring 1953 I was a regular visitor — to George to talk about Poetry and Life, but enjoying as well the pleasures of a cheerful and welcoming family house.

My life at that time was rather becalmed. With a general B.A. in Greek, German, and philosophy, and a father anxious to see me equipped for a job, I'd settled for library school as something that might let me work in a university. When the library school arranged a class trip to introduce us to the great Toronto public library system, George said I must visit his friend Norrie Frye at Victoria, and wrote a note to introduce me. Frye was at the time, and for some ten years, the poetry reviewer for the *University of Toronto Quarterly*'s "Letters in Canada," and I was by then the author of an extravagantly slender volume. However, I emerged from the interview with Frye — held mainly in Murray's, as he was escaping a meeting — with the offer ringing in my head that if I could get myself to Toronto he would "teach me Blake" — by myself, as he wasn't otherwise giving the course. Only now, writing this down, do I begin to wonder what George said in that note.

Back I went to George to discuss how I could spend the next year in Toronto — presumably in some library job. George wouldn't hear of it: I must go as a regular student and study English. He wrote another letter, to Norman Endicott, secretary of the graduate department of English, and I was given provisional acceptance as a make-up student: in those days, because all the institutions were small, things were both more flexible and more personal.

Having done all that, George thought of a further device to smooth my way: Old English would be required, so he would teach me Old English. Summer evenings, once a week, I proceeded to George's house on Second Avenue in the Glebe for this purpose. I can't recall much about it — only that he was very patient, and gradually his love for the subject rubbed off on me, to my later benefit. At the same time we had a little project to earn ourselves some money: we planned to sell a poetry series to the CBC to replace the horrible mood-flow sessions with background organ that they used to go in for, and practised reading indispensables like "Kubla Khan" and "The Daemon Lover" at each other. A recording did go off to Robert Weaver, but he for no doubt excellent reasons turned us down. — Let me record here what I was less aware of at twenty-two, Jeanne's great generosity in letting me impinge on so many quiet hours after the young folk had been coaxed into bed.

That fall I arrived in Toronto with a Nonesuch *Blake* given me by George and Jeanne. And with a bank balance, after fees and transportation, of 40 dollars — not the kind of thing that deterred one in those days: I spent my first year there hungry but happy. The result of George's taking my life in hand in that constructive fashion was several years of practically unmixed bliss as a graduate student, and thereafter, with the bliss more mixed but pretty steady, a lifelong job at Victoria, George's beloved college where at one time he'd hoped to teach himself. But his life, I can thankfully say, has been lucky too.

Christopher Levenson

TECHNIQUES OF INTIMACY IN THE OCCASIONAL POETRY OF GEORGE JOHNSTON

IN ONE SENSE, most poetry is occasional: there can be few poems for which the initial impulse comes from abstract speculation rather than from some external impulse — witnessing a particular event, hearing a snatch of song, looking at a view — that is identifiable at least by the poet. Generally, however, unless, as is often the case with W.B. Yeats, for instance, where the autobiographical impulse for the poem becomes (self-)consciously the introduction to the poem, this "occasion" for the poem will remain hidden.

Now, when we use the term "occasional poetry" it implies something different, less a poem written *on* a particular occasion and prompted by it, than a poem written *for* a particular occasion, generally a public one. Of this the history of English poetry provides many examples, ranging from, say, Marvell's "Horatian Ode upon Cromwell's Return from Ireland" to Tennyson's "Ode on the Death of the Duke of Wellington" (most elegies being by definition occasional poems).

But there have been at least as many poems written for personal occasions, such as births, birthdays, marriages, graduations, or retirements, where the sub-genre shades over into *vers de société*, or what in the Victorian era was often termed "keepsake verse," the kind of production burlesqued by Philip Larkin in his poem "Born Yesterday":

> Tightly-folded bud,
> I have wished you something
> None of the others would:
> Not the usual stuff
> About being beautiful,
> Or running off a spring
> Of innocence and love —
> They will all wish you that,
> And should it prove possible,
> Well, you're a lucky girl.
>
> But if it shouldn't, then
> May you be ordinary.

On the other hand, in such poems as Samuel Johnson's "On the Death of Dr. Robert Levet" (which I always associate with Goya's famous and moving self-portrait with his physician, Dr. Arrieta) the poet does not so much write *for*, as make use *of*, an occasion in order to bring out pre-existing sympathies, ideas, or states of mind. The occasion itself, then, may be fortuitous, but not so the basic moods or attitudes in whose service it is enlisted.

It is to this second type of "occasional poetry" that many of George Johnston's poems belong. Their typical subject matter and themes are not in any public sense remarkable, but that is precisely the point: unlike, say, Yeats, whose "In Memory of Major Robert Gregory" is intent on establishing its subject publicly as a twentieth-century version of the Renaissance man, or W.H. Auden, whose "In Memoriam W.B. Yeats" is again a public assessment and celebration, a summing up in public of a public life, for the most part George Johnston presents his judgements as it were peripherally, as asides or murmured afterthoughts.

In fact the term "judgement" seems misleading: in keeping perhaps with Johnston's views as a convinced Friend (a Quaker, that is, by conviction), he suggests or affirms shared values and concerns rather than imposes judgements, and his value and originality as a poet derive at least in part, as I hope to demonstrate, from the way he is able to devise techniques for suggesting intimacy without on the one hand becoming "confessional" or on the other succumbing to grand gestures or mere phrase-making.

Such a demonstration will involve mainly the later work, for although Johnston establishes his characteristically understated sly and often whimsical wit already in his first two books, *The Cruising Auk* (1959)[1] and *Home Free* (1966), and although the eponymous first section of *Happy Enough* contains three poems that could be termed "occasional" in the present restricted sense — "Eugene Thornton," "F.H. Underhill, 1889-1971," and the *tour de force* "Convocation Address: Queen's University, 29/5/71" — it is to his two subsequent books, *Taking a Grip* and *What Is to Come*, his most recent work, which appeared in 1996, that we must turn for the main examples of his skill in this sub-genre.

Here we will find that the occasional poems, when not dedicated to family members whom we have met in earlier volumes, are addressed mostly to old friends, old in both senses, ex-colleagues such as Rob McDougall or Munro Beattie, both of the Carleton English Department, or George Whalley, fellow-poet and critic, late of Queen's University. Sometimes the poems are directed

---

[1]Page references are to *Endeared by Dark: The Collected Poems* (Erin, Ontario: Porcupine's Quill, 1990), except for poems taken from *What Is to Come* (Toronto: St. Thomas, 1996), where a page reference is preceded by *WITC*.

to other friends identified for most readers only by the occasion, as is the case with "Kent Doe's Ordination." Then again there are some poems, such as "Brigid, Newly Arrived" (*WITC* 37), that seem *too* simple without implications of further meanings, or others, such as "Church Christmas Festivities" (*WITC* 38), that do not seem to go significantly beyond attractive compliment.

There is, however, a nucleus of poems — "Goodbye, Margaret," "Elegy for George Whalley," "Barney in Bliss," "For Bob McRae on his Eightieth Birthday," "A Letter to Hans Jonas," and "How Aged Was That?" — where we find a fuller, more deliberate celebration of certain admired qualities: praise of one's friends' virtues is, after all, an oblique but effective way of affirming one's own values. Thus in "Elegy for George Whalley" (*WITC* 16) the subject is honoured for precision, endurance, friendliness, and courage in face of a long illness, while "Barney in Bliss" (*WITC* 26) records matter-of-factly the ups and downs of an eccentric ex-Stalinist, ten years Johnston's senior and now dead:

> Henceforth out of one cheap
> room into another
> fetching up on the top
> floor of a city tower
> for aged indigent

but including also those intimate moments when "you cried in / Russian films / and when our kitten died." In both these cases, as also in his poem to Frank Underhill (153), whom he praises for being "stubbornly the same, stubbornly / himself," and in "For Bob McRae on his Eightieth Birthday" (*WITC* 30),

> One horrendous day on the beach at Dieppe
> has given your warp its own peculiar thread
> which probably yourself can hardly tell how
>   it is woven in
>
> with the genial, scholarly, fatherly
> eighty-year-old husband, traveller, greenhouse
> horticulturalist that we have loved and put
>   up with all these years

we find the same stress on integrity, courage, idiosyncrasy, and wit.

But such virtue, or rather, the praise of such virtue, is not of itself necessarily memorable or even remarkable. What usually makes the poems so in Johnston's case is a blending of three interrelated technical skills: an ability to use colloquial language tautly, a truly lyrical command of variation in cadence, and an intricate patterning of internal rhyme and assonance. George Johnston once remarked to me of a famous Canadian poet that she had "a tin ear." That at least is not a charge that can be levelled at him. One suspects that Johnston's skill in these areas is more the result of long practice than of serendipity. Either way he deserves the credit, for even what comes unbidden as a gift has to be recognized before it can be used.

The first of these skills, an ability to use colloquial language, might not nowadays seem any great achievement: after all, at least since Ginsberg's *Howl* in 1955 there have been no further taboos as regards level of language. But the trick is rather to use colloquial language so that it counts while maintaining some rhythmic suspense, rather than simply throwing away the lines in a misguided democratic mateyness. "Goodbye, Margaret" (216) provides a good example of the way Johnston follows Wordsworth in using "a *selection* of the real language of men." In the very first stanza

> It turns out to be, *as how*
>   *could we know*, our last walk
> and talk together

the italicized phrase by suggesting spontaneous intrusion both establishes an informality and keeps the rhythms delicately off-balance. Further on we find

> One day
>
> we come to our beauty,
>   terrified or serene
> or beyond both, *more likely*

and toward the end of the poem he asks

> What became of them all?
> Sometimes I wish I knew.
> *Dear God, perhaps I shall.*

Such phrases as those in italics, though not themselves highly charged as poetry, are nevertheless crucial in evoking a tone of voice, a directness and simplicity and intimacy that can, in the final stanza, build to an impressively understated climax:

Yet I cant not be glad
  that when you were sent for
and your days were yet good,
nights not yet bad
  you went.

As perhaps only practising poets know, it is hard to be that simple.

All this is not to imply, however, that Johnston's diction is consistently so colloquial. In the "Convocation Address" (169), for instance, in addition to such lines as "dont kid yourselves that you dont / kid yourselves," he tries on, in the spirit of good-humoured pastiche, other gaudier, more "literary" levels of speech, such as

Connubiality, heavenly maid,
  descend,

as well as elsewhere, with in my view mixed results, archly employing such bureaucratic or legalistic jargon as "wherefore," "therein," and "thereof." We see the same principle at work when in "Delay" (*WITC* 8) he writes, "The garden yields its not / unqualified foison," but more interesting in my view is the surprise effect of a word like "umbrage," which he restores to its original, literal sense of "shade" in the lines "hazy with new green and pink the growth / offers no umbrage yet" ("Between," 178). Thus although with Johnston we are always in the presence of a speaking voice, his poetic persona can easily adopt other modes for a few lines at a time, just as in a more language- and class-conscious society such as England's people will slip into accents associated with particular regions or classes in order ironically to distance themselves from certain kinds of statements. While I would, then, characterize Johnston's diction as eclectic rather than uniformly colloquial, he has over the years crafted for himself a quirkiness of language that can modulate easily and unself-consciously in and out of the colloquial.

The second element, the command of cadence and verse movement, is perhaps more difficult to discuss, because even among literary critics there is little shared vocabulary. However, since it is the control of verse movement in a poem that first captures and holds our attention, I must at least try.

To begin with, it is interesting to note that whereas Johnston's earlier work fell into what looked like and for the most part indeed were stanzas with regular metres, the last two volumes experiment with syllabics. This is a system, best exemplified by Auden, Marianne Moore, and at times also by Dylan Thomas, of avoiding the predictability of the iambic beat, and especially the fatal attraction of the iambic pentameter, by arbitrarily arranging lines by syllable count rather than by stress. Such is the case, for instance, with "Cat on the Roof, for Laura" (*WITC* 35-36), as also with the poem for Bob McRae quoted above, and "Creation, for Gerald Trottier" (*WITC* 19), which observes a nine-syllable line. The effect of syllabics, at least in short-line stanzas, is usually to impart an air of meditated precision, precisely the dominant effect of much of Johnston's work. We have already examined the final stanza from "Goodbye, Margaret" in terms of its colloquial diction, but at least as important is the way in which the main verb, "you went," is suspended across four lines (three of six syllables and one of four), and that those four lines keep us on the *qui vive* by their disruption of normal rhythmic expectations, so that we read, I suggest,

> Yét I cánt nót be glád
>   that whén you were sént for
> and your dáys were yét góod
> níghts not yet bád,
>   you wént.

Now of course unexpected inversions and in general the disruption of metrical expectations are an inevitable part of the liveliness of any good verse: it is one reason why for instance Marvell is so memorable in such ostensibly iambic lines as "to a gréen thóught in a gréen sháde," or again "róses withóut, lílies withín," and we find many comparable effects in Crashaw, and Henry King. But the analogy with Marvell may in fact go further: if we look at "A Letter to Hans Jonas, aet. 1905-1993" (*WITC* 31), which serves also as a — thankfully premature — valediction to Johnston's own life and experience, we find a tone strangely similar to that of Marvell's Horatian Ode, especially in the concluding final couplets of each stanza:

> Your searching Jewish eye
> Scanned my belief that on the Judgement Day
> What I had thought was truth might prove awry;
> Christian humility, as you would say,
>   Not doubting I might know
>   God's truth as well as you.

> My so-called humbleness —
> A form of pride — has hardly changed since then;
> Nor does my faith in your good words grow less
> For all that we would argue all again
>   If we were face to face
>   In heaven, or any place.

Whether or not he learned it from them, Johnston shares with the Metaphysical poets an ability to keep the reader off kilter, as here in the unexpected enjambement of that last couplet.

Almost inseparable from his dexterity with cadence is a third element, the intricate patterning of rhyme. Except occasionally for light, satiric verse, rhyme (especially end rhyme) is out of fashion in most contemporary Canadian verse, the problem again being its predictability. But there are ways around this too. One is the increased use of internal rhyme, and especially of half-rhyme such as "choirs" / "bars," for example, in "Church Christmas Festivity" (*WITC* 38); another is exemplified by the second section of "Brigid Newly Arrived" (*WITC* 37):

> Dear wordless little girl,
> forgive our words, we live
> by them as you soon shall.
> Choose wisely as you grow
> into your wording age
> among their worn meanings
> some you will surely need
> and we bleed to give you:
> luck, charity, courage.

Apart from the full internal rhymes such as "forgive" and "live," "need" and "bleed," and the half-rhymes of "girl" and "shall," or "grow" and "you," when full end rhyme is used, in pairs such as "age" and "courage," the stress in the two-syllable word falls on the non-rhyming element. So too in "Church Christmas Festivity" we find "revels" rhyming with "bells," and "cheer" with "headgear." Not that this is unique to Johnston, far from it; but he uses such devices and others frequently enough and consistently enough that the intricacy of his word music effectively offsets any suggestion of cloying sweetness or *simplesse*. In the above quotation, for instance, we can detect a repetition of certain vowel sounds and consonants not close enough together to be called assonance or alliteration but conspiring nonetheless to create a closely knit texture of sound. Thus "wordless ... words ... wisely ... wording ... worn" is parallelled by "girl ... forgive ... grow." Again this is hardly new, but the frequency with which such effects occur suggests that Johnston, like W.H. Auden and in Canada Earle Birney, may have picked up a trick or two for his own use from the Icelandic and Norse alliterative sagas he has so skilfully translated. If there is any doubt about this it would be dispelled by his exercises in alliterative verse originally published in the volume *Ask Again* (Penumbra Press, 1984), notably "Ecstatic" (265) and "Boon" (266).

We encounter an even more highly crafted example in the final verse paragraph of his "Elegy for George Whalley" (260):

> Fingers of the disease wrought
> artistry of your deep
> resources, made you ghostly,
> exquisite, still the same hid
> wistfulness always in your
> eyes, inward of the way you
> looked out from your bridge. That
> lingers.

Apart from the internal chiming of "wrought," "resources," and "your," and the way the "st" of "ghostly" is taken up by "wistfulness," just look at the insistence of the short "i" sounds in "fingers," "artistry," "exquisite," "still," "wistfulness," "hid," "inward," "bridge," and "lingers." And such a list does not begin to explore other sounds, such as the "w" of "wistfulness," "inward," and "way," or the long "a" of "made," "same," "always," and "way."

What, then, do all such details add up to? I am not for a moment claiming that Johnston necessarily consciously chose particular words for the sake of internal rhyme or assonance: rather, the fact that such choices were made attests to the craft that by this stage in his poetic career had become second nature. Technique for the artist, surely, means being able to say all that one wants or hopes to say; it is a process of individuation, of being fully oneself while being at the same time fully in control of one's medium. What I have tried to indicate is that George Johnston's apparently unbuttoned, intimate, and quirky style succeeds not because it is in fact colloquial and easy-going, but rather because it is based on a very skilful weighing and sifting of such technical aspects of language as cadence, verse movement, and sound patterning. Only the most accomplished poets can afford to look that casual.

Robert MacNeil

FROM *WORDSTRUCK*[1]

ONE COURSE WAS memorable because the professor's enthusiasm was so infectious. It was a small seminar in Chaucer, given to four students by George Johnston, a thin man with large eyes and a prominent adam's apple. A poet himself, he brought such a sense of fresh delight, such spontaneity to Chaucer, that I caught it like a virus. The principal works we had to study became a joy, particularly *Troilus and Criseyde*. Johnston read aloud a lot and, with his accent in my ear, I read to myself. The delicacy, psychological subtlety, and atmosphere Chaucer managed within the disciplines of his verse form, and the sweetness of his expression, left a lasting impression. There is no more beguiling scene in English literature than when Pandarus at the last insinuates the two lovers together in the night, with the heavy rain falling outside, adding to their intimacy.

What caught my imagination, because Johnston stressed it, was the word *daunger*, Chaucer's term for the demeanour of a woman who is not available; her modesty, her reserve, translated today as aloofness, coldness, disdain.

Pandarus, encouraging Criseyde to be warmer to Troilus, says,

> So lat youre *daunger* sucred ben a lite
> (Let your aloofness sweeten up a little),

and warns her that old age will break it down in the end:

> And elde daunteth *daunger* at the laste.

And when they are finally entwined in each other's arms — as Chaucer describes it, like honeysuckle twisted about a tree — he declares,

> Awey, thow foule *daunger* and thow feare,
> And lat hem in this hevene blisse dwelle,
> That is so heigh that al ne kan I telle!
> (Away with reserve and fear
> And let them dwell in this heavenly bliss
> That is greater than I can describe.)

[1]Robert MacNeil. *Wordstruck: A Memoir*. New York: Viking, 1989. 180–82.

Chaucer's meaning suddenly hit me because I was having direct experience of the ability of a woman to transmit receptivity to advances or indifference, alternately, like an invisible magnetic field force — suddenly on, suddenly off. It is a mechanism by which a woman restores her privacy and, in a sense, restores innocence. Criseyde was a widow, yet projected the aura of an innocent girl.

It intrigued me then and still does that, despite our abundance of words to describe psychological states, we no longer have a term for this most common human experience, fundamental to relations between the sexes. *Daunger* survives only as an obsolete form of *danger* and, for the curious, in Chaucer.

The years at Carleton would have been worth it for that alone. Chaucer is not an author one cracks easily, without expert guidance and inspiration.

Sean Kane

THE ONE WHO HEARD

"THREE APPLES FELL from heaven: one for the teller, one for the listener, and one for the one who heard." So goes an Armenian saying — you will hear it quoted often in the great revival of storytelling that is happening today in many places. The teller? The listener? That's easy. They make up the storytelling act. But who is "the one who heard"? I imagine someone who transcends the storytelling act altogether, an insider to what story conveys in its arcs of almost uncatchable truth, someone half inside their oral culture and half out there with the Muse, daughter of the weathergod and the spirit of a mountain. One feels storytellers speaking in code here. Who are they speaking to precisely? What kind of singular individual is "the one who heard"?

First of all, that someone is a wholly mythic person. By mythic person, I mean an individual formed so entirely on the values conveyed by traditional stories that he or she will go out to live their truth. This is stretching the term "myth" a bit, because not all oral literature is myth. But storytellers are the first to assume that the values of the mythtellers pass into the other traditional story-forms, and are kept in suspended animation in them. Mythic knowing passes especially into the wondertale, so in talking about mythic values I mean also, with a spin on them, wondertale values. And I mean to a lesser degree hero-story values, even nursery-rhyme values. They are all mythic. I mean the whole unformulated philosophy of life that is implied in oral tradition. Let us call it mythic, and ask if there is any way we can still go out and live its truth.

What are mythic values? Most broadly defined, they are the values that evolved from thousands of years of people's living on the Earth on the Earth's own terms — not in terms of some record of human history. There is an Earth-relatedness in myth that is still echoing in the wondertale.

Myth typically involves two worlds, with a boundary between them. The one world is the world of human ingenuity. The other world is what we can call the Otherworld of spiritual ingenuity. The two ingenious worlds behave quite differently — they have different thinking styles — but when they meet memorable things happen. Power is passed from one world to the other, for the other to use. The two worlds pursue their own concerns behind their domain-walls, but sometimes they play trick-or-treat with each other: they borrow or steal or exchange or leave gifts, always with the fortuitous outcome of ensuring the balanced survival of both worlds — the ingenuity of human culture and the world of Earth's nurture.

Myths, holding this double-universe together in narrative, project a basic plot involving passage from one world to the other. Then back again — because it is a prime directive of myth that beings cannot live long in the habitat that is not their own. So the plot may propel a human from this world to the Otherworld to bring back something valuable to humans. That something valuable may be the spirit of a person departed before her time, or it may be knowledge of where the bear is to be hunted, or knowledge of the weather and the right time for planting, or some other divine knowledge. In myth, such passages usually entail an animal guide, or the seeker's assumption of an animal form, first in order to cross the boundary, then to negotiate with the animal-spirits. You will recognize this passage across a boundary as the archetypal plot of the shaman's dream-quest or, in agricultural myths, the underworld descent. That plot is still going strong in the wondertale and fairy tale. The goddess of the boundary is still there, though she may be reduced to a talking mouse; the Otherworld deities have been reduced to ogres or witches or trolls. Yet the hero, like a shaman, brings something back, even if it is a princess awakened from a spell. Jack brings back from the sky-giants of the beanstalk a harp that sings with a human voice and a hen that lays golden eggs — the gifts of the gods: music and fertility.

Movement can be the other way too. A spirit-being from the Otherworld comes to live in this human world for a spell, like the goddess Étaíne of ancient Irish literature. She leaves behind the gifts of fertility before she is recalled to her higher duties. "Tonight you have heard the music of Faërie," Étaíne tells Eochy, King of Ireland, "and echoes of it shall be in the harpstrings of Ireland forever." In this telling of the myth by the wondertale artist Alice Kane, Étaíne has "put into one year the joy of a lifetime" — but she has to go back. In mythic narrative, you have to go back to your side of the boundary.[1]

If this is myth's structure, then myth's values are those that help one live completely in the everyday while negotiating with the mysterious Others. I won't sketch a whole ethics of mythic values. You know from traditional stories what

[1]"The Golden Fly," in Alice Kane, *The Dreamer Awakes* (Peterborough: Broadview Press, 1995), 83–92, at 92. This is a retelling of a story of the same name by Ella Young in *Celtic Wonder Tales* (1910, reissued Edinburgh: Floris Books, 1985, 127–41). For the original form of the story, see Sean Kane, *Wisdom of the Mythtellers* (Peterborough: Broadview Press, 1994), 90–101, where the myth is used to illustrate the concept of boundary.

they are — a heart for adventure; a sense of one's own singularity; generosity to creatures in need; an openness or flexibility or dreaminess or courtesy of mind that you see in the wondertale simpleton; above all, courage and cunning. Mostly, it is not being possessive of what you have — your name, your identity, your destiny, your spiritual or material wealth. You do not hoard things. This injunction against hoarding is strong in hunter-gatherer myths, which reason that hoarding ends spontaneous exchange with an earth who can usually be trusted to provide. Even in the wondertale, the villains are the ones who hoard — the witch counting her victims' skulls or the troll counting his gold. There are other values too — but these are the well-springs of what I will call a mythic ethical sense. And my question is: can these values — should these values — be lived in today's society?

First, can they? And then, should they?

Can they? I say — yes, they can! I know this having been raised on myth and wondertale. Now this upbringing may not seem like anything special and worth sharing. Probably all of us who write or study literature were raised on the old storybooks. We know the old stories by heart. We are full of their values. But I was a sort of test-case of the captivated listener. That is because I was brought up by Alice Kane and her stories — not only her stories, but stories by my aunt's colleagues in the Boys and Girls' Division of the Toronto Public Library during its golden age.

Is the golden age of children's librarianship still within the reach of common memory? I hope it is. George Johnston at his eighty-fifth year, and Alice Kane at her ninetieth, give us cause to remember — to remember how the librarians worked their complex magic on children. How each librarian was an academic specialist in some branch of literature for children: Alice Kane specialized in the literary wondertale; Helen Armstrong, trained by W.P. Ker at Edinburgh, handled epic and saga. These specialists in story would present research papers to each other in the hours before the children came in. Each librarian had to learn to tell three new stories a week, from the best versions available. The librarians had to lie flat on their backs with the Toronto Telephone Directory on their abdomens, and try to raise it three inches. I'm sure none of today's revivalist storytellers do that! In short, they were, as someone has said, a guild of women artists masquerading as children's librarians.

They were my babysitters. Because my mother was often sick, and died when I was young, I was babysat by the staff of the Toronto Public Library Boys and Girls' Division — but chiefly by Alice. I felt as the young King Arthur must have felt, educated by the faerie Otherworld.

Yes, I'm sure they practised their pernicious theories of oral literacy on me, their captive subject. I believe I was provided with just the right story at just the right age. I'm certain that the storybooks came flowing in artfully planned succession. The combined lore and witchcraft of the T.P.L. Boys and Girls' Division was tried and tested on my uncomprehending innocence.

For I was the ideal subject, you see. I was the ideal subject for an education in story. That is to say, I was imaginative and alienated. It is the perfect preparation to be the product of myth. I will say something about imagination and alienation later on. But first I must mythify my childhood some more.

I don't want to mythify it excessively — but you should see that not having a mother, and having a father who was powerful and remote, put me naturally in wondertale space. I was the perfect wondertale hero in the making. King Arthur was like me. Odysseus was like me. The children in Grimm and Asbjørnsen and Afanas'ev were like me. All my heroes were like me. I had no other ideal of proper behaviour except to be a hero and transgress the norms of the social. That is what I mean by imaginative and alienated. Never far away was Aunt Alice, or one of that sisterhood from the realm where things come true. In the serendipitous style of the faerie Otherworld, they kept — they still do keep — appearing and disappearing when needed.

So you see? I am a sort of ideal specimen.

What did that total education in story do for me? Well, I learned all about trolls. Do you know about trolls? Even today, you have to learn the rules for dealing with trolls. The fact about trolls is this: they can do only one thing — their own thing — well. They're good at the tasks they do, so you should never try to argue with them on their own ground. They are in charge of monotonous repetitive functions. For example, near the Faroe Islands, Christian Matras says, there is the weather troll who makes all the fog in the North Sea. In George Johnston's translation:

> Now it is winter and almost night
> and the troll sits and cards batt
> in some stone that winds hug
> and sucks man-marrow and chews rag.
>
> And the troll cards and the troll cards
> and heaps up gray stuff yards and yards,
> wind lays about and slings troll-gray,
> and has a feel that is all coal-gray.[2]

[2]"Weather Troll," by Christian Matras, in *Rocky Shores: An Anthology of Faroese Poetry*, compiled and translated by George Johnston (Paisley, Scotland: Wilfion Books, 1981), 8.

Do you hear the monotony of it? They kill you with monotony before they eat you.

Trolls are everywhere. You can't move on this planet without running into a troll. The government accountants who reject your income-tax return — they're trolls. The entire management of the modern university from the dean up — they're trolls too. The claims adjusters who terminate your home insurance unless you replace the more than one-quarter of your plumbing which is non-copper — more trolls. The student loans officers at the bank — they're all trolls. The administration of a nursing home for senior citizens — still more trolls! They're everywhere. Sucking the marrow out of your bones and spreading thick gray fog.

And, as I say, you don't argue with them on their own terms, or they just grow more heads. You don't ask them why they think they own that bridge. Instead you say to them something like this: "You want me to pay back my student loan? But look at the guy behind me — he owes more. Get him!" And then the person behind him says, "Me? What about the guy behind me? He owes tons more." You see? You tie them up in their own bureaucratic hunger. You can't cut off their heads because they'll just grow three more — that's what bureaucracies do — but you can get those three heads arguing with each other while you steal away. That's cunning — one of the qualities of the folktale hero. The cultural theorist Walter Benjamin calls it *Untermut* — under-spiritedness. It is one of the jujitsu-like powers flanking tricksterism.[3]

Then there's the other flanking power — courage, *Übermut*. It leads to over-spirited situations. At the age of seven, I got lost in the mountains of British Columbia. My mother, never happy east of the Rockies, took me to a ghost town in the Kootenays. There, in a cottage halfway up the mountainside overlooking the abandoned silvermines, she collected flowers and wrote poetry in the margins of books. The first night there, we walked along a forest path to the ruined smelting mill, with the river hurtling straight down behind it. "Don't go off the path," she said.

Now, readers of the tale of adventure and transformation will at once recognize these words as a form of the negative injunction or prohibition. In myth, they warn of the boundary you cross at your peril. Prohibitions, of course, exist to be broken. That's what prohibitions are for. I have a homespun

[3]"The Storyteller: Reflections on the Works of Nikolai Leskov," in Walter Benjamin, *Illuminations*, edited by Hannah Arendt, translated by Harry Zohn (New York: Schocken, 1968), 83–109, at 102.

theory about this, based on my checkered career as a parent.

The theory is that at any stage of parenting, the parent will underestimate the child's actual age. Simultaneously, the child will overestimate the parent's actual age. The ongoing communication gap that results is called "growing up." "Don't do this," the parent says. And immediately the child goes and does the forbidden thing. He has to find out the meaning of life for himself. She has to earn her own freedom. Because freedom can't be given — the novelist Margaret Laurence used to say that, in relation to leaving a marriage: you can't ask for freedom; you have to take it. Then the child, trapped like Adam and Eve in an infantile paradise, reaches for the one thing that is forbidden. Growth. The freedom to find your own destiny. To freely choose good over evil.

That long night in the Kootenay mountains I learned fear. There is a Russian wondertale about "The Boy Who Learned the Meaning of Fear." I learned the meaning of fear that night. I have never really been afraid of anything since — least of all trolls. And I have never felt lost since.

I learned something else too. This came around midnight or so, after I had skirted mine shafts and glacial rivers, learning the meaning of fear. Another outlook took hold. I made a lean-to for myself, right out of the children's book *Wildwood Wisdom*. I found a small pinetree root that made a perfect club. (The reporter for the *New Denver Daily* found this poignant: when asked what the club was for, the boy replied that it was in case he met a wolf.) Then I slept. In the morning, I climbed the tallest tree and looked around the mountains. There was a logging road down there. Where there's a road, there's people. Remember, the books say, it's not you who are lost, it's your camp that's lost. So I spent the morning moving down through the forest, reaching that road. "Heel first on moss, toe first on rock." Pause and be still for five minutes; listen if any animal is around. By some instinct, I turned right instead of left, and walked into town from the direction of the Slocan Valley.

I joined the back of the crowd of a search-party that was being instructed by a Mountie. Shot-guns and tracker-dogs. "Johnny comes marching home again after night in the wilderness" was the headline on the New Denver paper.

I survived. You see — I simply became a wondertale hero. I had a trust, which the wondertale gives, that lost children will usually be found, that adventures turn out all right in the end.

I went back to that place of initiation last summer. Sandon is still there — a ghost-town in the mountains; in fact, it was a ghost city: during the silver boom, it had three hotels, several churches, two hundred prostitutes; it was the first city in British Columbia to have electricity. Now, the place is suspended in the timelessness of the mountains: the wooden store-fronts, the rusted ore buckets, the sharp smell of minerals in the tailings.

I found the road where the Mountie carried me home to my mother on his shoulders — I remembered how disappointed I was that he was not wearing a scarlet tunic. I found the cottage on the mountainside where my distraught mother — her hold on reality tenuous in the best of circumstances — waited on the porch. The roof has caved in, and it is covered with moss, but the antiquated refrigerator is still there on the porch. I found the path to the mill. I found the precise place where I left the path to try to take a shortcut home to surprise my mother. And I retraced the first part of that journey I made years ago, when I was seven and crossed the boundary into the forest of the Mysterious Others. I knew every step of the way.

I say "boundary" because I became a person of myth as well as of wondertale. I crossed from the human world into the dark unknown of the animal powers. In effect, I behaved like an animal there — I trusted my wits and instincts. Perhaps I became a mythic person.

Yes — mythic values *can* be lived in our time — but you have to be thrown into a certain situation to live them. The larger question is should they? Should mythic values be deliberately lived in our time?

My opinion, for what it's worth, is that we live increasingly in a world very much like that of the folk wondertale. We have to use our wits to survive. We're up against powers that are bigger than ourselves. They are morally ambiguous; things that are bad for you these institutions present as good. Call them corporations and banks; Saint Paul called them "principalities and powers." They make themselves too shadowy to overthrow. Yet their actions are as capricious and arbitrary as any aristocrat riding his horse over your vegetable patch. Or any Grendel bursting into your home. Beside them, we are little people. Little people from broken families — there are so many broken families again nowadays. When a student asks me, what is a little person, I say: someone who owes the banks a student loan of twenty-four thousand dollars is a little person.

There are no wolves in the wilderness now, nor highwaymen — but in our urban peasant world the news is all of rape and abuse and murder. We have in our midst ogres like Paul Bernardo and his accomplice.

The peasant wondertale counsels a spirit of ironic resourcefulness. Tricksterism, as a way of survival, has no illusions about an apocalyptic overthrow of the powers that be. Instead, tricksterism works within the system, turning its vanities and superiorities to the trickster's advantage.

The myths and wondertales do something else too — all this is such a secret that I'm not sure I ought to give it away. But this is how the old stories work their magic on the uncomprehending innocent. They seek out the most imaginative and the most alienated among us, and they give that special individual a sense of her own uniqueness. This is the great untold right-under-your-nose secret of literature. I will tell you that secret now. Literature is a *subversive elitist activity*. Literature is elitist because essentially it involves insiders conspiring with insiders: literature is alienated people with imagination speaking in code for other alienated people with imagination.

Consider how deviously this system of recruitment works.

A young boy, for example, has lost his parents. So many of the oral myths begin this way — with the orphan as hero. He is isolated from the other children playing in the village. He hears a myth about a powerful shaman or a hero who also lost his parents when he was young. That listener will feel picked out especially by that story. He will feel it was meant just for him, and he will go on to live its mythic truth. Or a day-dreaming girl, held in subjection by her older worldly sisters, and seeing her mother's face in the ashes of the fireplace, hears a wondertale about another Cinderella just like herself. The listener will feel the story was meant privately for her ears. It is just for her alone. The ones without imagination, of course, hear nothing special in the entertainment. They are never allowed to know that a special magic went on just out of the range of ordinary hearing.

In literature, whether it is told or written, there are the tellers and there are the listeners. But, let me quote the Armenian saying again: "Three apples fell from heaven: one for the teller, one for the listener, and one for the one who heard." There is also and always "the one who heard." That singular imaginative and alienated soul is the real one the stories are after. That person will go out and live the truth of the story as a hero. If the person lives long enough, he or she will become a storyteller. Thus an elite minority is recruited from generation to generation among the small minority of the human population that is fully imaginative. I mean the small minority in any sub-population — English professors or garbage collectors.

This Reception Theory of literature I will call the Anne Shirley theory, because in her empowered singularity Anne "with an e" is one of the literature's most typical products. Anne of Green Gables believes that all of literature was meant just for her ears alone. So, of course, does every other avid and alienated imaginer.

Wayne Grady

ON BECOMING A TRANSLATOR,
OR BLESS THEE! THOU ART TRANSLATED

A FEW YEARS ago, I was asked to contribute a short essay to a collection being put together to raise money for a local literacy program, and I wrote a piece entitled "How I Became a Translator." It is a true story. One day, I wrote, I was driving to Montreal along the 401, listening to Radio-Canada, the French-language CBC-FM station, when the announcer came on the air and said she was going to play "'Les Feux d'artifices' par Georges Frédéric Handel."

"Feux d'artifices," I said to myself, possibly aloud. "What is that in English, I wonder?"

Just at that moment, I happened to be passing a large red-and-white building almost exactly at the border between Ontario and Quebec. In the parking lot of the building was an 18-foot trailer also painted white, with huge red letters on the side. It was functioning as a kind of billboard, and the letters said, "FEUX D'ARTIFICES — FIREWORKS."

"Thank you," I said, vaguely wishing at the time that I had asked a more profound question, something like "Will the Blue Jays win the World Series this year?" But I hadn't. I had asked to be a translator.

I always feel a bit diffident about being a translator. In fact, the feux d'artifices story is only partly true (as all stories are), because I had been translating for quite some time when it happened. Like many translators, I had more or less fallen into translating. (As Octavio Paz puts it, "I didn't decide, really [to become a translator]. It was — well, as always — an accident.") In 1981, I was editing an anthology of Canadian short stories for Penguin (it eventually became *The Penguin Book of Modern Canadian Short Stories* — I more or less fell into editing that, too, but that's another story), and I wanted to include in it several stories by Québécois writers, and since Penguin had no budget for translating (it was not "a wholly Canadian-owned publisher" and so could not get money for translating from the Canada Council), I took a deep breath and translated the stories myself, gratis. And thus became a translator.

No, not even that is the whole truth. I had, after all, lived in Montreal for five years, and before that in Ottawa, and before that in Sept-Iles, a mining town on Quebec's north shore a few inches up the map from Baie Comeau. Although I would not have called myself bilingual in any of those places, I would have said I spoke French *pas couramment, mais comme il faut*. (I now say I can read French better than I speak it, but that is also true of my English.) Montreal in the seventies was a heady time for translators: street names were being made politically correct, for example. In Montreal, someone changed Mountain Street, named after Jacob Mountain, who in 1793 was the first Anglican bishop of Quebec, to rue de la Montagne. It made me wonder why Peel Street wasn't changed to rue de la Pelure, and Guy to rue Zèbre.

Perhaps in response to this transitional atmosphere, I had tried my hand at translating. Certainly it wasn't so much a conscious decision as something more akin to osmosis. Robert Fitzgerald, an American poet and translator, has talked about "the other and more serious way" of becoming a translator, in which "one finds in poems and language some quality one appropriates for oneself and wishes to reproduce." For Fitzgerald it was François Villon, whose lines rattled around in his head for nine years before he took a notion to set them down in English. For me, it was a poem by Emile Nelligan, "La Romance du Vin," an unabashed ode to the studied accidie of an adolescent poet that fit my own mood at the time:

> This beautiful May night. This merry night in May.
> Somewhere a church organ's cold, monotonous chords
> Pierce the day's heart with such melancholy swords
> That it of course dies, releasing a sour bouquet.

I was also interested in the purely technical challenge of retaining the poem's original metre and rhyme-scheme — the alexandrines and the abba — which in English produces such a satisfying tension between the expansiveness of prose and the parsimony of poetry, and this tension, I thought, reflected the contrast between the delights of spring and the poet's own sense of imminent doom:

> But as long as the heavens are studded with hope,
> And one hymn for gilded youth can strike a refrain,
> Though the day croaks out its last breath, I won't complain,
> Not I, who through this dark, hellish springtime must grope.

It wasn't a huge or distinguished body of work — there were also some poems by Marie-Claire Blais and Ronsard with which I will not detain the reader — but when the Penguin anthology came along, the idea of translating some stories for it didn't come entirely out of ignorance and cheek. I went to work and produced, *à coup de dictionnaire*, two tolerably readable versions of stories that I particularly liked, Jacques Ferron's "Les Chroniques de l'Anse St.-Roch" and Gérard Bessette's "Romance."

The immediate repercussions were mild to the point of nonexistent. No one, it seemed, noticed, or cared, which I took to be a good sign, an indication that at least the translations did not cry out in their awfulness. When I showed my translated version of "Romance" to Bessette, his only comment was that I had mistranslated "dix-huit jours" as "eighteen hours," which I excused as a kind of mental typographical error: jours into hours. The two words have the same false association as "time" and "tide," which have little in common but three letters and a disinclination to wait for man. But that was it for feedback.

The long-term consequences, however, were more important. For one thing, I began to feel like a translator. They were my first published translations. I had, of course, no theory of literary translation (I still haven't, although at least now I've heard a few). But the process itself was eerily familiar to me. I had enjoyed it. I felt I had become closer to two writers I had not formerly known. I also felt closer to another culture, one that I had known only peripherally, as a kind of looker-on. For I had definitely been a looker-on. I remember, for example, one of the last St.-Jean-Baptiste Day celebrations to take place in Place Jacques Cartier, in Old Montreal, in the early 1970s, just after I'd moved to Montreal. I'd gone down to watch the festivities. When I got there, the square was full of people, singing patriotic songs, sitting on cases of beer, passing joints around, laughing, minding their own business. I felt very comfortable, leaning against the wall of the Hotel Iroquois, watching the crowd. Suddenly, at the north end of the square, in front of l'Hôtel de Ville, a line of policemen began to form. Each cop was wearing a white helmet and carrying a rubber night-stick and a plexiglas shield. When the line stretched the entire width of Place Jacques Cartier, it began to move into the square, pushing everyone in it down toward the river, squeezing them out of the square and into the small side streets. I was standing about half-way down the square when the line of policemen began moving toward me and, to my everlasting shame, it never occurred to me to get out of the way. It wasn't my affair. The cops were clearing the square of québecois protesters, not English on-lookers. When the end cop swung his night-stick at me and pushed me into the crowd, along with everyone else, I felt like saying he had made a mistake. I wasn't part of this culture. I hadn't yet become a translator.

Years later, after the Penguin book came out, my friend Fred Wardle, who was then president of Methuen Publications in Toronto, returned from the Frankfurt Book Fair with the English-language rights to a novel by

Antonine Maillet, *Christophe Cartier de la Noisette, dit Nounours*, and he and
I were having a celebratory drink in the Montreal Bistro. He asked me if I
knew of any translator who might be interested in taking it on.

"What about me?" I asked.

"You?" he replied, surprised. "Are you a translator?" As I've said, fallout
from the Penguin book hadn't been thick on the ground.

"Yes," I said, "I am."

Feeling like a translator is a kind of private pleasure. Translators in Canada,
I found, enjoy a relatively subdued reputation — relative to other kinds of
writers, relative to translators in other countries, and relative to the status
they ought to enjoy in any country — and I've often asked myself why this
should be so, especially in an officially bilingual nation. In 1988, I was invited
to Norway to attend the Annual General Meeting of the Norwegian Translators
Association, to participate in the workshops and to deliver a paper on
translating in Canada. My paper was about how the Canadian system worked.
The Norwegian system, I learned, is an extremely interesting one, and one
that ought to be emulated in Canada. All writers' associations in Norway —
associations of poets, playwrights, novelists, screen-writers, journalists, and
translators — belong to a single umbrella organization, the Norwegian Writers
Union. All are housed in a single building — one of the oldest buildings in
Oslo, a beautiful, huge, rambling, post-and-beam or maybe mud-and-wattle
warren of secretariats, meeting rooms, and closets — not a long walk from
the Grand Hotel, where Ibsen drank tea daily, although not while I was there.
(I did, however, buy a second-hand copy of *A Doll's House* and, while drinking
beer at what was reputed to have been Ibsen's table in the Grand, flog away
at it with a pocket dictionary, to absolutely no avail.) The associations all
share such costly items as Xerox machines and coffee-makers, and their
funding comes entirely from Norway's version of the Public Lending Rights
Commission — in other words, every time a Norwegian takes a book from
a library, a few kroner are dropped into the coffers of the Writers Union. This
amounts to about 250,000 kroner a year. The Union takes 10 percent off the
top for administrative expenses, and the rest is put into a trust fund from
which member associations provide grants and even loans — to buy
computers, for instance — to Union members. This seems to me to be an
admirable arrangement of things.

Having just spent a year as Treasurer of the Canadian Literary Translators
Association, I had a fairly good idea of how things worked in this country,
and reason to be envious of the Norwegians. The differences are instructive.

For one thing, it is not only possible for a Norwegian translator to earn a living by translating, it is customary, it is expected. Translators are paid for their work by publishers — not by the government, as is the case in Canada. They are full members of the Writers Union — not a sort of subspecies in the literary ecosystem, as is the case in Canada, where translators are not even allowed to become associate members of the Writers Union. And they are not paid by the word, as we are in Canada, but by the quarto sheet (a printers' proof of 16 pages), so that someone translating poetry, or a novel with a lot of meaningless and monosyllabic dialogue (Samuel Beckett, say), earns as much as someone translating Kierkegaard or Sontag, who fill their pages to the edges. Applicants to the Norwegian Translators Association must have published two book-length translations — not one, as is the case here — and the quality of the translation is judged by a committee established by the Association. They must be literary translations; no translator of Harlequin Romances or even Barbara Cartland need apply.

I gave my talk on how things worked in Canada. Canadian translators must have a contract with a publisher — a wholly Canadian-owned publisher — in order to receive the government grant. The work must be Canadian, either from French into English or English into French. If the Council accepts the application, the translator receives 10 cents per word, half of it up front, 40 percent upon submission of an acceptable manuscript, and 10 percent when the book is published. All this was so familiar to me that I explained it almost without thinking about it. For an average-sized novel of 80,000 words, which would take the better part of a year to translate, we would receive over a period of about 18 months a total of $8,000. No one, obviously, could live by translating full-time.

What was worse, I said, translators in Canada worked almost anonymously in many cases: it had only been within the last few years that some of us could expect to see our names on the covers of the books we translated. Usually they were buried on the acknowledgement page somewhere below the name of the person who had sharpened the cover-designer's pencils. Translators did not normally receive royalties for the sale of their translations. Translators were not often mentioned in reviews of the books they had translated. They were not then eligible for Canada Council reading grants (they are now, as long as they are reading along with the original writer — to give their translations legitimacy), and so they were (are) almost never invited to read from their translations. And, although translators were given a Governor General Award each year, until 1989 those awards were presented at a different time and in a different city than the same awards for fiction, poetry, nonfiction, and children's-book illustration. Translations, in short, were not considered the literary creations of the translator, perhaps not as literary creations at all, but rather as somewhat lesser versions of the original book, a kind of second edition, a sort of necessary evil occasioned by the unfortunate but temporary fact that many English Canadians had not yet had time to learn how to read French. In the unspoken hierarchy of literary production (poets as CEOs, novelists as vice-presidents, short-story writers as managers, and so on), translators figured somewhere down in the typing pool.

I thought I had delineated the plight of the Canadian translator in a very satisfactory manner: underpaid, undervalued, neglected, disenfranchized. After the talk, however, the first question from the audience completely stunned me. It seemed, at the time, almost irrelevant.

"Do you mean to say," a listener asked, "that Canadian translators spend all their time translating other Canadians?"

The question instantly clarified for me the situation of the Canadian translator. In Norway, translators spend all their time translating non-Norwegians. Since something like 80 percent of all the books sold in Norwegian bookstores were originally written by non-Norwegians, translators in Norway perform an extremely important function, and one that is recognized as such by any literate Norwegian, of whom there is an extremely high proportion. Without Norwegian translators, no one in Norway would be able to read any book that had not been written by a Norwegian writer.

(This is not literally true, since many literate Norwegians can also read Danish and Swedish, and some can read Finnish and German, and quite a few can read English and French. But I am sticking to my point because reading a book in a language that is not in one's mother tongue is not the same as reading one that is, and most Norwegians prefer to read translations rather than the original works. There is also an argument to be made for the idea that reading a book in a language that is not one's own is in fact an act of translation.)

The situation in English Canada is exactly the opposite. As English-speaking people, we are a small island in a vast archipelago of English-speaking peoples. We can read books written in the United States, Great Britain, Australia, New Zealand, much of Africa, and parts of the West Indies. Currently, 85 percent of the books sold in Canadian bookstores are written by non-Canadians and imported from foreign countries, but all of them were originally written in English or have already been translated into English. And of the 15 percent of books sold in Canadian bookstores that are Canadian books, almost all of them are written in English. Figures from the Canada Council Translation Programme show that only about 40 literary books a year are translated from Canadian French into English. Of foreign books sold in Canada that have been translated into English from some foreign language, then, almost all of them are translated for us by translators from other countries, usually the United States or England. It is tempting to say that, in economic terms at least, we don't need translators in Canada at all. We don't need Canadian translators of, say, Spanish books, because some American will eventually translate them; and if translations of books written in French by Canadians were to disappear from the bookshelves tomorrow, only eighty people would notice. No wonder Canadian translators feel anonymous, undervalued, beleaguered, and belittled. In the economics of the marketplace, they are.

But ought they to be? After all, the same may be said of Canadian writers (and, during the NAFTA talks, it was said of Canadian culture in general — not what is it, but who needs it?). Let us return to Norway for a moment. Every book read by a Norwegian has been either written or translated by a Norwegian. It is impossible to overstate what this does for a Norwegian's sense of his or her cultural self. Norwegians know who they are. They have no difficulty distinguishing themselves from, say, Swedes, and will do so at the drop of a cheese Danish. Upon the Danes, by the way, they cast a regal and baleful regard, even though — or perhaps because — Norway was a province of Denmark until 1814. Few English Canadians are likely to agree with Ibsen's remark, in *An Enemy of the People*, that "the minority is always right." And it is no accident that Knut Hamsun's greatest novel, *Mysteries*, is about a young man for whom all contact with other people is painful and meaningless except in its effect upon his own mind. When a Norwegian reads a book by, say, Italo Calvino, he or she reads it in the words, idioms, phrases, expressions, and cultural assumptions supplied by a fellow Norwegian.

When we read a novel by Italo Calvino — say, *If on a Winter's Night a Traveller...*, published in Toronto by Lester & Orpen Dennys in 1981 — we are ingesting the words, idioms, phrases, expressions, and cultural assumptions of its American translator, William Weaver. Now, Weaver is a fine translator, and I am not going to commit the tedious folly of going through his text and pointing out how a Canadian might have rendered such-and-such a line or expression. Weaver is, however, an American, and Americans do not speak the same English as English-speaking Canadians speak. Americans do not live in a Canadian cultural context, and it is in a cultural context that translations, no less than poems and novels, exist. A great many Canadians would no doubt ask themselves what I can possibly mean by that, which merely demonstrates the depth and seriousness of the problem. Many of us think there is no linguistic difference between the United States and Canada, and where there is no linguistic difference it is hard to postulate a cultural difference. And part of the reason we think it, is that the vast majority of our written cultural artifacts — books and translations of books — come to us from outside Canada.

This has produced a kind of numbness in us when we talk about Canadian works. When, for the 1993 season, the Stratford Festival decided to present Rostand's *Cyrano de Bergerac*, it initially chose a new translation by Canadian translator John Murrell. In late January, the theatre suddenly announced it had changed its mind, and was going to use an older translation by Anthony Burgess. No reason was given for the switch. Murrell's translation, performed in Edmonton with Canadian actor Brent Carver as Cyrano, was hailed as "a heroic masterpiece" by critic Urjo Kareda, so it probably wasn't a question of calibre. Stratford quite simply didn't see the difference.

"Translation," says the American translator Edwin Honig, "is an activity that in its purposes lies at the root of all art." What are those purposes? And what does it do to our cultural identity when most of that activity takes place for us in another country? Isn't it just as important to have Canadian translations of foreign texts as it is to have Canadian texts? Perhaps even more important, since all writers read a great many books before they begin to write. Translations may be the first line of defence against invasion by a foreign culture. How can we have a sense of who we are, of how we differ from other cultures, if in order to read literature from another culture we have to do so through the filter of yet another culture?

There are signs that this is changing. A few years ago the Ontario Arts Council set up a system (since cancelled) modelled loosely on the Canada Council's, except that it was aimed at translators who translate from non-official languages into English. There are many Canadian translators who translate from languages other than English or French. David Helwig's translations of stories by Anton Chekhov were published in Canada; George Woodcock's translation of *À la recherche du temps perdu* is eagerly awaited; George Johnston's translations of the Norse and Icelandic sagas as well as of modern Norwegian poets are universally admired, as I learned during my stay in Norway. Is there something in Johnston's northernness, in his shared experience, that makes him a fitting translator of Scandinavian verse, and a perfect interpreter of Norse reality to a Canadian audience?

Mentioning George Johnston made me realize I was lying again when I said that "La Romance du Vin" was my first translation. Many years ago I took a course in Old English from George, and produced for him at the end of it a translation of "The Seafarer." It is certainly true that something about the ancient mariner's experience of cold and ice touched a deep chord in me, and it may have been because I am Canadian, and know something about ice:

> Mæg ic be me sylfum   sodgied wrecan,
> siþas secgan,   hu ic geswincdagum
> earfodhwile   oft prowade,
> bitre breostceare   gebiden hæbbe,
> gecunnad in ceole   cearswelda fela.

The force and immediacy of the poem (when, thanks to George, I was finally able to read it) struck me between the eyes. Old English is a tough, rock-strewn, wave-bashing, no-nonsense sort of a language, and this anonymous poet had managed to make it sing and live. I was appalled by the standard 1902 translation by Alfred Cook and the unfortunately named Chauncey Tinker. As Messrs. Cook and Tinker confessed in their introduction, their translation "does not represent any particular theory of translation to the exclusion of others," and indeed the poem could hardly be said to have been translated at all, except in the sense that Bottom was. Here is the beginning of their "Seafarer," the same lines quoted above:

> I can sing of myself a true song, of my voyages telling,
> How oft through laborious days, through the wearisome hours
> I have suffered; have borne tribulations; explored in my ship,
> Mid the terrible rolling of waves, habitations of sorrow.

Yikes. The poet's furious (and almost Modern English) "bitre breostceare" becomes "I have suffered." No wonder he lived in habitations of sorrow. Ezra Pound's version was better:

> May I for my own self song's truth reckon,
> Journey's jargon, how I in harsh days
> Hardship endured oft.
> Bitter breast-cares have I abided,
> Known on my keel many a care's hold,
> And dire sea-surge.

At least Pound kept some of the poem's alliteration: "Bitre breostcaere gebiden hæbbe" is, literally, "bitter breast-care / have I abided." But even Pound soon flew off into his own stratosphere: at one point he rendered englum (angels) as English (Anglos?). How would he have fared as a street-sign translator in Montreal?

I still have my own stab at translating "The Seafarer." It starts out relatively sedately:

> I tell my own   true story,
> of my trials   my days of toil,
> and soothsay   how I suffered sore,
> how bitter breastcare   I have borne.

It goes on for a while in much the same vein. I still like the split lines, the alliteration, and the simplicity of the language. It isn't as good a translation as Pound's, in the long run, of course, but I'm working on it. It got me an A in George's course, but it got me much more than that in the end: it got me going as a translator.

Chris Faulkner

LETTER TO GEORGE (ABOUT
GRAVES, ROBERT AND PARIS, FRANCE)

HI GEORGE. HOW are you and Jeanne doing?

It's been a long time since we've seen each other, years even. Certainly it has been years since we passed comments about poetry, you and I. Years and years since we did our thing with David Jones, when Bill Blissett, "friend of poets," came up from Toronto and we had that little exhibition and a reading with the stuff Bill brought up from Toronto in a wooden box. There weren't many there but we read well and we all shared a passion for David Jones and his talents and I still have my modest David Jones collection and the poster from the event. I often wondered whether you liked him especially for his calligraphy because of your own deliberate hand. And I remember taking the exhibition materials in the wooden box (did it have a top) in my car on to George Whalley at Queen's whom I met then for the first time and with his parrot. Nervous, I was, nervous about meeting George and the parrot (noisy bugger, and spoiled rotten with George feeding him crackers while we tried to eat tomato soup that lunch four of us counting the parrot I remember). But in the end it was good, because we talked about wood engraving and there were lots of examples including David Jones to show. "Gruesome combination, knowledge and thought," as the poet said.

You know I got interested in David Jones because I was interested in the literature of the First World War and Robert Graves. And it was still Graves that I wanted to work on, even when I learned about David Jones and Sassoon and Owen and Blunden and Rosenberg and Ivor Gurney and all of the others those two years I sat wearing gloves without fingers in the library at the University of Manchester it was so cold and so damp it never ended. When I got to ask you what poets you liked after I came to Carleton you mentioned all kinds of people from David Jones to Cid Corman but I don't think you ever mentioned Robert Graves. I couldn't make sense of that reach of yours until I worked it out that why one likes some poets has nothing to do with science. Of course, that's not working it out exactly, is it? But there's the beauty. "I think we only learn / what is already there / in the grain."

I've been talking about film in the classroom for over twenty years now and I only discovered recently like a brick fell on my head that what obsesses me about film is what obsessed me about Robert Graves and the First World

War and that I've been talking about the same stuff all my life. That's not so bad as it sounds, actually. But it does mean that what I want to tell you about Robert Graves tells you just as much about why I was drawn to his work as it does about the work itself. Ditto for film. It's all about language really or languages, and one's own head, and then there's the world. It's not deep, it's just that you discover what obsesses you and you can't help going on with that even if you don't realize you're going on with it all the same. So now I go to Paris and watch movies. That is the capital of my Norse land, those are my sagas, with their tales of courage and retreat, trust and betrayal, treasure and waste.

I

GRAVES, ROBERT (IN ONE ANECDOTE)

I want to quote a passage from *Good-bye to All That* (London: Jonathan Cape, 1929). Graves is an instructor at the Bull-Ring, Le Havre:

> I was feeling a bit better after a few weeks at the base, though the knowledge that this was only temporary relief was with me all the time. One day I walked out of the mess to begin the afternoon's work on the drill ground. I had to pass by the place where bombing instruction was given. A group of men was standing around the table where the various types of bombs were set out for demonstration. There was a sudden crash. An instructor of the Royal Irish Rifles had been giving a little unofficial instruction before the proper instructor arrived. He had picked up a No. 1 percussion grenade and said: "Now lads, you've got to be careful with this chap. Remember that if you touch anything while you're swinging it, it will go off." To illustrate the point he rapped it against the edge of the table. It killed him and another man and wounded twelve others more or less severely. (243–44)

In this passage one can observe Graves' easy and inevitable style, its economy of phrase, its freedom from extravagance. The continuing appeal of *Good-bye to All That* is due in part to the clear, personal voice that comes through, without rhetorical overtones, without moralizing. Here, with the quickness of a man talking, is a vernacular English freedom, no solemn rhythms, no periodic structures, no romantic appeal, colloquial without being vulgar. Graves' is a paratactic style, sentences made up of independent clauses without much subordination. It is a feature of this unadorned and anti-rhetorical prose that it does not invite the reader to draw breath at his or her recognition of a "literary" device or a clever stroke of "style." Graves says of his prose that it was learned from a prep-school master, "a good man, who had taught me how to write English by eliminating all phrases that could be done without, and using verbs and nouns instead of adjectives and adverbs wherever possible. And where to start new paragraphs, and the difference between O and Oh. He was a very heavy man. He used to stand at his desk and lean on his thumbs until they bent at right angles" (41). (I like that, about his thumbs bending at right angles.)

Graves never interposes between the reader — or rather between himself — and the report of his experiences any stylistic virtuosities or contrivances. His prose is distinguished, instead, by a power of literal observation. It is suited to the description of actions, of persons and things in movement. It is not designed to describe or promote reflection, contemplation, introspection. It will not communicate intensity of feeling. Its intentions are self-defensive.

Now in itself a power of literal observation in the plain style is not enough to raise anyone's prose above the level of general competence. It certainly does not suffice to distinguish what is compelling about Graves' portrait of himself and his experiences in *Good-bye to All That*. So to talk of Graves' plain style, and to praise the power of observation that it allows, is not to say that the book writes itself, or that the author's presence is not marked. There is a definable tone which establishes Graves' relationship to the material he is dealing with. In the passage I have quoted concerning the accident with the No. 1 percussion grenade there is a matter-of-fact flatness effective for the purpose in hand. The anecdote is recounted to illustrate the omnipresence of death in or out of the trenches. The description ends bluntly, as the best means of conveying the consequences of the explosion and the indelibility of the scene. But that is not all. What is especially memorable about this passage is the folly of the "unofficial" instructor, because Graves draws attention to it by quoting his showy remarks. Unlike Edmund Blunden, say, whose *Undertones of War* (1928) is no less justly famous, Graves is interested in people, not landscapes. And not only their foibles, as here, but their strengths as well. Contrast, for example, the would-be instructor's foolhardiness with the bravery of Captain Samson who, when wounded in No Man's Land, "had forced his knuckles into his mouth to stop himself from crying out and attracting any more men to their death. He had been hit in seventeen places" (206). He was discovered in this attitude, dead.

But in the end, it is Graves' taste for the curious that distinguishes the human focus of *Good-bye to All That* (a man stuffs his knuckles into his mouth). And instead of lengthy description in the ruminative manner of Blunden, or of Siegfried Sassoon and his *Memoirs of an Infantry Officer* (1930), a quick sketch of "sights, faces, words, incidents" does the job ("Trench History," *The Nation and Athenaeum*, December 15, 1928, 420). Graves has said that "neither rhythmic repetition, adjectival profusion, nor quaintness of metaphor will convince a reader nearly so easily that such and such a house was disgustingly dirty and its proprietor an old wretch, as a simple, unemphatic anecdote of what happened early one Monday morning between the kitchen and the backdoor" (with Alan Hodge, *The Reader Over Your Shoulder* [New York: Macmillan, 1961], 38).

Good-bye to All That is really a succession of anecdotes, as Graves himself once acknowledged: "it was already roughly organized in my mind in the form of a number of short stories, which is the way that people find it easiest to be interested by the things that interest them" ("Robert Graves Replies," in *The Daily Mail*, December 16, 1929, 10). Some of these stories, like "Old Papa Johnson," found themselves outside the autobiography proper. Graves has been a prolific writer of short stories or, more accurately, of extended anecdotes, which are invariably sketches of slightly bizarre incidents or conversations, with himself directly involved: "Pure fiction is beyond my imaginative range," he said ("Introduction," to *Collected Short Stories* [New York: Doubleday, 1964], ix).

In *Good-bye to All That*, not surprisingly, the emphasis in one anecdote after another is invariably upon the contrast between one's shocking proximity to death and the ordinary or the everyday. It is this circumstance which, for Graves, "characterized the times." Given the supra-normality of the situation, incongruity becomes the master strategy for lending one's terrors a redemptive value. The recognition of incongruity may be the necessary safeguard against hysteria. That seems a legitimate response to the inscrutable absurdity of one's fate in certain circumstances. For Graves, the true measure of the response comes down to a matter of the risks one dare take with language in the face of lived experience.

What I have been trying to talk about, with the illustration from Robert Graves, is what is at stake in the wrestle with language, the risks involved in getting it right, for which the foolhardiness of the "unofficial" instructor with the No. 1 percussion grenade is the anecdotal equivalent, in life as in words. At one extreme, there is the danger of "volubility"; at the other, we lose "self-possession": yet we cannot do without "the cool web of language." Language is safeguard and obstacle. Robert Graves' best poetry deals with emotional vicissitudes for which his yard-stick is the shocks of war: "Warning to Children," "The Chink," "A Former Attachment," "Lost Acres," "The Legs," "It Was All Very Tidy," "Despite and Still," "The Shot"; and there are others. All of these poems are also about the necessities of poetry itself.

In the long run, one can only write about that which is always getting in, that which always will get in (the water in the hold, the shadow cast in brightest sunlight, the dust on one's shoe). That which threatens to make writing impossible also makes it necessary. Silence is not an option. Don't get me wrong. Writing doesn't contain; containment would be meaningless. Writing doesn't hold off the flood or the shadows or the dust; if it did we wouldn't need it. Even for those of us who mostly teach it rather than write it, in words or in images, it is not difficult to understand why one ought to take language very seriously indeed.

II

PARIS, FRANCE (IN FIVE ACTS)

1. ARRIVAL

The first time I went to Paris with my imperfect French, I came up out of the Métro (line no. 10, direction Austerlitz) at Place Maubert, and on breaking the surface experienced that spatial disorientation familiar to all underground travellers. I was simply at a loss for coordinates. To reach my destination down what I knew to be a little side alley somewhere nearby, I had to choose between six or seven streets big and small leading off the square. Was I to go east or west, right or left? Time had passed, too, since I had plunged into the comfort provided by the temporal emptiness of the Métro ride and an early darkness now obscured an unfamiliar quarter.

A young woman approached as I fluttered with indecision about which way to go. Boldly, I asked for my little side alley. She turned back, and pointed off into the artificial light and dark, apparently in the direction from which she had just come, and said, politely, "Normalement, c'est la deuxième à gauche." I thanked her, took one step, and a couple more, in the direction her finger indicated, then stopped, puzzled. What did she mean, "Normalement"? Did she mean that sometimes the little side alley is there and sometimes it isn't? Was the geography of the city but a phantasmagoria? Or did she put it that way because she didn't want to take full responsibility for what she had just said, in case she were wrong? Was knowing one's way in the city a moral as well as a geographic challenge?

2. MEETING

Victor Hugo's house is no. 6, Place des Vosges, in the south-west corner of the square. He is said to have bought this house in 1832 because Marion de Lorme had lived here, and he wished to write a play about her in the house in which she had once lived. As a 1929 guide to Paris slyly points out: "The wish was not difficult of accomplishment, for there is hardly an old house in Paris that did not have Marion de Lorme for a tenant — if the legends are correct." (Written by an Englishman to be sure.) Marion de Lorme was a seventeenth-century French courtesan, reputed to have had a long list of lovers that included the Marquis de Cinq-Mars, the Duke of Buckingham and the Great Condé. She died in mysterious circumstances at the age of 37, just like Marilyn Monroe. In Paris, people often arrange to meet in front of Victor Hugo's house. I discovered this first-hand as I waited long minutes for my friends and with nothing much to do watched expectant loiterers greet eager companions. As the twilight approached, I walked out of the damp arcade in front of no. 6 and crossed the road to the corner opposite the park situated in the middle of the square. Here, with my back to the house, I leaned on a metal street barricade at the sidewalk's edge and looked through the barred gate into the park with its plane trees, its sandboxes, and its children's play structures. People passed in front of me and turned the corner. Dog-walkers. A woman with two string bags stuffed with baguettes. A man with a little girl. Baby carriages. More dog-walkers. Snatches of conversation drifted with the passers-by. Then a couple came toward me who were definitely not French. Definitely. She was blonde, in her thirties, and wore a knee-length red coat. He was in his late thirties, stocky, spectacled, balding, and wore jogging pants and a grey sweat shirt whose sleeves came down over his hands so that they could not be seen. As they passed, I heard her say clearly, in American English, "Well, to tell you the truth, I got married last year." "Oh," he said, followed by three measured beats. "Then you're here on your honeymoon." A pause. "No," she said, "I'm here on business, actually." And off they went, out of earshot, lost to me, and their story lost to me as well. My friends arrived almost immediately thereafter.

Would a moving picture be truer than a snapshot?

3. DREAMING

Wrecked on the fringes of the city there are the ZACs. Concrete not stone, white not brown, in the 13th and 14th, the 18th and 19th and 20th arrondissements, apartment living for immigrants mostly, they press down on the metal roofs and skylights of the traditional city. Seen from below, their tops cut chunks out of the sky. At the level of the street, waste paper, scraps of wood, old clothes, wash up against their sides, blown there by the tunnels of wind in the streets.

An African man, a black man from sub-Saharan Africa, about six feet tall, not largely built, in his late fifties, wearing a brown trench coat below his knees, open, shuffles his feet back and forth, back and forth, to a rhythm in his head. Arms dangle by his sides, all but free of his body. He is oblivious to everyone around him, who pay him no attention in any case, on this street corner in Paris, under a grey sky. Is he somewhere else, transported by the rhythm in his head? The movement of his feet does not suggest he is in this place, Paris, on this day. On this day Paris will not hold him as he moves to the rhythm of some elsewhere. I watch for five minutes or so, behind him, and then suddenly he stops shuffling his feet and he lifts his arms from his sides slowly and spreads them slowly the trench coat opening under his arms as though he were lifting, about to lift himself off the sidewalk and into the air, effortlessly.

Enough.

I am sure he is right, in his act of faith, this man from Africa under a grey sky on a street corner in Paris.

4. NAMING

Historically, the city of Paris has always expelled its waste to its outskirts, its disagreeable sights and smells, the screams and agonies of its disabled and its dispossessed. The famous prison La Santé ("Health!"), Salpêtrière the psychiatric hospital, the Hôpital Ste. Anne the asylum for the insane, the Hôpital Cochin which treated communicable diseases, the Hospice des Enfants Assistés the Paris orphanage, the Maison d'Accouchement de Port-Royal the lying-in hospital for single mothers, and the place of capital punishments were all (and most still are) to be found between the working-class fourteenth and thirteenth arrondissements on the south-east edge of the city. Many of these institutions are all on the same street, the rue de la Santé, a street whose course becomes a cruel metaphor of the social passage from life to death of many of the city's inhabitants. As recently as the 1950s, one could be born, orphaned, imprisoned, diagnosed as tubercular or syphilitic, be executed for one's crimes, or go mad and die a painful death, all within the space of a ten minute walk on a more or less direct route from the boulevard de Port-Royal along rue du faubourg St. Jacques, across boulevard Arago, and down the rue de la Santé south as far as rue d'Alésia.

The Hôpital Ste. Anne, also known as the Clinique des aliénés, the clinic of the alienated ones, is a little city within the larger city, with its own streets and passageways, its own ghostly inhabitants. The *clinique* is a walled city, with its gates and gatekeepers, but its streets and passageways are not found on any map or guidebook. The paper substitute for these streets of the mind is a patch without detail on the Paris map. To discover the streets and their names one has actually to enter the phantom city.

In the small, green gardens inside the walls, isolated figures in white stand or sit, propped against tree or bush or falling lawn. Beside the gatekeeper's house, a small boy beats a soccer ball over and over against the wall with his foot to the same thumping rhythm. Huge, beautiful, silence-inducing plane trees and chestnuts hang over the streets of the *clinique*, all of which it turns out are named after various artists: Artaud, given to bouts of madness, institutionalized in the latter part of his life; Kafka, tubercular, in and out of sanitoriums in his last years; Verlaine, alcoholic, ended his life in institutions; Van Gogh, confined at various times, alleged to have been mad; Baudelaire, succumbed to a general paralysis; de Maupassant, syphilitic, went mad; Gérard de Nerval, given to bouts of insanity, a suicide; André Breton, preoccupied with mental disorder; Camille Claudel, confined to an asylum for the last thirty years of her life; Robert Schumann, mad, died in an asylum;

Appollinaire, died of influenza; Edgar Allan Poe, struck down by a delirium on a street in Baltimore. Mad, all of them, mad or obsessed, and most of them institutionalized. Perhaps this act of naming was meant to be redemptive and prophylactic, and not just another instance of the city's uncanny.

5. DEPARTURE

The walls of the prison, La Santé, are very high, perhaps thirty feet, and they encompass its entire perimeter around an irregular city block of four streets in the 14th arrondissement. On two sides, on rue Jean Dolent and rue Messier, the walls do not, however, rise up to the windows of the uppermost cells. The rows of cell windows are clearly visible from the sidewalk opposite the prison wall. Towels, bits of clothing, soft drink tins, bottles of shampoo and the like can be observed between the bars on the window ledges. On a bright October afternoon I walked up rue Messier and a man stood on the sidewalk opposite the prison and called to another man inside. I heard the man on the street say, "So what do you do all day?" The answer came back: "Well, I walk to the right, then I walk to the left, and sometimes I hear music and I think it's birds singing." And then the prisoner said to the man on the street: "And you, you out there, what do you do all day?" "Well," came the reply, "we too, we walk to the left, and then we walk to the right, and sometimes we hear music and we think it's birds singing." And the insider commented: "At least you have a little more room than I do." I passed on the sidewalk and said to the man, is that your friend, and yes he said. Yes.

Regards to Jeanne. All the best, Chris.

Thomas Dilworth

SMILE

If you sit alone by the side of a lake
and smile, you will feel lonely.
A river is more company, unless
the lake waves at you. The experience
may be improved by ceasing smiling.

Smiling at strangers in the morning,
especially young women, is rewarding.
You sometimes get one back. If not,
there is fresh light. That makes
you feel smiled at.

The unrequited smile — who dares to
risk it? You walk the world waiting to be
smiled at first — of many curses, this
the worst, unless you are depressed
or very ill.

It might be a mistake to offer in hospital
a course on the literature of illness.
What would go on the syllabus? unless
you specialize in madness. There's lots
of that.

Oops, I forgot the smile. So much
for consistency, and returning to it
now makes for an awful unity —
the emptiness of form for its own
sake.

Quick, back to life, a cutting word
that rhymes with knife and is a mystery.
You can express what it contains —
smiles and history — not what contains it,
emptiness.

William Blissett

THINGS UNATTEMPTED YET IN PROSE OR RHYME

I

ALEXANDER POPE AT twenty-five had already published his *Essay on Criticism* and was just embarking on the translation of the *Iliad*, a labour of six years. As a joke and a corrective — not against taking epic too seriously but against pedants and dunces — he drew up "A RECEIT *to make an* EPICK POEM," which appeared in the *Guardian* of 10 June 1713. It climbs to the grand and undisputed claim of Rapin, made famous in England by Dryden, that the epic is "the greatest Work Human Nature is capable of," and then rolls merrily downhill. The French critics, he writes,

> have already laid down many Mechanical Rules for Compositions of this Sort, but at the same time they cut off almost all Undertakers from the Possibility of ever performing them; for the first Qualification they unanimously require in a Poet, is a *Genius*. I shall here endeavour (for the Benefit of my Countrymen) to make it manifest, that Epick Poems may be made *without a Genius*, nay without Learning or much Reading.

The recipe, in brief, is to take the fable from some old poem, history book, romance, or legend, and having chosen a hero for the sound of his name, and placed him in the midst of adventures, contrive a fortunate conclusion in conquest or marriage; superfluous adventures to be supplied as episodes; moral and allegory to be extracted afterwards, at leisure. As for "machines,"

> Take of deities, male and female, as many as you can use. Separate them into two equal parts, and keep Jupiter in the middle. Let Juno put him in a ferment, and Venus mollify him. Remember on all occasions to make use of volatile Mercury. If you have need of devils, draw them out of Milton's *Paradise*, and extract your spirits from Tasso.[1]

In this context of playful scepticism it will do no harm to list the conventions of the classical epic — what most readers, led by teachers and critics, have over the centuries agreed to expect of most poems so termed; later we may try to determine what they really want and need and will settle for. Moving from gross anatomy to fine, and from structure to function, we recognize in epic a poem of magnitude: if recited, recited at length on a special occasion, the bard in his singing robes; if read, read deliberately, not casually; long enough to possess an architecture, to be divided into books or cantos or both. At the outset it states its subject and intent, and it often invokes the Muse or otherwise admits that the enterprise is beyond normal human powers. Pervasively, though not always in every detail, the action is serious, the persons of stature, the style adequate to the great subject. Instead of chronicling events, as in annals, it thrusts into the midst of things, following in this regard good teaching practice, which begins where the learners are and brings them from the proximate to the deeper concerns of the subject. A teaching or edifying function is always present, openly or by implication. The auditors or readers learn what they need to know of the religion and history of their people — not all there is to know, but more than the bare essentials. An epic is a poem for a lifetime, a poem to grow up within, to keep returning to, as one returns to live a liturgical year. A poem for edification that can be quickly absorbed will be quickly discarded: it must yield only after long resistance; and a poem for edification is itself an edifice — a long time in building and built to last. Epics regularly contain references or allusions to earlier epics, and in some the poet identifies himself by a sort of signature.

Something like that, as I see it, is the conventional wisdom about the epic. In the *Poetics* Aristotle was chiefly concerned with a form brought to perfection in the time of his grandparents, and so he defined tragedy as a genre and analysed its best specimen. Epic was a lively topic in antiquity but produced no great critic: its models came down from the remote past and were fully absorbed into general culture long before criticism got to work. Other tragedies fit more or less snugly into the definition devised for *Oedipus*; but if epic is flatly stated to be "a poem written on the model of the *Iliad*," difficulties arise at once: the *Odyssey* will not fit. For all its similarities and overlappings with the *Iliad*, the *Odyssey* is a poem of movement, of steering, of aiming, not of force and combat; its most memorable episodes are not heroic but marvellous, and its tone without being unserious is comic. Northrop Frye went so far as to divide his profession into *Iliad* critics and *Odyssey* critics and to enrol himself among the latter.[2]

Wise young Telemachus explains to his mother that listeners always prefer a "new song" — this in the first book (lines 351–52) of a new epic. What we call primary epics, the shaping spirit of imagination bringing together oral constituents, always, as if effortlessly, convey a sense of a new beginning;

but every successful secondary or literary epic must work to a new end and achieve, in the grand phrase of Ariosto taken into English by Milton, "things unattempted yet in prose or rhyme."[3] "Make it new" has always been the motto of the artist, hidden or proclaimed; and surprise, already inherent in the most mundane unfolding of events, is sharply concentrated at the appearance of "the new, the really new," among the existing monuments of the arts. Curiously, we now expect surprise in the form of "shock" or "outrage" (produced by recipe), probably because we have been instructed to believe that all innovation in the arts has regularly been rejected on first appearance. By censors, critics, and claques, yes, often, but the record shows that most new work of lasting value has been greeted by the alert section of the general public as the very thing they had been waiting for: it has so thwarted expectation as surprisingly to fulfil it. There is always a first time, happily, and if a new song is a surprise, a new epic is a big surprise, mind-stretching, marvellous, daringly different; and it continues to surprise. It comes just at the time when the working definition, the workaday definition, of epic is "the sort of great poem it is no longer possible to write."

To narrow the field, let us consider some of the problems poets and readers have wrestled with, in Antiquity, the Renaissance, and Modernity, so that the difficulties facing David Jones in his epically conceived *In Parenthesis* (1937) and *The Anathemata* (1952), and our difficulties with them, may be seen in context. Chief among these are the perennial question of convention and innovation, the question of the heroic fable in the Christian world view, and the question of the possibility of an extended poem within the strictures of Modernism.

II

We cannot know exactly when Homer, whoever he was, became "the educator of Greece," but we know it was so, and that when a body of writing takes on canonical or quasi-scriptural character it immediately generates problems of two sorts, as Homer's did: call them the problem of what is there and the problem of what is not there. If Homer is to be at the heart of the curriculum, he must be assumed to be an intelligible whole, historically true and ethically edifying (or at least true enough and edifying enough) — and he must be worked on until he proves so. Hence the beginnings in Antiquity of the historical and moral allegory that has ever since kept pace with epic, hence too the great Socratic debate on poetry. But what if the teacher's and the student's interests are not really literary or historical or ethical at all? What if they want to talk about the weather or the nature of being? They must then pretend that in singing of Hera or Poseidon Homer says what they want him to say about the elements of air and water; or they find, as Porphyry did, in the Cave of the Nymphs (*Odyssey* 13) a lesson in occult wisdom.

In this welter of interpretation the epic impulse spent itself in devising supplementary songs of gods and heroes, but no third epic appeared. Alexander the Great, tutored in the epics by Aristotle, visited the site of Troy, carried the *Iliad* with him on his campaigns, and identified himself with Achilles, but found no Homer capable of celebrating his unexampled heroic exploits. One Choerilus of Iasos made an attempt, but Alexander said he would rather be Homer's Thersites than Choerilus's Achilles. In the Hellenistic world, epic on the Homeric model was to all intents and purposes dead. The most learned and gifted of the Alexandrian poets, Callimachus, scorned the epic recipe and the adulation of captains and kings. His famous dictum, that a great book is a great evil, is not an attack on Homer but an assertion that, after Homer, small is beautiful and the merely big, boring. He used all the devices of literary art, some of them daringly surprising, to achieve concentration so that the part could serve for the whole. The one surviving epic poet of Alexandrian civilization, Apollonius Rhodius, compressed his well-honed *Argonautica* into four (rather ample) books, not the Homeric twenty-four. This reaction against the epic as an impossible task will recur and, as we shall see, is at the centre of Modernism. We recall "These fragments I have shored against my ruins"; we recall the subtitle of *The Anathemata*, "fragments of an attempted writing."[4]

It is impossible to think of the two Homeric epics except as coming out of the deep past, and this was as true for Virgil as it is for us. The *Aeneid* reaches back to the heroic age so as to avoid the complications of the long civil wars just ending, the establishment of the principate, the consolidation of empire by marching legions; but in it we have a poem composed, with Alexandrian artistry, in a datable present, in historic time, after the Alexandrian settlement of the epic question. It was eagerly awaited by a reading public. By systematically parallel episodes and characters and by countless subtle allusions, always with arresting dissimilarity as well as similarity, the *Aeneid* approaches, embraces, takes leave of the *Odyssey* and the *Iliad*, by which it is inspired and all but overwhelmed. Moreover, it attempts, beginning now, to perform the same educational function for the Romans that Homer had long performed for the Greeks. The shadowy Homer neither provided nor expected annotation, commentary, *scholia*, but Virgil probably did: they certainly came soon enough.

There have always been jealous Homerists and scornful Alexandrians who find Virgil's endeavour impossible or impermissible. They raise the perennial question of secondary or literary epic, the admissibility of the heroic poem in an unheroic age, an age where artist is conscious of epoch. Approved or not, most secondary epics are poems written in imitation of the *Aeneid*. They are written in the expectation of their being studied. Didactic, yes, in having something momentous and demanding to impart; didactic, no, in not being pedantic or domineering. The *Aeneid* could not be the epic it is, could hardly have been an epic at all, if it had been, *in toto* and in detail, a glorification of Augustus, of Rome, of the imperial idea. The poem is Augustan, with pius Aeneas as princeps and pontifex; but the whole Odyssean first half is Trojan, not Roman, Dido and Turnus die unappeased, and for all the sorties and raids and combats, Marcus Agrippa might well have asked, "Virgil, where are my legions?"[5]

Occasion does not serve for more than a mention of mediaeval poems in which the epic impulse reappears without epic conventions, though David Jones knew many of them and must have taken heart from them. He knew the resplendent *Dream of the Rood* and the sunlit *Song of Roland* (so grandly translated by his friend René Hague), with its rocklike conviction that the Christians are right and the paynims wrong. He made no headway with Dante, the supreme exemplar of the unexpected great poem, despite the urgings of friends like Hague, Harman Grisewood, and T.S. Eliot. He did know Aneirin's *Y Gododdin* and the Welsh heroic romances of the *Mabinogion*, and the British historical poem, Layamon's *Brut* (also known to Charles Doughty and Ezra Pound and to how few others), and the vast forest of Malory, the later chapters of whom take on the dimensions and direction of tragic epic. Each of these deserves a place in a larger study of epic purpose and achievement, especially if Jones is involved, but their mere mention will reinforce the first basic point of my argument — the unpredictability of epic and the fluidity of its contours. And they point to our second concern, the heroic poem in the Renaissance with its urgent question of Christian epic substance.[6]

III

The formal classical epic is a Renaissance phenomenon, and it was in the Renaissance that critics attempted to match Aristotle's theory of tragedy with a fully worked out theory of epic and to recommend the comprehension of a genre, not merely the imitation of an example. Most, though not all, Renaissance epics have a Christian theme and Christian heroes. Petrarch's *Africa*, the prototype of the humanist epic, is an exception in this regard, dealing as it does with the victory of Scipio Africanus in the Second Punic War. This first epic on classical lines, by the first modern man, is a signal example of how not to do it. Petrarch's most ambitious work, spread over most of his active lifetime and left (like Virgil's) unrevised at his death in 1474, *Africa* perishes from two quite reasonable miscalculations. He chose to write it in Latin, thinking the language of Eternal Rome to be the language of the future; and he reached back through the Dark Ages, and Christian Antiquity, and Imperial Rome, to the Roman Republic for his epic hero, judging Scipio to be the noblest Roman of them all and therefore the noblest human being. With the best will in the world, Petrarch could only produce a willed epic, patriotic, with a willed patriotism not rooted in one dear perpetual place but in an imaginary Rome for which Spain, Sicily, and Africa are no more than battlefields. Though always on the move, Petrarch never visited the scene of the epic action, and he was quite unacquainted with military life. His Scipio, though based on history and true to character, comes across as a figment of the imagination; and the poet's "signature" at the end, where the future singer of the *Africa* is seen to crown himself with laurel and to sit down beside the laurelled Scipio, will strike most readers as more a threnody than a diapason.[7]

More successful than the *Africa* is the *Lusiad* (1576) of Luis de Camoens — indeed one of the great poems of the world. Virgil is Camoens's model in structure and detail, as he was for Petrarch; but Virgil is plangent and melancholy, Petrarch rather dogged, whereas Camoens is buoyant and spirited. The poem embraces the whole history, and sings the exalted idea, of Portugal, while relating its most marvellous exploit, the voyage of Vasco da Gama round the Cape of Good Hope to India, a voyage only one generation removed from the time of the poet, who had himself voyaged as far as Goa and Macau. It is rare indeed in being based on such recent events, but this major departure from epic convention had compelling causes: the events were unquestionably heroic, and the rôle of tiny Portugal in world history is astounding; they involved no civil strife and so could enlist and not divide their original audience; they were far removed in place if not in time, and yet the antagonistic force was the historic foe, Islam. Vasco da Gama takes the Church and the Gospel with him and is under the protection of saints and angels, as well as of Venus as patroness of Western civilization in conflict with Bacchus as patron of Eastern barbarism, but the *Lusiad* is much more an epic of Portugal than of Christendom. And it is more a patriotic than an imperial epic, the poet being at pains to place at the outset of the voyage an emphatic early warning of the moral dangers of the imperial venture.[8]

If an epic is truly "the greatest work which the soul of man is capable to perform," why should not the Christian poet, inspired by a divine afflatus, meet the problem of heroism head-on? Surely the grandest and most heroic story is the Gospel itself, which conduces to the instruction and edification of the people of God as a royal priesthood. Why not put it into epic form, in the grand style? This is what Marco Girolamo Vida attempted in his Latin epic, the *Christiad* (1535). Not now well known, though greatly admired for more than a century, it needs brief description. Beginning with an invocation of *Spiritus alme*, it plunges *in media res* by recounting in the first of its six books the later events of Christ's ministry — the raising of Lazarus, the cleansing of the Temple, the Transfiguration — using the Temple episode as the occasion for a "grand epic in marble," a lengthy description of the friezes depicting the creation of the world and the biblical stories from Adam to Moses. The second book begins with the plot against Jesus and ends with the arrest: the gathering of the people for the Passover allows the description of the twelve tribes, their territories, their history, their worthies. In book three the apostle John and the aged Joseph seek out Pilate to plead for the accused man, and Joseph relates the story of the birth and boyhood and youth of Jesus as far as the marriage feast at Cana. In book four John takes over, expounding first (from the opening chapter of his Gospel) the doctrines of the Trinity and the Incarnation and then relating his account of the ministry and miracles; he is interrupted when the enraged mob bursts in. Book five begins with the warning dream of Pilate's wife and is then given over to the elaboration first of Satanic allegorical figures, then of divine allegorical figures and the spontaneous mobilization of legions of good angels, who are stayed by the Father so that the sacrifice of Calvary may proceed. The last book relates the interment, the harrowing of Hell, the resurrection, the ascension, and pentecost. The Latin verse (so far as I am able to judge) is correct, concise, eloquent; the organization is economical, the pace rapid but not hurried. Why then does this Gospel gift-wrapped in a sumptuous epic parcel not have the staying-power of *Paradise Lost*? The answer I think is this. The attentive reader of the Gospel itself tries to relate what he reads, first to his understanding of scripture as a whole and the teaching of the church, then to his experience of life. The reader of the *Christiad* much less strenuously remembers previous readings and hearings of the Gospel: yes, here comes Nicodemus, here is Elizabeth, here Simeon. I find I remember best some little invented details, such as the unkempt beards of the fishermen-apostles or Pilate's wife's dream of a white lamb. The Ministry, the Passion, the Resurrection really went without saying. Milton must have pondered such ready responses as these in determining his oblique course, altogether scripturally based but not at all in substitution or rivalry with scripture. So too David Jones: he relates no scriptural stories, but every rifle-stock, every ship's keel, every tree, partakes of the wood of the Cross.[9]

Unhappy Tasso, a man of genius and troubled Catholic faith, acclaimed early and encouraged by all but a few pedantic critics, seized upon a great subject for a Christian epic — the conquest of Jerusalem in the First Crusade, with the noble Godfrey as its blameless Agamemnon, the spirited Rinaldo as its erring Achilles. How much more grateful is this subject than *Italia liberata dai Goti* (1547), by Gian Giorgio Trissino, for who cares now about the vanished Goths and who does not care about the perennial world debate of Cross and Crescent? The idea of heroic virtue has never been foreign to the Christian mind, though on the question of bearing arms the division of opinion has been lasting and profound. The Christianization of epic and of the heroic ethos is mediated by the *pietas* of Virgil and Aeneas. The idea of Christendom (as distinct from St. Augustine's two cities and from St. Paul's "whole armour" of the Christian soldier) took form in answer to Islam, as the Crusade answered the Islamic Jihad. This momentous theme, together with chivalry, heroic love and melancholy, a rich and coherent allegory of outward and inward conflict, and wondrously contrived "marvels," all conjoin to make *Jerusalem Liberated* (1581) blaze out as a perilously achieved Christian epic — just the sort of poem that had been hoped for and despaired of.[10]

As well as the good example of Godfrey and the preaching of Peter the Hermit and the regular channels of grace in the sacraments, Tasso reached out to the "conflict stupendous" of spiritual forces, allotting to it the formal place of the supernatural machinery of classical epic: it is God and his angel messenger who inspire Godfrey at the outset to lay siege to Jerusalem; it is Satan and his agents who counter that move. Strangely, for more than a century of neo-classical critical and theoretical activity no strong objection was raised to this practice, to which the added example of Milton gave increased authority. Then, in 1674, an eminent critic, whom Keats (who had not read him) was to call "one Boileau," asserted the exclusive claims of classical mythology in epic:

> In vain have our mistaken authors tried
> To lay these ancient ornaments aside,
> Thinking our God, and prophets that he sent,
> Might act like those the poets did invent,
> To fright poor readers in each line with hell,

And talk of Satan, Ashteroth, and Bel.
The mysteries which Christians must believe
Disdain such shifting pageants to receive;
The Gospel offers nothing to our thoughts
But penitence, or punishment for faults:
And mingling falsehoods with these mysteries,
Would make our sacred truths appear like lies.

He goes on to name Tasso without respect, and in so doing, as lawgiver of classicism, marks the first turn of the tide against the long favour of Italian epic, and poses a problem for defenders of Milton. Epic may be living in Homer and Pope's Homer, living in Virgil and Dryden's Virgil; but its modern successors — the "tinsel of Tasso," Spenser, who "can please an understanding age no more," even Milton, who may be praised for everything but writing an epic poem — show the impossibility of continuing the line. If Christian substance is to be excluded from a poem that must include everything, the epic is indeed dead.[11]

IV

Tasso survived, not as a creator of Christian epic but, in the eighteenth century, as a source of plots for opera and, in the nineteenth, as a romantic figure, noble, erotic, excessive, driven to melancholy and madness. In the time of Revolution and Romanticism there occurred a sharp reaction against Virgil, for so many centuries the pattern of the epic. He was dismissed, by those who had studied him in school, as politically subservient and poetically unoriginal, inferior in all respects to Homer — or even Ossian. The primitive, or primitivist, rhapsodies of the supposed Ossian, if taken seriously — as they were taken with the highest seriousness by such readers as Goethe, Napoleon, and Jefferson — could hardly help dissolving any clear conception of what an epic might be.[12]

What Boileau was to neo-classicism Edgar Allan Poe is to be, specifically to Symbolism, more generally to Modernism — the man of the hour, refutable but not refuted. At the start of his essay on "The Poetic Principle" (1850) Poe wrote this: "I hold that a long poem does not exist. I maintain that the phrase, 'a long poem,' is simply a flat contradiction in terms." His words in France, with Baudelaire's championship and Mallarmé's, were fighting words, words of victory. The French, remember, have no *Jerusalem Liberated*, no *Lusiad*, no

Paradise Lost. Their one notable heroic poem is the rough, clangorous, early *Song of Roland*. Ronsard worked on his *Franciade* under orders from Charles IX to include the deeds of every one of the royal ancestors; no wonder he gave up after four books. Efficient Voltaire, a free classicist aware of modern developments and untroubled by Christian imperatives, knew all that was needed to be known about Henry of Navarre and about concocting an epic. He completed his *Henriade* (1723–24), and it occupies a not dishonourable minor place in his oeuvre, but it never would be missed, and that is hardly the accolade the true epic poet lives and dies for. Long French poems are held together by narrative and by rhetoric — rhetoric, "the common, teachable element in poetry," in Gerard Manley Hopkins's phrase — a subject at the lycée, at which every clever schoolboy could become an adept. So much was this the case that the *poète maudit* Paul Verlaine exclaimed, "We must take rhetoric and wring its neck" — which is, ironically, a highly rhetorical gesture intended to end an argument in victory. This resolution was applauded on many sides and in many countries. And yet the poets of symbolist Modernism, having assented to Poe and Verlaine, yearn nevertheless to reach out and include a whole world, to say something momentous without telling a story and, above all, without arguing, without having a palpable design on the reader.[13]

Some poets who have entered the symbolist garden find it a prison courtyard and long for a wider scope and more resonant historic depth — a "poem of some length," a "poem including history," to use famous phrases of T.S. Eliot and Ezra Pound. One way of accomplishing this was the adoption of what Eliot in championing Joyce called "the mythic method," whereby a myth, or thoroughly assimilated story, a story that goes without saying, takes over the narrative function, and realistic detail chosen for its symbolic quality (what Joyce calls epiphanies) takes over the function of persuasive rhetoric. *Ulysses* is not exactly instantaneous, being longer than the *Odyssey*, whose *mythos* it adopts, but Joyce (like one of his masters, Wagner) is an "exquisite miniaturist." Eliot himself practises the same method in *The Waste Land*, at 433 lines "the longest poem in the language," in Pound's words. Something closely akin to this is to be found in St.-John Perse's *Anabase* (1924, translated by Eliot, 1931) — one of the few modern poems that David Jones read closely and admitted as an influence.

When I said that Poe was refutable but not refuted, I meant that he was not, in advanced literary circles, seen to be refuted and driven from the field. The shelves of Milton criticism (to which Milton himself contributed one page, a note on the verse: all the rest he must have considered self-explanatory) and such compilations as *The Spenser Encyclopedia* rest on the firm assumption that the long poem does exist and deserves prolonged and close attention.

Early in this century a highly influential critic, A.C. Bradley, author of *Shakespearean Tragedy*, published as one of his *Oxford Lectures on Poetry* (1909) an essay on "The Long Poem in Wordsworth's Age." He has this to say in reply to Poe and the Symbolists:

> Naturally, in any poem not quite short, there must be many variations and grades of poetic intensity; but to represent the differences of these numerous grades as a simple antithesis between pure poetry and mere prose is like saying that, because the eyes are the most expressive part of the face, the rest of the face expresses nothing. To hold again that this variation of intensity is a defect is like holding that a face would be more beautiful if it were all eyes.... And to speak as if a small poem could do all that a long one does, and do it more completely, is to speak as if a humming-bird could have the same kind of beauty as an eagle, the rainbow in the fountain produce the same effect as the rainbow in the sky, or a moorland stream thunder like Niagara. A long poem ... requires imaginative powers superfluous in a short one; and it would be easy to show that it admits of strictly poetic effects of the highest value which the mere brevity of the short one excludes.

One of the strongest words of critical rejection among those who reject the long poem is *voulu*, "willed." (I have used it here in discussing Petrarch's *Africa* and implied it in connection with Voltaire's *Henriade*.) In an arresting moment in his useful book on epic, E.M.W. Tillyard reminds us that it is an "exercise of the will and the belief in it" that "help to associate epic poetry with the largest human movements and solidest human institutions. In creating what we call civilisation the sheer human will has had a major part." The will to power, the imperial idea, the triumph of the will, all show how appalling and destructive the dark side of this urge can be, but it has a positive side, and any poetry ample enough to require "disposition" rather than "fusion" of its constituents, that enlists the powers of the architect rather than the jeweller, is bound to be "willed."[14]

There appeared, also in the first decade of this century, as if in proof of Bradley's assertion, a poem slightly less in bulk than *The Faerie Queene* but longer than the two Homeric poems together: it is a grandly conceived and I think grandly executed reconstruction of the forming of British culture and character from the most primitive beginnings to the coming of Roman hegemony and the Christian religion — anticipating in this respect *The Anathemata* by half a century. This is Charles Doughty's *The Dawn in Britain*.

The declared motive for Doughty's going into Arabia Deserta and later writing the massive book of that name for which he is now chiefly remembered was to rescue the English language from the "vility" into which it had fallen since the time of Spenser. *The Dawn in Britain* was what he deemed his true life-work, a work of "deliberate valour" — "willed," if you like, not with a dry self-conscious rhetorical will, but with an architectonic will in the service of a poetic vision. Though read aloud by Ezra Pound to W.B. Yeats, though praised by Bernard Shaw and Hugh MacDiarmid, by Edward Thomas and W.H. Auden, Doughty is a scandalously neglected and ignored poet. One of the sad stories of literary history is that David Jones would have read *The Dawn in Britain* if the six volumes had been on an open shelf, but he did not want to take them from his patroness's glassed-in cabinet.[15]

V

And so, with the epic missing and presumed dead but with the need for something like the epic undiminished, we arrive at David Jones, who attempts, twice, to rise to two massive challenges, impossible or just about impossible: to deal with Christian epos and to write a long poem in the idiom of literary Modernism. We began with a recipe for writing a conventional epic without genius; we now turn to *In Parenthesis*, which T.S. Eliot called "a work of genius," and to *The Anathemata*, which has been similarly acclaimed, to see how far from convention an epic impulse may depart.[16]

Analogous questions have been asked and answered before, in connection with comedy and tragedy. The term *comedy*, first defined as a dramatic form, has without confusion been stretched to include on the one hand such narratives as the *Divine Comedy* and on the other *Tom Jones* and *Pride and Prejudice*, and in ordinary language it reaches beyond that to laughable incidents in fiction and life. Again, *tragedy*, originally a closely defined dramatic form, has been legitimately stretched to include such narratives as *Clarissa* and *Nostromo* and (here, I think, illegitimately) painful, pathetic, and pointless incidents. By the same token it should be permissible to consider *War and Peace* along with the *Iliad*, *Moby-Dick* or *Ulysses* along with the *Odyssey*, or to add *In Parenthesis* or *The Anathemata* to their company as being just as "epic" as any and more recognizably a "poem." They may be *quasi*-epics: they are not *pseudo*-epics.

Neither beginning at the beginning nor ending at the end, the *Iliad* includes the whole Trojan War so as to make it the archetype of life as conflict.

Similarly, *In Parenthesis* includes in one "intelligent song," telling the story of one infantry company from Christmas 1915 to the Battle of Mametz Wood in the summer of 1916, the whole of the Great War on the Western Front, that "first clarst bollocks and murthering of Christen men." That last phrase, fusing cockney and Malory, is an instance of the historic depth of the writing, of which Jones gives a foretaste and early warning in his Preface:

> I suppose at no time did one so much live with a consciousness of the past, the very remote, and the more immediate and trivial past, both superficially and more subtly. No one, I suppose, however much not given to association, could see infantry in tin hats, with ground-sheets over their shoulders, with sharpened pine-stakes in their hands, and not recall
> > ' ... or may we cram
> > Within this wooden O ... '
> But there were deeper complexities of sight and sound to make ever present
> > 'the pibble pabble in Pompey's camp'
> Every man's speech and habit of mind were a perpetual showing: now of Napier's expedition, now of the Legions at the Wall, now of 'train-band captain', now of Jack Cade, of John Ball, of the commons in arms. Now of *High Germany*, of *Dolly Gray*, of Bullcalf, Wart and Poins; of Jingo largenesses, of things as small as the Kingdom of Elmet; of Wellington's raw shire recruits, of ancient border antipathies, of our contemporary, less intimate, larger unities, of *John Barleycorn*, of 'sweet Sally Frampton'. Now of Coel Hên — of the Celtic cycle that lies, a subterranean influence as a deep water troubling, under every tump in this Island, like Merlin complaining under his big rock.

Read on: what is promised here is delivered, the poet himself in his notes providing the necessary *scholia* to throw light on "unshared backgrounds."[17]

If *In Parenthesis* has a wide historical embrace, *The Anathemata* has a yet more (shall I say?) epic ambition: to gather in a vast meditation the story of the Island of Britain and by implication the whole human story, under the image of voyage, with the Cross as both mast and keel, and, under the image of combat, with the Holy Table, Calvary, and altar as place of victory. Voyager and Victor are hidden, discerned, and proclaimed as Christ. *In Parenthesis* narrates events within a definite parenthesis of time and place, and for all its fullness of allusion has a bony structure of "straight reporting," sharing with other narratives of war the sequence of embarkation and arrival, marching to the base and to the support trenches, the sound of bombardment, the first shell, the front line, its routine of boredom and danger, comrades and friends, the approach and arrival of zero hour, the stunning confusion of battle. *The Anathemata* is of similar scope, requiring ample time to read, and has divisions that are architectural wings, not jewellers' facets; but it is described in its subtitle as "fragments of an attempted writing," and the great accumulations from which it and the poems of *The Sleeping Lord* have been extracted are called "quarries." The opening lines of *The Anathemata* seem to be hewn from rock:

> We already and first of all discern him making this thing
> other. His groping syntax, if we attend, already shapes:
>   ADSCRIPTAM, RATAM, RATIONABILEM ... and by pre-
> application and for *them*, under modes and patterns altogether
> theirs, the holy and venerable hands lift up an efficacious
> sign.

The making of something other, setting it apart, signing it, is an "action" in the strictest sense, and the characteristically human action, whether done "already and first of all" by the most primitive and inarticulate human being or by the *sacerdos* at mass. These words weigh as decisively in the ensuing poem as the wrath of Achilles or the return of polytropic Odysseus do in theirs.[18]

Some ingredients — a surprising number — of the old epic recipe reappear in Jones's work if we think to look for them. Compared to *The Waste Land* or *Anabase* or Hart Crane's *The Bridge*, the dehydrated epics of High Modernism, his poems, as we have noted, take ample space and require ample time to read. There is no formal invocation of the Muse, but few modern writers show so keen an awareness of the feminine tutelary spirit as inspiring all great undertakings. *In Parenthesis* tells of the Great War less than twenty years after its conclusion, and so Jones is closer to his subject even than Camoens, that other poet "who can look a common soldier in the face," but the Great War was so uniquely unintelligible that proximity makes no difference; its issues are not debated, and through its barbed wire entanglement we look with the poet at an intelligible past — the Homeric and Biblical world, Caesar and Marlborough and Napoleon, Aneirin and the Mabinogion, Malory and *Henry V*. *The Anathemata* in contrast ranges from geological and prehistoric origins to the time of Jones's grandfather, Ebeneezer Bradshaw, a Thames-side mast- and block-maker, and ends at the centre, steadying the whirl on the pivot of the Cross — *stat Crux dum volvitur orbis.*[19]

Both writings possess what Matthew Arnold calls high seriousness, enlivened by wit and humour, and both sing of heroic actions: "poetry is the song of deeds," Jones wrote in 1953 in reference to *The Anathemata*. *In Parenthesis* is not a "glorification of war," neither is it a denigration of the soldier and the soldierly virtues. Of his comrades the narrator says, "They're worthy of an intelligent song for all the stupidity of their contest," and if this "noble fellowship" (in the words of Malory) is "wholly mischiefed," it is seen, cumulatively, as a noble fellowship. Jones's princes are "secret princes," his epic not a celebration of captains and kings but of enlisted men and, hidden among them, the *plebs* of God. The heroic deeds lying behind the multifarious goings and comings of *The Anathemata* (really a single deed) are the docking to schedule of the Bark of Salvation and (to use the terms that the poem itself makes resplendent) the action of the young prince of glory in the "upper cave of bread" in Sherthursday and on Skull Ridge on Venus Day.[20]

In both, the reader is trained, armed, and edified, so that at the finish he is better able to soldier on, or, like the Ancient Mariner's wedding guest, released to go his way. Jones writes in the Preface to *The Anathemata*,

> My intention has not been to 'edify' (in the secondary but accepted and customary sense of that word), nor, I think, to persuade, but there is indeed an intention to 'uncover'; which is what a 'mystery' does, for though at root 'mystery' implies a closing, all 'mysteries' are meant to disclose, to show forth something. So that in one sense it *is* meant to 'edify', i.e. 'to set up.'

Both poems have an encyclopedic character — as Homer had for the Hellenic and Hellenistic world, Virgil for the Romans and all their Western successors, Camoens for the Portuguese in the time of greatness and tribulation, Tasso for the Catholic Reformation, Spenser and Milton and Doughty for God's Englishmen. They have, as they need, extensive annotation by the poet; they have a historic depth at first bewildering and always impressive, and a religion that makes sense of the whole. These are major epic qualities.[21]

To be sure, the consistent grand style of the classical hexameter, the stanza of Tasso or Camoens, the English blank verse of Milton or Doughty, is altogether abandoned. Nevertheless, many passages of *In Parenthesis*, almost alone in the vast literature of the Great War, ring out with a fullness and resonance far beyond the reach of ordinary prose narrative. I am thinking first of Dai's Boast, so memorably read by Dylan Thomas:

> My fathers were with the Black Prinse of Wales
> at the passion of
> the blind Bohemian king.
> They served in these fields,
> it is in the histories that you can read it, Corporal — boys
> Gower, they were — it is writ down — yes.
> 　Wot about Methuselum, Taffy?
> I was with Abel when his brother found him,
> under the green tree.
> I built a shit-house for Artaxerxes.
> I was the spear in Balin's hand
> 　　　　　　　that made waste King Pellam's land.
> I took the smooth stones of the brook,
> I was with Saul
> playing before him.
> I saw him armed like Derfel Gatheren.
> I the fox-run fire
> 　　　　　consuming in the wheat-lands.[22]

And I am thinking of the more impassioned parts of the narrative, as delivered by Richard Burton, in Douglas Cleverdon's superb radio adaptation, but not only of these. A university class or an informal group of readers, I can report from frequent experience, will rise to the variety of pace, the richness and energy of vocabulary, the syntactical demands, the sweep of allusion, the differentiation of voices, as to a challenge with rewards, immediate as well as long-term. In *The Anathemata* Eb Bradshaw defies a temptation to scamp a job with the eloquence of Abdiel defying Satan. And the long rigmarole of the cockney Lady of the Pool has a grand demotic freedom:

> 　　　　　　　　　Come buy!
> Come buy, good for between the sheets, good for all ails o'
> the head an' nerves.
> B' the bell'd clout o' Martin, you'll owe me only five farthin'.
> Buy m' livid flower
> 　　　　　　　　　　　there's good souls!
> There ducks!
> 　　　　an' a' extree sweet bunch from the Sud Ridge

for a pretty boatswain's boy. There's a poor curly — and
fairish for a Wog — not a' afreet but a' elfin!
                    Plucked with his jack bucket from
the Punic foreshore b' a bollocky great Bocco procurer, or
I weren't christed Elen Monica in Papey Juxta Muram. 'V'a
mind to sign him Austin Gregorians in Thames-water, an'
ransom him with m'own woman's body.[23]

This freedom balances the hieratic grandeur of the description of Queen
Gwenhwyfar:

                    If her gilt, unbound
(for she was a consort of a *regulus*) and falling to below her
sacral bone, was pale as standing North-Humber barley-corn,
here, held back in the lunula of Doleucothi gold, it was
paler than under-stalks of barley, held in the sickle's lunula.
So that the pale gilt where it was by nature palest, together
with the pale river-gold where it most received the pallid
candle-sheen, rimmed the crescent whiteness where it was
whitest.[24]

The attempt to write *In Parenthesis* and *The Anathemata*, and the attempt
to write them *so*, was a heroic attempt.[25]
    The inclusiveness of epic begins by including other epics, as Virgil was the
first to do, with Homer, as Tasso and Camoens and Milton were to do with Homer
and Virgil. *In Parenthesis* does this systematically by incorporating epigraphs from
the early Welsh heroic poem, Aneirin's *Y Gododdin*, and more sporadically by
frequent references to the *Mabinogion*, Malory, and *The Ancient Mariner*. *The
Anathemata* reaches back to touch Troy through Homer and Virgil and the
mediaeval Matter of Rome the Great — a labyrinth or Troy-game of references.[26]
    One last observation. Both poems are signed, as Virgil was long believed
to have signed the *Aeneid* in four introductory lines rejected by his literary
executors; as Spenser signed *The Faerie Queene* when Colin Clout (his name
as a pastoral poet) pipes to the dance of the Graces in his last completed book;
as Milton was to sign *Paradise Lost* in the great invocations. Add the name
of David Jones to fame's eternal beadroll. A bombardment just at tea-time:

    This nasty type of flamboyance makes you light an-
other cigarette from the stub-end of the one before — makes

Fatty sing loudly of the Armentieres lady — makes '79 Jones,
in his far corner, rearrange and arrange again a pattern of
match-ends.

This is the modest sign-manual of 22579 JONES, WALTER DAVID 2 JAN 15 – 15
JAN 19 TRADE OR CALLING, ART STUDENT, as quietly (do not say compulsively)
he "makes this thing other." And at the end of *In Parenthesis* he takes for his
own some phrases of the author of *The Song of Roland* (who is anonymous)
as the voice of the serving man: "The geste says this and the man who was
on the field ... and who wrote the book ... the man who does not know this
has not understood anything."[27]

The Anathemata likewise contains a signature, the poet's personal
recollection or *anamnesis* of Christmas 1915 in the trenches, attracting to
it Caesar's *Gallic Wars* and by implication all the annals of conflict:

On this night, when I was a young man in France, in Gallia
Belgica, the forward ballista-teams of the Island of Britain
green-garlanded their silent three-o-threes for this I saw
and heard their cockney song salute the happy morning; and
later, on this same morning certain of the footmen of Britain, walking
in daylight, upright, through the lanes of the war-net
to outside and beyond the rusted trip-belt, some with gifts,
none with ported weapons, embraced him between his *fossa*
and ours, exchanging tokens.

("Him" — the enemy front-fighters — so termed also by Tolstoy in his *Tales
of Army Life.*) The speaking voice of the epic continues:

And this I know
if only from immediate hearsay, for we had come on this
mild morning (it was a Green Christmas) back into the rear,
two or three hundred paces behind where his front *vallum*
was called, by us, the Maiden's Bulge, and ours, the Pontiff's
Neb, between which parallels, these things, according to
oral report reaching us in this forward reserve area, were done,
BECAUSE OF THE CHILD.[28]

NOTES

[1]Alexander Pope, *The Prose Works*, ed. Norman Ault, Oxford, Blackwell (1936) 115–20.

[2]Aristotle, *Poetics*, ch. 23–24; W. Macneile Dixon, *English Epic and Heroic Poetry*, London, Dent (1912) 1.

[3]Ariosto, *Orlando Furioso*, first stanza; *Paradise Lost*, I.16.

[4]"Homer the Educator of Greece," the opening chapter of Werner Jaeger, *Paideia: The Ideals of Greek Culture*, tr. Gilbert Highet, New York, Oxford UP (1945) I. See also Howard Clarke, *Homer's Readers*, Newark, U of Delaware P (1981); Robert Lamberton, *Homer the Theologian*, U of California P (1986); John Kevin Newman, *The Classical Epic Tradition*, Madison, U of Wisconsin P (1986).

[5]See W.R. Johnson, *Darkness Visible*, U of California P (1976); J.K. Newman, *The Classical Epic Tradition*; Brooks Otis, *Virgil: A Study in Civilized Poetry*, Oxford, Clarendon Press (1964); Kenneth Quinn, *Virgil's Aeneid: A Critical Description*, Ann Arbor, U of Michigan P (1968). David Jones met and corresponded with W.F. Jackson Knight and possessed these books of his: *Cumean Gates*, Oxford, Blackwell (1936); *Elysion*, London, Rider (1970); *Roman Vergil*, London, Faber (1953) ("given to me by Tom Eliot"); *Vergil Epic and Anthropology*, London, George Allen & Unwin (1967); *Vergil's Troy*, Oxford, Blackwell (1932).

[6]David Jones's library, the catalogue of which, edited by Huw Ceiriog Jones, is published by the National Library of Wales, Aberystwyth (1995), is, as one would expect, notably strong on mediaeval Britain, especially Wales, its languages, literature, and history. In the context of our discussion, it is weak in Homer, strong in Virgil, Milton being the sole representative of the Renaissance epic, St.-John Perse of the modern. Jones knew the work of Eliot and Joyce from the 1930s, but Pound only from the 1960s — well after the publication of *The Anathemata*. Many of his books were presentation copies: he was the sort of person one likes to give books to. Nancy Sanders, whose translation of the earliest epic, *Gilgamesh*, he knew and possessed, gave him Guy Davenport's Archilochus, and George Johnston gave him *The Saga of Gisli*.

[7]Petrarch's *Africa* has been translated with an introduction by Thomas G. Bergin and Alice S. Wilson, Yale UP (1977); see also E.H. Wilkins, *Life of Petrarch*, U of Chicago P (1961); and S. Bernardo, *Petrarch, Scipio and the 'Africa'*, Baltimore, Johns Hopkins UP (1962).

[8]The spirited translation by Sir Richard Fanshawe (1655) has been edited by

Jeremiah D.M. Ford and published by Harvard UP (1940). The anglicization of the poet's name and the poem's follows Fanshawe and subsequent translators.

[9]*The Christiad*, ed. and tr. Gertrude C. Drake and Clarence A. Forbes, Carbondale, Southern Illinois UP (1978).

[10]*Jerusalem Liberated*, tr. Edward Fairfax (1600), ed. John Charles Nelson, London (1963). See also Tasso, *Discourses on the Heroic Poem*, ed. and tr. Mariella Cavalcrini and Irene Samuel, Oxford, Clarendon P (1973), especially discussion of epic magnitude, variety, and the marvellous.

[11]Boileau, *Art of Poetry*, tr. Soame, quoted in Albert S. Cook, ed., *The Art of Poetry*, New York, Stechert (1926) 195–96; A.F.B. Clark, *Boileau and the French Classical Critics in England*, Paris, Champion (1925) 308–09, for general acceptance of Christian "machinery" before Boileau. It may be noted that Milton himself feared that he may have come in an "age too late" (*P.L.* IX. 44): see W.J. Bate, *The Burden of the Past*, Harvard UP (1970) 50; two alert contemporary critics think the epic ends in Milton's time: Colin Burrow, *Epic Romance: Homer to Milton*, Oxford, Clarendon (1993) 288; David Quint, *Epic and Empire*, Princeton UP (1993) 10.

[12]Donald M. Foerster, *The Fortunes of Epic Poetry*, n.p., Catholic University of America (1962) 37, for the "exhaustion of epic" in the early nineteenth century; 84, for Jefferson on Ossian: "I am not ashamed to own that I think this rude bard of the north to be the greatest poet that has ever existed."

[13]Edgar Allan Poe, *Essays and Reviews*, New York, Library of America (1984) 71–73; Paul Verlaine, "Art Poétique," line 21, "Prends l'éloquence et tords-lui son cou!"

[14]A. C. Bradley, *Oxford Lectures on Poetry*, London, Macmillan (1909) 203–04; E.M.W. Tillyard, *The English Epic and Its Background*, London, Chatto and Windus (1954) 10; see also Jackson Knight, *Roman Vergil*, 81–82.

[15]Charles M. Doughty, *The Dawn in Britain*, London, Duckworth (1906), especially his "Post Illa," vol. VI , 241–44; also my memoir of David Jones, *The Long Conversation*, Oxford (1981) 87.

[16]*In Parenthesis* (1937), *The Anathemata* (1952), *Epoch and Artist* (1959), *The Sleeping Lord* (1974), and *The Dying Gaul* (1978) are all published in London by Faber and Faber; *The Roman Quarry*, London (1981) is published by Agenda Editions.

[17]"They're worthy of an intelligent song for all the stupidity of their contest," *I.P.* 88–89; "bollocks ... fellowship," 138; consciousness of the past, Preface xi. See also my "*In Parenthesis* Among the War Books," *University of Toronto Quarterly*, 42 (1973) 258–88; Colin Hughes, *David Jones the man who was on the field*: In Parenthesis *as straight reporting*, Manchester, David Jones Society (1979).

[18]*The Anathemata*, 49.

[19]Roy Campbell, "Luis de Camões," *Collected Poems*, London, Bodley Head (1949) 159. *"Stat Crux ... ,"* the motto of the Carthusian order, often cited by David Jones.

[20]"The song of deeds," from "Past and present" (1953), in *Epoch and Artist*, 138, used as the title of a study of *The Anathemata* by Neil Corcoran, Cardiff, U of Wales P (1982); on the matter of his alleged "glorification of war," see Paul Fussell's chapter on Jones in *The Great War and Modern Memory*, New York, Oxford UP (1975) and my review article in *University of Toronto Quarterly* 45 (1976) 268–74. *I.P.*, 138, "noble fellowship"; "secret princes," dedication and 185; "upper cave of bread," *Ana.* 242, fuses the "large upper room" of the first Eucharist with Bethlehem ("house of bread") and the cave of the Nativity; "Skull Ridge" (241) is Calvary, "the place of a skull," thought of as a Great War battlefield.

[21]*The Anathemata*, 33.

[22]*In Parenthesis*, 79–80.

[23]*The Anathemata*, 166–67.

[24]*The Anathemata*, 196–97.

[25]This stylistic decision of David Jones is no more (and no less) a thing "unattempted yet" than Dante's decision to write in vernacular stanzas. *I.P.*, 79–84, "Dai's Boast"; 66, "To groves always men come both to their joys and their undoings"; 162, "sweet sister death"; 185, "The Queen of the Woods"; *Ana.* 118–21, Eb Bradshaw's *aristeia*; 124–68, The Lady of the Pool; 194–97, Gwenhwyfar's Mass of the Nativity.

[26]The epigraphs from Aneirin were added late to the manuscript, but it is now hard to imagine *In Parenthesis* without them.

[27]*I.P.*, 108, 187.

[28]*Ana.*, 216.

Yesterday here sat a bird
in the branches of a tree outside my window;
but I have not seen him since
and I missed him all day long.

Edith Pahlke
Icelandic Poem
by Thorsteinn Gislason
linocut 12 x 12 inches

Marius Kociejowski

A THUMBNAIL SKETCH OF GEORGE JOHNSTON

WHEN I WAS a student in Ottawa in the late sixties, occasionally I would see George Johnston walking in the distance. There was something so finely polished in him, so imbued with purpose, that even now I see him as he was then and as I still imagine him to be. Always in a pale mac and black beret, beard and locks startlingly white (could they have ever been otherwise?), hands thrust in pockets, he stood an inch or two above the general populace. If my eyes, these eyes that memory has, do not deceive me, George wore a strand of gold wire spiralling through his earlobe. What one heard of him bespoke a man of many deep kindnesses. The sad fact is, I never mustered sufficient courage to speak to him. More foolishly still, and this remains one of the great regrets of my life, I neglected to enrol for the course he gave in Icelandic literature. Also, I knew from high school his much anthologized poem "War on the Periphery," and it seemed to me incredible that its author could be found at such close quarters. A genuine, breathing poet was for me almost unimaginable.

Some years later, I was passing Leicester Square tube station when up from London's gloomy depths rose George. We spoke, for the first time, for five, no, perhaps eight minutes. It was a chance meeting that would engender a warm, though occasional, correspondence that has lasted ever since. George's letters, written in a beautiful, almost mediaeval script on oblong pages, each measuring four by six inches, look as though they ought to be preserved beneath glass. Although a man's letters are private, and this holds particularly true in a world where everything is, as Rimbaud says, for sale, I hope it would not be betraying George if I were to divulge a couple of things found in them. They reflect aspects of character self-evident to anyone who has read his poems.

First, George is, to a profound degree, a family man, and from where he writes, and by this I mean his poetical centre, his wife Jeanne, his children, and their children are always close. It is this being so warmly ensconced at the centre of his familial tribe that informs much of his poetry. Then there is a second circle, the tribe that constitutes his several deep friendships. It has been my good fortune to know one of his most stalwart allies, Bill Blissett, who shares with George the civilized values of men who have had to forge a space for them. If theirs is a professorial air it is one few students will ever again be able to breathe. I do not mean to strike too elegiac a note, but they both are of a generation for whom the enlarging of young minds was rather more than a profession — it was almost a religious duty.

Most striking, although really it ought not to be, George and Jeanne dwell in a televisionless state. Now, what do people of the late twentieth century who do not own televisions do? Why, they read, that's what they do. What's more, George and Jeanne read *aloud* to each other. *What* they read gives further pause for reflection — Tyndale's translation of the New Testament, Spenser's *Faerie Queene*, and *Paradise Lost*, to give but three examples. This is the most abiding image I have of George and his wife, swapping passages in a room I have never seen.

The event to which my poem obliquely refers, and not even its dedicatee would guess at its nature, is an outdoor poetry reading that was held in the backyard of the Victoria Hotel in Byward Market, Ottawa, on the evening of June 29, 1972. George had been scheduled to read but for some reason was unable to attend. The organizer phoned him where he was, somewhere deep in the countryside, with the bright notion of putting the microphone up to the telephone's earpiece. If the technology was crude, the product was sublime. George read three poems, "Poor Edward" being one of them. If his fine disembodied voice provided the evening's most magical moment, the magic was assisted by the appearance, most unusual for the time of year, of the Aurora Borealis.

* * *

AURORA BOREALIS
for George Johnston

Who dares pick a bone with Aristotle?
The ghostly light he describes is like smoke,
A burning of straw in the countryside.

Wise Pliny made the world his catalogue,
Says when the Lacedaemonians lost Greece
An aurora mocked their galleys in flames.

The Vikings, of whom Johnston may be one,
Saw blond Valkyries swooping through battle,
Their brief to gather up the dying heroes.

What science says, a jongleur may endorse.
A solar wind brings Sun's charged particles;
They gather above earth's magnetic pole.

What happens then, the elements collide.
The electrons knocked sideways, as by love,
Warm the ions to a tremulous state.

Three pounds of starstuff childishly simple
When compared to a flickering in the nerves
Which may, with luck, translate into image.

This elderly gentleman with young eyes,
A gold wire spiralling through his earlobe,
A Viking in pale mac, speaks his verses:

Whose hat is moving on the water's face?
Alas, *poor Edward's* (stanza one, line three):
We must pray *for Edward and his trouble.*

We never get to make his acquaintance,
Yet what one watchful in his craft does is
Construct, with as few words as possible,

A sly dirge for the man of misfortune,
An asylum where he may dry his clothes.
We pity him who perhaps never was.

A dab hand he makes his art look simple,
Although Valhalla knows the wild tumble
With the Muse, a soul covered with bruises.

While sadly he maps poor Edward's absence
The northern lights sway above our heads like
A woman sashaying down heaven's catwalk.

Whether they really do move as a whole,
Or rather, their atoms, gathering strength here
And dimming there, play upon our senses,

As they do, so dance the lords of language.

Kathryn Hunt

MACTAQUAC BEACH IN AUGUST
for my grandmother

I remember a spray of light.

Sky blue, dark blue, and green across the lake
and red and white buoys.

I remember water droplets in a fanning arc
catching the sunlight like a cut glass chandelier.

I remember the hands catching me,
and the feel of a smile on the face of a tiny woman
with eyes the same colour as the sky.
I remember ducking in cool-warm water
down over my waist — dangerous depth —
I couldn't swim. I was two.
The water could never close on me
though it rushed up around my body
her hands always caught me
and up I went again,
laughing.

I only remember this:
one swing up, one anticipated immersion in the water.
I am hovering in my memory at the top of the arc,
in a spray of light.

Richard Carter

HOME

First, split earth: ditches, spilling mounds
shovelled aside against the gorse. Next, the wood
in massive logs, braced against foundations.
Then caulking, the rap of hammers and hoarse
teething of a saw to shape the planks
to floorboards, length and width. Soon, a
sloping roof, slated about the chimney
carted down from Huntsville, fitted smoothly
between highbeams. November now, the chimney
smoking evenly. Below, the first snowpatches
dappled on the field, impaled and caught
on the crooks of pines. Pines and spruces
crowd the empty spaces. Hawks hover over
their flocks by night. Inside the cabin,
flames joust with shadows. A sagging line
of crumpled clothes dries above the snapping
hearth. Cheeks glow. The fireplace flicker
jumps. It is a hand that touches the room —
a metal basin, folded blankets on the pallet,
two stools. And there in the corner, a spade.

Fish

Edith Pahlke
Fiskur
linocut 12 x 12 inches

James Downey

HOME FREE, OUTPORT STYLE

At the same time as Ian Cameron was writing to ask if I would contribute to a book marking George Johnston's eighty-fifth birthday, I was sending Ian a copy of a talk I had just given at a homecoming dinner in Winterton, the Newfoundland outport where I was born and bent. George is one of the wisest, kindest, and most gifted people I have known, and one of my dearest friends, and I was anxious to accept Ian's invitation. Before I could get started on a good fret about what I might write, however, Ian was in touch again to say that he thought my Winterton piece would suit the unusual kind of tribute he and fellow editors Gurli Woods and Douglas Campbell had in mind, which was to be a volume "in the spirit of George Johnston" rather than a scholarly festschrift about his work and times. Ian knew that my favourite book of George's poetry has always been the endearingly autobiographical Home Free, *and thought my own autobiographical musings were in the same spirit. I have not edited the text for publication, believing that whatever value it may have lies in the occasion and audience for which it was prepared.*

When I was installed as president of the University of New Brunswick, George wrote and declaimed an ode in my honour. Had I his gift for poetry, I would gladly reciprocate. Since I do not, I offer this bit of self-reflection in tribute to a man whose finest poem is his own beautiful life.

WHAT OTTO TUCKER has suggested I do tonight is something at which I have not had nearly as much practice as he. He has said that I should bear witness and give a brief personal testimony. That, as you will recognize, is the language of the Salvation Army. We were always much more reserved and inhibited in the United Church, and I still find it hard to talk about myself in public.

Nevertheless, as a boy growing up I was attracted by the Army's way of worshipping. After attending my own church on Sunday evening, I sometimes went over to the barracks, where the service was just warming up. The hymns were livelier, the young female officers were irresistibly attractive in their navy uniforms and red-banded bonnets. But the most engaging part was the testimony meeting, when those who had been saved confessed to their formerly sinful ways and bore witness to what great things God had wrought in their lives. It was there no doubt that Brother Tucker learned his eloquence and shed some of his inhibitions. As an unredeemed United Churchman all I could do was to sit and marvel and wait for one of those young female officers to put her arm around me in hopes of getting me to the penitent altar. Alas, it wasn't to the penitent altar I wished her to take me, and so I never learned to testify.

Your invitation to speak tonight has, however, released a flood tide of memories and feelings about my childhood in Winterton, of the people and events and experiences that profoundly influenced my life. I have tried to distil some of that into a few observations, not so much about myself, as about what Winterton has meant to me and some of the indebtedness I feel. I hope in doing so I speak for more than myself, though each of us would of course express common sentiments differently.

The first debt I wish to acknowledge is that Winterton fostered in me a powerful sense of the past. Not because people dwelt on the past in any self-conscious way or thought of it as history, but because life had a seamless splicing of the present with what had gone before.

I grew up in the forties and early fifties, when Newfoundland was still on slow time. The pace and pattern of life were closer to that of eighteenth-century Dorset than to twentieth-century Toronto. Economic and social organization had not changed much for more than a century: cod fishing was still largely done by handline, and the catch was dried on flakes. In fact, the Winterton I was born into was still lined around its harbour with fishing stages and flakes. The employment rhythm of the year for many men consisted of fishing in the summer, the lumberwoods in the fall, and the seal hunt in the spring. In between, there was firewood to be gathered, snaring, trapping, and hunting to be done. Some men still coopered in the winter, and a few built boats.

For the women there was vegetable gardening, knitting, mat-hooking and quilting, besides the endless round of household chores and helping with the curing of the fish. The technology too was largely unchanged from a century before. In my father's shed, which we called "the store," there was no implement his great-grandfather would not have been able to pick up and use: an axe and a chopping block, a wood horse and saw, a plane, an auger, an awl, and a few garden implements; nothing that depended on electricity to power it. With these now antique tools my father, like other men in the community, performed an impressive variety of functions necessary to the comfort and security of his family.

And if the technology my father worked with was the same as had been used for generations, so too for the most part was the technology my mother used in our house. Water had to be fetched from a well, human waste had to be carried to the brook that flowed into the harbour at the foot of Downey's Bank, cooking was done on a wood-and-coal stove, which also served to heat as much of the house as got heated; a broom, a mop, a bucket, and a scrub-brush were the only instruments of cleaning. Electricity had arrived in Winterton, but only lights and radio had made much of a difference to the pattern of life.

This connectedness with the past shaped my psychology in a couple of ways. First, it fostered a profound respect for those who had gone before. It is commonly believed, or at least commonly observed, that life has become more complex and stressful in our time, and that we need many more sophisticated skills than in the past to succeed. The assumption that so often lies behind this is that our forebears may have been more noble and courageous than we are but they were backward in their technical knowledge and skills. I think this is wrong on both counts. There is no evidence that those who went before were morally superior, but the range of skills they needed to survive was certainly greater than those we need today, living as we do in a time when electricity and electronics enable us to plug it in and switch it on with minimum intelligence and know-how.

The repertoire of competencies of any one of our fathers was impressive. He was by turns fisherman, farmer, woodsman, hunter, and carpenter, not to mention all the roles he played in his church, his lodge, and his community. Nor was this less true for our mothers. If anything the range of their skills was greater, for not only did they perform all the traditional household and church and community work of women, but because husbands were often away for much of the year women also needed to carry out many of the tasks normally assumed by men.

Don't get me wrong, I have no wish to romanticize that past. I don't regret that technology has brought immense comfort and efficiency. I remember very well the terror engendered by a North Atlantic storm, especially if there was someone still out fishing; I remember how hard it was to wrestle a few annual vegetables from the thin, recalcitrant soil; I remember the vulnerability of people and families to illnesses in the absence of adequate medical care; I remember the economic insecurity that affected all but a few families year after year. It was an arduous and stressful life, but it was none the less complex than our own, none the less demanding of sharp minds, quick wits, sophisticated skills, imagination, and a sense of adventure, and none the less textured and nuanced with pleasure and pain, rapture and despair.

In the second place, this active presence of the past engendered in me a sense that we move toward the future as a rower rows a boat, not as a driver drives a car. Paradoxical as it may seem, it is our past that is always in front of us; our future is at our back. We get our bearings and set our course from where we've been, occasionally looking over our shoulder for reefs and cliffs and shoals. This way of thinking is not very popular in an age that stresses fast-forward movement and sets a premium on visioneering and long-range planning. In the end, however, I believe that knowing whence we have come is the most important part of knowing where we can and should be going.

But in this, I suspect, I may be a typical Newfoundlander. Others have reflected on how maritime as opposed to agricultural environments foster this mentality. In his book, *In Search of the Newfoundland Soul*, Cyril Poole contrasts the psychology of the farmer with that of the fisherman. "To till the soil is to enclose it against the beasts of the forest; to spread lime where there is acid; to fertilize when it is deficient; to irrigate against a drought and to ditch against the flood. In a word, to till is to thwart the laws of nature or at least to bend them to one's will. But the fisherman can do none of these things. It is not given to him to still the waters" (93).

Then Poole quotes what an old fisherman had once told Farley Mowatt on this subject: "Ah, me son, we don't be takin' nothin' from the sea. We has to sneak up on what we wants and wiggle it away." Poole concludes: "The land can be tamed to man's purposes, but we cannot enclose and cultivate the sea. We are capelin fishermen casting our nets on wild, exposed beaches, casting over our shoulders for the yet more furious comber rolling in unobserved or poised to dash us against the rocks. He who casts his net must sneak up and wiggle his catch away" (93).

It is this spirit, which I have inherited in spades, that has made me mistrustful of strategic planning either for myself or the organizations I have had the honour to lead. It has always seemed to me dangerous and delusive to think we can foresee the future well enough to take our bearings from that. But lulled into presumption by what science and technology have accomplished, people seem to exaggerate what we imagine we can control and orchestrate. I think it is still good advice to consider the lilies of the field and not take too much thought for the morrow. Generally, I prefer tactics to strategy; they keep you focussed on what is actually happening now, and they give you more wiggle room. I suspect I owe this preference, like so many others, to growing up in a Newfoundland outport.

But I don't wish to suggest that we should be preoccupied with the past, only that we give it the respect and the careful attention it deserves. And here may I digress a moment to say how much I have valued what has been happening in recent years in this regard, and note especially the many fine books that have appeared devoted to Newfoundland culture and history. And may I also say how admiring I am of the work of Otto Tucker and his colleagues in the Newfoundland Wessex Society for reconnecting so many of us to our own historical provenance. It was a matter of personal delight to me that Memorial University awarded Otto an honorary Doctor of Literature at its spring convocation. Together with Rhoda Maude Piercey, whose wonderful book, *True Tales of Rhoda Maude*, I have read several times, Otto has done more than anyone else to make us aware of the richness of our Winterton history. We are all in his debt.

I myself was born on the cusp between an old way of life and a new. Of course, in a sense this is true of everyone, everywhere, but more sharply so, I believe, in the case of Newfoundlanders of my generation. Confederation was a watershed in this respect. It accelerated the pace with which Newfoundland moved toward the modern world — a world of greater social security, more educational opportunities, and a different economic pattern of life. I was ten when confederation came about; by the time I was finishing school six years later, going to university was starting to become an option for those whose parents were willing to make real sacrifices.

Not that my generation was the first in Winterton to be represented in university. Elias Andrews and Bert Green and Otto Tucker and one or two others had already demonstrated that it could be done, with exceptional talent and determination. From the mid-fifties on, however, the road to university would be gradually widened. Regrettably, it meant that most of those who took that road would not return to Winterton to live, but it did allow them to make contributions to their province and country in other ways.

To come of age in a Newfoundland outport in the fifties was to experience acutely the juncture of two worlds: the one I have described and a new one aborning. The people I grew up with and I were able to take an active part in each. We pitched buttons in the spring, played tiddley in the summer, in the fall built and raced flat wooden carts, their wooden wheels greased with the cod liver oil we were given in school and expected to swallow, and gallied on pans of ice in the harbour in winter — games engaged in for generations. But we also rode bicycles, played baseball on the Guide's Ground and hockey on Clark's Pond, and listened to Hockey Night in Canada with other Canadians.

Like generations before us, we took part in Christmas concerts, attended the "times" that were held, and went jannying (as mummering was called in Winterton) as often as our mothers allowed. But we also read the same comic books being read by children all over North America, listened to radio

programs heard across Canada, saw movies now and then in the Fisherman's
Hall, and ordered clothes from Eaton's and Simpson's when we could afford
them, which was much less often than we wished. We sang the hymns of our
ancestors, but we also, thanks to radio, sang the same songs as other young
people across the continent.

In a sense we were bi-cultural. We were also bi-lingual. We became
aware that there was an old way of speaking and a new. There was the idiom
of Winterton, which hadn't changed much in several hundred years, and
which harkened back to the dialect of West-Country England. You know
the idiom of which I speak, but let me remind you by reading a few verses
from a Newfoundland version of the Arthurian legend. It was modelled on
the Tennysonian original by Paul Sparks, who is, I suspect, writing in the
Upper Island Cove version of the idiom, to judge by some of the expressions
he uses. This is the part where a dying King Arthur requests noble knight
Belvedere to throw the magic sword Excalibur into the lake as he (Arthur)
has promised. For a moment, however, Belvedere is overcome by the
temptation to keep this priceless sword for himself. The poem is entitled
"How Arter's Sard Was Trode Away."

> So 'ee looked 'ard at 'ee's sard
> (Which were 'ee's pride)
> And addressed 'eeself to Belvedere:
> "This 'ere be full of diamonds.
> Take'n down to the pond,
> Swing'n round yer hid
> And have'n out in the water."
>
> But when Belvedere seen the diamonds
> In the sard, 'ee tinks to 'eeself,
> "That's wonderful clever to be trowed away —
> 'Tisn' every day Morris kills a cow."
> So 'ee keep'n to show the youngsters.
>
> Well, when Arter heard tell the sard weren't
> Trode away, he gets powerful fierce at
> Belvedere and says to'n, "I knowed 'ee'd
> Fargit a dyin' king. If 'ee don't git out dere
> And trow out me sard, I'll kill 'ee!"

'Course that feared Belvedere and 'ee run
To the pond, grabbed up the sard
And trode'n out farthwith.

Well my lard, if an arm didn't come up out'n
The water, covered in the best piece of chintz
You ever seed, an' cotch aholt of the sard, an'
Swingd'n around a spell and drawd'n under.
She was gone, b'y, sunk, narry a sine!

That was the old lingo, and we spoke it fluently. There was creeping into our speech, however, new vocabulary, expressions, and pronunciations — the result of the new textbooks we were reading in school, the greater number of visitors who came from away, and the radio announcers who spoke a more standard English. Mind you, we had to be careful when and how we used the two registers of speech; it was as easy to be accused of being stuck-up ("I knows you idden some proud to be talkin' like dat") as of not talkin' proper when you should. It was mostly one's peers who accused one of the former, and teachers, ministers, and occasionally parents who chastised us for the latter.

It was inevitable for those of us who went away, and even for most who stayed, that standard English would gain sway as time passed. Television would finish what radio began in homogenizing culture. But I shall always be grateful for growing up in a place where an older and, in some respects, richer form of English was spoken. It gave me a sense of the sinew, the flexibility, and the music of language, which, combined with the storytelling and oral entertainment which were such a vital part of Winterton life, led me to the study of English literature and a lifelong fascination with how language serves to inform, inspire, and delight.

It also made me aware of other powers and potentialities of language. If I have made any contributions of value as an educator and educational leader, it is not by virtue of my innovative ideas, for I have had very few. It has been through my modest ability to engage people's interest and win them over by telling them old truths in fresh ways — by using the techniques of storytelling and the endlessly inventive resources of language that were a matter-of-fact part of the community and culture into which I was born.

A powerful sense of the past as a living part of the present and a guide to the future; an appreciation of the charm, the grace, and the potency of language are two of the gifts Winterton gave me, and for which I am grateful.

A third gift is harder to define but perhaps the most valuable. Winterton has helped me to understand what it means to be a community. Not because it was a perfect or ideal community itself. Not because its social organization didn't leave something to be desired. Not because its citizens were all noble and honourable people. Like everywhere else, the Winterton I knew was an amalgam of good and bad. But there was enough common interest, enough competence, enough tradition, enough pride, enough faith, hope, and charity to make a community.

Especially charity. It is no accident that, as measured each year by Revenue Canada, Newfoundlanders are the most generous givers to charitable causes. Considerably more generous than fellow Canadians in much richer provinces. The reason for this is rooted in the communal nature of Newfoundland society. For much of Newfoundland history hospitality was not an expression of social graces; it was the means whereby people responded to each other's needs; it was charity's protocol. That tradition, blessedly, lives on, and warms and impresses nearly everyone who visits Newfoundland. It is the load-bearing beam of community.

I have spent nearly all of my professional life teaching and working with young people. It is perhaps natural that I should end this talk with some words for them.

And let me begin with a confession. It took me a while to learn to be proud of my roots. I never denied or disguised my origins, but as a young man I was reluctant to declare them. Everywhere I lived, it seemed, was more prosperous, more sophisticated, and more modern than where I had come from. Newfoundland, and especially a Newfoundland outport, didn't seem to have much cachet. There was an assumption, or so it seemed, of backwardness and dependency. Some of that was in my own mind, but some of it was also in the minds of others. Like most young people, I was anxious to be accepted and not be stereotyped.

There was of course a reason many young Newfoundlanders had a bit of an inferiority complex. For years after confederation Newfoundland seemed an orphan who had been adopted by the kind Canadian family. The orphan had some talents, all right, everyone agreed, and a cheerful disposition, but it had queer and quaint ways of talking and doing things, and it didn't show much promise of ever being able to get a steady job and support itself. Then came the Newfie jokes, and they only seemed to confirm all this.

For me, however, Newfie jokes were the beginning of a recognition that Newfoundland and Newfoundlanders were being acknowledged as a distinctive part of the Canadian mosaic. These were the same jokes as had been told about French Canadians, and about Irish, Polish, Italian, Ukrainian, and other large immigrant populations. In a sense Newfoundlanders too were a large group of immigrants who entered Canada all at once. We may have spoken the same language as other Canadians, more or less, but we were still sufficiently different in our traditions and ways to constitute a visible minority (or perhaps, more accurately, an audible minority). The jokes were a kind of hazing that newcomers had to endure before they became full members of the club.

Oh, yes, there was something childish and humiliating about it all, but what it signified in a perverse way was acceptance. The jokes have long since passed on to other groups, and the image of Newfoundland has in the meantime become more attractive, thanks to the many talented men and women who have contributed to every important aspect of Canadian life and culture — from politics to business to the arts, the media, law, religion, and, yes, education.

There are only 24 or 25 major universities in Canada, and four of them at present are being led by Newfoundlanders. I say this, not to boast, but to encourage the young people among us this evening that there should be no restraint on your ambition and your aspirations because of where you grew up. There are various kinds of advantages conferred by one's place of birth. What Winterton lacked, and perhaps still lacks, in sophisticated facilities and organized activities was more than made up for by the attributes of which I have spoken this evening, and, above all, by the strength and warmth of character of the people.

To you young people I may seem very sure of myself and all I say — like someone who had an ambition and set sail to achieve it without ever straying off course. It actually wasn't like that at all. Looking back it all seems rather unplanned and mostly accidental. After all, if you think about it you'll quickly realize that no one sets out in life to be a university president. There is no recorded case of any child, anywhere, who when asked what he or she wanted to become in life, ever answering "a university president."

No, like nearly all my mates (Lorne Parrott, Willy Jacobs, George Hiscock, and the other boys with whom I lugged my skates to Clark's Pond), I wanted above all to be a hockey player. When ability and opportunity conspired to frustrate that ambition I experimented with the things my talents and opportunities allowed: teaching, the ministry, university professorship, and finally, university administration. There was nothing inevitable about any of this; there was no overwhelming ambition or outstanding ability that made it all happen. Opportunities arose and I tried enough things to discover what I was reasonably good at, and having discovered what I was good at I worked hard to get it right, blessed with good health, a supportive family, and generous friends.

Woody Allen says somewhere that ninety percent of life is just showing up. He may have exaggerated the importance of just showing up, of trying out, of volunteering, but not by much. I made up my mind early, inspired by the precept and practice of my mother and father, that I would make a habit of showing up. I haven't always succeeded at the things I showed up for, and there have been many occasions when I have had to force myself to show up at all, sometimes because I lacked confidence. And of course there have been a few things for which I might have showed up but consciously chose not to. But I have made it a practice of putting my talents to the test. That is the only advice I would presume to give to you tonight: put your talents to the test. Make a practice of showing up. Leave the judging to others. You may be pleasantly surprised at the results.

Make the most of what's left of your time in Winterton, enjoy the comforting embrace of its simple traditions, take time to observe the rough-hewn beauty of its landscape and seascape, listen for the music and inventiveness in the language still spoken here, store up memories for a lifetime, and be mindful that you have a unique vantage point from which to observe the past and launch into the future. When it comes to fortunate places to be born in this world, you have won the lottery. Winterton is a fine place to come from. It's just as fine a place to come home to.

Gurli Aagaard Woods

THE OLD ICELANDIC SAGA READING CLUB

ONE ROLE THAT really suited George Johnston was that of mentor and gently guiding force of the Old Icelandic Saga Reading Club in the 1970s. The Club seems quite unthinkable without George, but it was not his idea to start with. The impetus actually came from Enoch Padolsky, who, following his Ph.D. studies at the University of California at Berkeley, had joined the Department of English at Carleton University in 1971. One of the bright ideas Enoch brought with him from California was that of forming a club, like the one at U.C. Berkeley founded by University Librarian Jerry James, where one could read Old Icelandic sagas for the fun of it. Enoch tells me that when he first suggested to his new colleague George Johnston that they should start an Old Icelandic saga reading club at Carleton, George answered "What's that?" Once he was told about the ten to fifteen years of tradition enjoyed by the club at Berkeley, George's enthusiasm was quickly ignited.

George remembers being told about the Berkeley tradition also by Mrs. Sigrid Peterson, who kept prodding him to "get on with it," that is, to talk to Enoch Padolsky about starting a club in Ottawa. Mrs. Peterson, then about 70 years old, was born and raised in Akureyri in northern Iceland. When she was fifteen, her father had left Iceland to homestead on Lake Winnipeg. She never lost her mother tongue and thus was the Group's one true native Icelandic speaker.

Enoch and George eventually had the talk that led to the first meeting of the Old Icelandic Saga Reading Club, on December 17, 1971. Present at that meeting were, according to George's diary, Enoch Padolsky, Ian Pringle, Mrs. Peterson (as we always called her), Susan Schultz, and John Hedley. Enoch remembers that eight or nine eager beavers attended, including students from George's Old Norse class.[1] The first text read was *Hrǽðars Þáttr*,

---

[1] Apart from students from George's Old Norse classes, the Carleton people who regularly participated in the Old Icelandic Saga Reading Club included Enoch Padolsky (English), Ian Pringle (English and Linguistics), Nan Griffith (Architecture), Alison Hall (Music Librarian), Gurli Woods (German and Comparative Literature), Pat Bethel (Ph.D. in Old Saxon), and Naomi Jackson Groves (Fine Arts, retired, from McMaster; later the recipient of an Honorary Doctorate from Carleton), at whose house on Highfield Crescent we celebrated several Christmas

which the Club was still reading in February or March, when Howard Woods and I joined. We had just arrived in Ottawa from our Ph.D. studies at the University of British Columbia. This newly established club was one of the first academic activities we engaged in that first year in Ottawa.

I remember the meeting of October 22, 1972, at George's incredibly cosy house on Second Avenue in the Glebe, now the home of professor of philosophy Randall Marlin and his family. Edith Pahlke, a recent immigrant from Germany who had spent eighteen months in Iceland in the mid-sixties, was also at that meeting. I believe Howard and I had told her about the Club at a Goethe Institute meeting earlier that fall. Edith became an active member from that day on, until the meetings stopped, after having become less and less frequent, about a year after George had retired from Carleton and moved away from Ottawa to his country home on Cook's Line in Athelstan, Quebec, right at the border with the State of New York. At one of the last meetings of the Club, which took place at George's Athelstan home, he and Jeanne told the group many an amusing tale about the Johnston family's border experiences. One end of their property actually extended into the United States. Being a Quaker, George found that this state of affairs suited his temperament just fine. To him, borders were nothing but artificial obstructions.

Thanks to Edith's notes, we have a rough record of the meetings between October 1972 at George's house on Second Avenue and one of the final meetings at his cottage in Athelstan in September 1977. We all took turns hosting the Group, and in this way our meetings provided considerable culinary delight, in addition to satisfying our appetite for Old Icelandic sagas read aloud. The meetings continued for only a short time without George and eventually ground to a halt. It just was not the same without his spirited comments and guidance. After all, having by now translated several sagas and taught Old Norse at Carleton for some twenty years, George had acquired

---

meetings. Members affiliated with the University of Ottawa were Hans Møller (Chief Librarian), John Jensen (Linguistics), and Margaret Stong Jensen (Post-Doctoral Fellow). Other participants were Mrs. Sigrid Peterson (retired school-teacher and native speaker of Icelandic), Edith Pahlke (graphic artist), Rhys Knott (bookseller), Howard Woods, and Michael Sutton (both of the last two from the Federal Language Bureau). According to Edith's notes, the texts this group eagerly devoured included *Orms Þáttr, Hænsa-þóris Saga, Gunnlaugssaga Ormstungu, Völundarkviða, Hrafnkels Saga Freysgoða, Víga-Glúm Saga, Sæmundar Edda, Þrymskviða,* and "Gylfaginning" from *Snorra Edda.*

a thorough knowledge of Old Icelandic language and literary practice. And just below the surface lurked the poet, who never missed an opportunity to express the poetic qualities of the old tales, in contrast to the rather pedestrian attempts of most of the rest of us. This is what was so enchanting, and what kept the group alive for all those years.

John Flood

KICKED BY A HORSE ON THE BLUE CHURCH ROAD

On that road crows gather in the treetops,
eyeing the spoils below. Sometimes
you can hear the honking of a swerving car, the screeching
of locked tires, and see the crows drop like anchors.
They plunge, almost recklessly
— the otherwise still air sucking through stiff wings —
and plunder the still-warm road-kill. Normally

they are lazy, almost human in that ready-made,
easily-rehearsed black act. Day-in-and-day-out. Year-after-year.

On that road horses loaf around the trees
marking the boundary. Sometimes they see crows
chasing dead things, almost inanely. If they were human
they would kick the crows, but
horses can be stubborn, sometimes stupid. You can see them
gazing stupidly with eyes as big as a crow's head
as the crows rollick and flinch, their gut-bloodied beady eyes a-frenzy.

Rosalind Conway

FROM "THE LONGER VERSION OF
GÍSLA SAGA: A TRANSLATION"

The Saga of Gisli *has survived in two versions, a shorter one, which George Johnston translated for the University of Toronto Press in 1963, and a longer one, which Rosalind Conway translated in 1976 under George Johnston's supervision. No English translation of the longer version has been published since George Webbe Dasent's of 1866, a translation that is weakened by borrowings from the shorter version and by indecorous archaisms ("I don't know what they are mooting, but methinks they are striving whether Vestein left only daughters behind him, or whether he ever had a son"). Conway agrees with Johnston that colloquial modern English is the best medium for translating Old Norse, but modern English, she notes, provides a translator with a dangerous playing field, thanks to the words drawn from Latin and Greek and the vogue words drawn from the sciences and social sciences that can dominate its vocabulary. Though negotiating the playing field with her own sense of language, she has followed Johnston's lead in her translation, favouring style patterns drawn from speech, preferring Germanic to latinate vocabulary, keeping the word-order and tense-shifts of the Old Norse, and parting with any of these tactics where they would produce self-conscious effects. The pages that follow contain her translation of the climax of the longer version of the saga. They will prompt readers who don't know Johnston's* Gisli *to seek it out and will provide readers who do know it with evidence for comparison.*

In the longer version, Gisli's fate is pervasively linked to the sword Greysides. Gisli's uncle uses Greysides to win a dangerous duel and much later to kill Greysides' owner, Kol. "This," Kol utters as he dies, "will just be the beginning of the bad luck that will be brought upon your kinsmen." Gisli's family, the Whey-Thorbjornssons, take Greysides to Iceland with them, but in pieces, for it was shattered in killing Kol. Years afterwards Thorkel, Gisli's brother, brings the pieces out of their chest, and Thorgrim, the husband of Gisli's sister Thordis, works them into a spear head. With the spear Thorgrim kills Vestein, Gisli's brother-in-law, the brother of his wife Aud, and with it Gisli in turn kills Thorgrim, avenging Vestein. At Thorgrim's funeral another Thorgrim, Thorgrim the Beak, who has magical powers, works a spell so that Thorgrim's murderer will have no help and find no rest on the land.

Before these disasters the Whey-Thorbjornssons and their in-laws live in friendship and prosperity. At the height of their good luck they attend the Thing,

*a local parliament, and spend their time feasting, having no legal troubles to
settle. Their insouciance and splendour provoke envious comment, to which Gest
the Wise, a man with the gift of foresight, replies, predicting the murders, "All
of those who are there now will not be of one mind three springs from now."*

*After the murders, Thorgrim's widow, Thordis, Gisli's sister, marries
Thorgrim's brother, Bork the Stout, and prods him into bringing legal action
against Gisli. The Thing declares Gisli an outlaw, an act that sanctions vengeance
against him. For six years he evades his killers. Then Bork gives 30 pieces "of
the finest silver" to Eyjolf the Grey to track Gisli down, and Eyjolf puts his
henchman, Spying-Helgi, to work. Gisli turns to his brother Thorkel, but Thorkel,
whose jealousy of Vestein lies behind the murders, refuses him help, but promises
to warn him whenever he hears that his life is in danger. It is here that the excerpt
from Rosalind Conway's translation begins.*

— Editors

32. GISLI'S DREAM WOMEN

GISLI WAS A wise man and a great dreamer and of all men his dreams were
the most prophetic. It is clearly said, about this, that Gisli had gone as an
outlaw the longest of all men, besides Grettir Asmundarson; most men say
that Gisli was an outlaw for eighteen years.

It is told that one fall Gisli tossed and turned in his sleep — and he was
at home at Aud's steading then — and she asks, when he awoke, what he
dreamt. And he answers: "I have two women in my dreams, and one wishes
me well and gives me good counsel, but the other always tells me things that
seem ill to me and she foretells evil for me; and now the worse woman has
come to me in my dream. I seemed to come to a great hall, and there, inside
the hall, were many of my friends and kinsmen; they were drinking beside
some fires; and there were seven fires and some were nearly burnt out, but
some were bright. Then the better dream woman came there, and spoke. 'Now
I shall do you a friendly turn, Gisli,' she says, 'I will tell you now how many
years you have left to live; these fires mark your lifetime; and I advise you,'
she says, 'that while you are alive, you must give up the heathen faith and
all other sacrifices; you must not take up charms or witchcraft, and you must
be kind to the blind and lame and lesser men than you; and I hope,' she says,
'if you handle things in this way, that it will help you; and you have as many
years left as there were fires that were not burnt out.' And afterwards, I
awoke." Then he spoke these verses:

Wave fire's earth, I came into a hall where one and six fires burned; they were there as a harm to me; Eir of gold, I saw both bench-crews greet me graciously, praise-dealer wished health to each man in the house.[1]

"Take note, generous metal-tree," said Vor of bands, "friend of Agdir men, how many fires burned in the hall; thus many winters you have left to live," said Bil of headcloth, "wielder of drinks of rock-Scylds, a short time until the better."[2]

Nauma of Idi's song said, "Bringer of moon-play of eagle's steak, become not swift to learn from skalds unless you hear all-good; they say few things are worse for a fire-diminisher of ship's road, tested shield of shield's fire, than to know evil.[3]

"Cause not a fight maliciously, you be untaunting at first with meeting-Njords of death, promise me this; ring-speeder, help the blind; think about this, shield's Baldr, they say mockery and harming of the lame is evil; help the handless."[4]

33. TRIPS INTO GEIRTHJOFSFIRTH

Now Bork holds a talk with Eyjolf when they meet; it seems to him that his search has not gone forward as he had promised, and the money that he had given him had not come to much, but he thinks he knows that Gisli was there, west in the Firths; he asks him to search, or else he would go after him himself

[1]Wave-fire = gold, gold's earth = woman: Aud, who is being addressed. Eir, a goddess, goddess of gold = woman: Aud, addressed here. Praise-dealer = skald: Gisli.

[2]Metal-tree = man: Gisli, who is being addressed. Vor, a goddess, goddess of bands = woman: the better dream-woman. Agdir, a county in Norway, friend of Agdir men = Norwegian: Gisli, addressed here. Bil, a goddess, goddess of headcloth = woman: the better dream-woman. Scylds = Danish kings, kings, rock-kings = dwarves, drinks of dwarves = poetry, wielder of poetry = skald: Gisli.

[3]Nauma, a goddess, Idi, a giant, Idi's song = gold, goddess of gold = woman: the better dream-woman. Eagle's steak = carrion, moon-play of carrion = feeding on carrion in dark delight, bringer of carrion-feeding = warrior: Gisli. Ship's road = sea, fire of sea = gold, diminisher of gold = generous man. Shield's fire = sword, tested shield of sword = warrior: Gisli.

[4]Njord, a god, meetings of death = battle, gods of battle = warriors. Ring-speeder = generous man: Gisli, who is being addressed. Baldr, a god, shield's god = warrior: Gisli, addressed here.

— "And this is a great shame to both of us, not to have killed Gisli, such bold chieftains as we are and think we are." Then Eyjolf promises to search for Gisli; and they part at this.

Now Spying-Helgi goes again and takes provisions with him. He is away for a week, and night and day he watches in case he might see Gisli. Now one day he sees where Gisli is going north from his hiding place, and he recognizes him; now he goes away with matters thus, and tells Eyjolf what has happened.

He now gets a trip ready with nine others. He goes into Geirthjofsfirth and calls on Gisli's farm, but Gisli is not there. They look for him in all the woods in the neighbouring parts, but they do not find him. Then they go to the farm, and Eyjolf says to Aud that he will give her a great deal of money if she will say where Gisli is; but that is of no use; and then he threatens her and tries to make her tremble with harsh words, but has no effect. Eyjolf goes home with matters thus and is not happy with his trip.

34. GISLI SEEKS HELP FROM THORKEL AND FROM GEST'S MOTHER

Now all is quiet during the fall. Gisli thinks he knows that the way matters stand nothing can help, and now he thinks that he will be taken if he stays there. Now Gisli leaves home and rides to Bardastrand to visit Thorkel, his brother, at Hvamm. Gisli knocks on the door of the sleeping-hall that Thorkel sleeps in. Thorkel greets him, and asks what he wants. Gisli says he now wants to know if he will consider his plight, and now says he is hard-pressed — "Brother, I have left you alone for a long while, and now I expect good help from you."

But Thorkel answers the same way as before, and says he will not give him help that would place himself or his property in danger, so that a charge might be brought against him. "And I will get you a cart and some silver, if you think you need it, and other things, as I have said to you before."

"Now I see," said Gisli, "that you will not help me, brother, in such a way that you would put anything of yours in danger. Now get me three hundred and sixty ells[5] of cloth, and I intend from now on seldom to crave help from you."

Thorkel now gives him a hundred ells of cloth and also silver, and they part after this, and Gisli said that he would not treat him this way.

[5]An ell is 45 inches. The cloth is home-spun, un-dyed, and of a fixed quality, because it was used as currency. See Jón Jóhanneson, *A History of the Old Icelandic Commonwealth*, trans. Haraldur Bessanson (Winnipeg: U of Manitoba P, 1974), 331.

Afterwards, Gisli goes out to Haga, to Thorunn, the mother of Gest the Wise, and he comes there before it is dawn; he knocks on the door there, and the woman comes out. She was often in the habit of taking in outlaws; she had an underground room, and there was one opening by the river that flows near the farm, and the other was in her hearth-room; and one can still see traces of this.

Thorunn welcomes him, and Gisli calls upon her for her hospitality. She says she would certainly shelter him for a time, if she could; but said that still it would only be a woman's help. But he states that he would take the risk and would willingly accept; he said that men had not been so good to him, that it would be unlikely that women would not be better. Gisli was there for the winter, and was never as well off as then.

35. THE WORSE DREAM-WOMAN

But when spring came he went west into Geirthjofsfirth; he can stay away from his wife no longer, they loved each other so much. He was there secretly for the summer and until it became fall. And soon it comes to the same thing, when the nights grow longer, that he always dreams that the worse dream-woman comes to him.

One time Aud asks what he was dreaming — "Now," she says, "your dreams are evil."

Then Gisli spoke a verse:

Sjofn of seams comes to me in my sleep; my dreams lead me astray, if point-foe shall await old age; though ale-Nanna gives not to poetry's arranger other stuff, pin bearer, that does not stand in the way of my sleep.[6]

And now he tells her that the worse woman always comes to him and wants to smear and redden him with blood and wash him in it, and she acts hideously to him. Then he said a verse again:

Good does not come about in each dream; Gefn of shields kills merriment for me, and words are granted to me about that; as soon as

---

[6]Sjofn, a goddess, goddess of seams = woman: dream-woman. Point-foe = warrior: Gisli. Nanna, a goddess, Baldr's wife, ale-goddess = woman: dream-woman. Poetry's arranger = skald: Gisli. Pin-bearer = woman: Aud, who is being addressed.

I doze, a woman, all in men's blood, comes to meet with me, and washes me with wounds' flood.[7]

And again he spoke:

I have told again to point-din's trees about my dream of when I shall leave; Eir of gold, I did not have few words; wakers of weapons' onslaught, hunters of bitter mail-coat's hate, they who had me outlawed, will have worse if now I grow angry.[8]

And now it is quiet for a while.

36. GISLI SEEKS HELP FROM THORKEL A THIRD TIME

This fall Gisli goes to Vadil again, to Thorunn, and was there another winter with her. And then in the summer he went to Geirthjofsfirth and was there over the summer until the fall. And now he goes again to visit his brother Thorkel, and comes there at daybreak. Gisli knocks on the door; and Thorkel does not want to come out, because he thinks he knows who has come. Then Gisli takes a stick and cuts runes on it, and throws it in a window that was in the house. Now Thorkel sees this, and looks at the stick. He goes out and greets Gisli and asks him the news. But Gisli says that he cannot tell him any — "I have come to meet with you, and I mean this to be the last time; and make the best of it, brother, and help me in some way, because I will not beg of you again."

Thorkel answers again the same way, he says he would not endanger his goods or himself, and offers him a horse or a boat if he wants to get away at all; and he accepts that, and asks him to launch the boat with him. Thorkel does this and gives him a six-oared boat and also four hundred and eighty pounds of food and a hundred ells of cloth. And when Gisli has gone aboard, then Thorkel is left standing ashore.

Then Gisli spoke: "Now you think you are safe and sound in the crib, and are the friend of many chieftains, and you do not fear for yourself; but I am

[7]Gefn, a goddess, goddess of shields = woman: the worse dream-woman. Wounds' flood = blood.

[8]Point-din = battle, trees of battle = warriors: men. Eir, a goddess, goddess of gold = woman: Aud, who is being addressed here. Wakers of weapons' onslaught = warriors: men. Hunters of bitter mail-coat's hate = warriors: men.

an outlaw, and I have hope of shelter and help nowhere; but I can nevertheless tell you this, that you will be killed before me, or else my prophesying signifies nothing; but I still would expect that that will have nothing to do with me. We will now part for the time being, and not with as great friendliness as there ought to have been; and I would never treat you this way, if you needed me as much, and we should both be the same way to each other."

"I do not care about your prophecies," says Thorkel, "though you are boasting of your manliness" — and now they part with matters thus.

37. GISLI GOES TO HERGIL'S ISLAND

Gisli now rows south toward Hergil's Island, which is in Breidafirth; and when he is a short distance from the island, then he takes the planking and the oars from the boat and the thwarts, and then he overturns the boat, and he lets the boat drive in against the headlands. And when the boat was found, men thought that Gisli must have been drowned, and must have taken the boat from his brother Thorkel.

Now Gisli goes to Hergil's Island. The man who lived there was called Ingjald; his wife was called Thorgerd. Ingjald was the son of Gisli's mother's sister, in kinship, and he had come out to Iceland with him. And when they met, then Ingjald offers to Gisli to stay there with him, and what other help he can give him. And Gisli accepts that, and he is there for a time.

Ingjald's slave, who lived there with him, was called Svart; and his bondmaid or bondwoman was called Bothild. Ingjald's son was called Helgi; he was as much a fool as could be and a half-wit. He had grown as big as a troll.

Gisli stayed there for the winter. He forged tools and many other things; it was better done than that which most other men did, and more skilfully. Now men wonder greatly at this, those who came there and saw the work, because men knew that Ingjald was not very skilful — but this was all made so that it by far outdid other workmanship. Gisli stays there for three winters altogether; but he is away in the summers, and is then in Geirthjofsfirth; and Ingjald becomes the one who gives him the best help; and now three years have passed of those that he had dreamt about, that the dream woman showed him he had left to live.

Now this seems suspicious to men, and men agreed now that Gisli must be staying with Ingjald, and must not have drowned as was thought; Ingjald now also has three new boats, all well-made. Now Eyjolf is suspicious of this, and now he sends Spying-Helgi so that he will learn more of this. Then he goes dutifully and comes to Hergil's Island.

Gisli has an underground room for himself, and he is always there when men come around. And when Helgi has been there for the night, then he lets on as if he were sick, and he does not look strong at all. Ingjald was out fishing during the day, and he had his slave with him, and Bothild the bondwoman. And during the day, as the time passed, Thorgerd the housewife goes to Gisli's underground room and gave him his food; but there was a panel between the sleeping-hall, which Helgi slept in, and the pantry; and when Helgi becomes suspicious of this, where the housewife must have gone, he climbs up onto the panel, and sees that a meal has been prepared for one man; and at that moment she goes out of the pantry; he jerks suddenly and firmly, and tumbles down from the panel.

Then she spoke: "Why do you go to bed in such a way that you climb up toward the roof like a thief, and are not quiet?"

"I am so mad with pain," he says, "that I cannot be still; and lead me to my room."

She does this; and after that she goes with the food and gives it to Gisli. Then Helgi rises, and follows her footsteps at once, and now sees clearly what had happened; he lies down after that, and is there for the day.

Ingjald comes home in the evening, and asks if Helgi is getting at all better. He says he is on the road to recovery. He is there the night. But in the morning he asks for a passage away from the island; he says he has an errand south along the firth; and he is taken south to Flat Island.

He does not stop until he comes south to Thorsness, and tells Bork that he has found out about Gisli, that Ingjald is keeping him on Hergil's Island. After that Bork gets ready to go away from home with fifteen men, and they go in a ten-oared boat and sail from the south through Breidafirth.

38. INGJALD AND BOTHILD HELP GISLI

Ingjald is out fishing again, and Gisli is with him; but the slave and the bondwoman are in another boat. They are lying off the islands that are called Stykkiseyar.[9] Now Ingjald sees the sail and the ship that sails up from the south, and said, "I can see a sight there that is not to my liking."

"What is that?" says Gisli.

"A ship is sailing north from Flat Island with a red-striped sail, and it is rather likely that Bork the Stout could be in it."

[9]The Shorter Version of the saga has *Skutileyar*.

"What is to be done, then?" says Gisli, "and now I want to know whether you are as wise a man as you are worthy."

"It is easy to find a plan now," says Ingjald, "but even so I am not a wise man. Let us two row home to the island, and go up onto Vadsteinaberg and defend ourselves from there, as long as fate grants it."

"This is bravely spoken," says Gisli, "but I will not place you in so much danger, and I want to take up another plan. You row home to the island now with the slave, and go up onto the cliff and show yourselves; and they will think that I must be the other man, when they sail into the sound. And I will exchange clothes with Svart, as I have done once before; and I will go in the seal-boat with Bothild. You two need not worry about us." And they do this.

"What shall we two do now," she says, "since we are parting with Ingjald?" Then Gisli spoke a verse:

> Prop of mill-stone, shield's tree now seeks a plan because we
> must part from Ingjald; I wake Sudri's mead; nevertheless, whatever
> happens, I will have what is fated for me, I do not grieve, poor swept
> doorsill of fire of blue-land's snow-drifts.[10]

"Now we two," says Gisli, "shall row straight south toward Bork and the others, and act as if we expect no trouble; and when we meet with Bork, then you say that the fool is in the boat with you, because everyone expects this; I will sit on the prow and imitate him, and I will make myself very like him; I will tangle myself up in the fishing-line, and nearly be overboard at times, and look as if I am quite mad. But if it happens that we get past them and they pay no heed to this, then we two shall both row as best we can, as soon as we cannot be seen clearly."

She does this, so that she rows south toward them, and very close to the boat. And when they meet Bork, he calls to her, and knew who she was, and asked if Gisli were on the island. She let on as if she did not know. "But I know one thing," she says, "that that man has been there for a while, who looks much bigger than other men."

"Will he still be there?" says Bork.

"He was there before I left the house," she says.

---

[10]Prop of mill-stone = serving woman: Bothild, who is being addressed. Shield's tree = warrior: Gisli. Sudri, a dwarf, dwarf's mead = poetry. Blue-land = sea, sea's snow-drifts = waves, fire of waves = gold, doorsill of gold = serving woman: Bothild, addressed here.

"That sounds good," says Bork, "but is Ingjald at home in the house?"

She says that he rowed home a short while before, and his slave with him, "or so I thought."

"That must not have been so," says Bork, "and that must have been Gisli."

"I must not make too much of it," she says; "but I thought this, that the slave was with him there."

"You behave well," says Bork, "but we can be sure that Gisli was there."

Bork and the others row after them quickly — "Because 'now the fish might bite, if a line is just dropped over the gunwale.' And when they rowed homeward to the island, Ingjald and Gisli must have seen the ship, when we sailed north, and set off as soon as he saw us; and now let us press after him, because now it shall all be one for him."

They say, "It is good sport for us to watch the fool, how he lets himself flop in so many ways" — and said that she was wretchedly placed, since she had to follow such a one.

"So it seems to me," she says; "but I only see that it seems laughable to you, not pitiable, but you are not harming me much."

They now part after that, and the men come to the island, and go ashore at Vadsteinaberg; but Ingjald and the slave are up on the cliff. Then Bork begins to speak: "It is advisable now, Ingjald, to give Gisli up or else to tell where he is; and you are a filthy swine, since you hide him here, the slayer of my brother, whereas you are my tenant, and you deserve trouble for such a thing."

Ingjald says, "I have poor clothes, and it does not mean much to me, even if I do not get to wear them out; and I shall rather give up my life than not give Gisli all the help I can or keep him from trouble."

And men have said that Ingjald had given Gisli the most help of all in his outlawry and it had been the most useful to him. Men have also said that when Thorgrim the Beak cast the spell, he stipulated that the help that men in Iceland offered him should not benefit him; but this did not enter his head, to include the out-lying islands; and thus this help lasts a good deal longer, though it was not complete.

39. GISLI GETS AWAY FROM BORK

Bork thought he could not attack Ingjald, his tenant, and said he did not feel like having him killed. Now they go to the house, and search for Gisli, and do not find him. They go around the island now, and now come to the place in a narrow glen where the fool was, eating grass, and there was a stone tied to his neck; and now Bork begins to speak: "Now both things are so," he says, "that much is told about Ingjald's fool, and also that he can divide off into more places than seemed to be a likelihood to me. And there is nothing to look at here — we have shown such a lack of wit, that it is enormous; and I do not know when we will get back onto the right path; Gisli must have rowed toward us today, when we thought it was the fool and the bondwoman with him. Let us hasten after them, and let us not let him get away now, and let us rescue this bungled trip at once."

Now they row after Gisli and the bondwoman as best they can, and soon they see that the others have come a good way into the sound, and have the current with them. And when Gisli and the bondwoman have nearly come to shore, then Bork and his men come into spear-range of them.

Then Gisli begins to speak: "Now we two will part here; and here are two gold rings, which you shall hand to Ingjald and his wife; you shall also bring him my greeting, and this with it, that I want Ingjald to give you your freedom, and also Svart, and bring this as a token; tell him that this matters a great deal to me, because you have given me my life, and I would like you to benefit from this."

And now they part. Gisli jumps ashore; and it was an island that he had then come to, but it is only a little way off the mainland; this island is off the coast of Hjardaness. Gisli runs across the island and into a certain cleft between two crags on this island. And Bothild rows away covered with sweat from the strain and goes out into the sound beside them; and Bork and the others pay her no heed, when they see her alone in the boat.

Bork and his men now row out to the island, and Lawsuit-Stein is the first ashore, and he runs across the island at once to look for Gisli; and when he comes to the cleft, then Gisli stands before him with a drawn sword, and brings it down on his head at once, and cleaves him down to the shoulders, and he drops dead to the earth at once. Bork and the others go ashore on the island and see these events. Gisli swims then, and intends to go to the mainland. Bork lets a spear fly at Gisli, and it strikes him in the calf, and that made a large wound. Gisli snatches the spear, but he loses his sword, since he is already very weary, and cannot hold onto it. Gisli comes ashore at dusk, because then it was growing dark, and he dashes into the woods; and there the forest had grown very dense. Now they row to shore, and search for Gisli, and surround him in the woods, because the woods were not very wide, and Gisli was very tired, so that he nearly could not walk. He now becomes aware of the men on every side of him, and he now knows that they are surrounding the woods. Gisli tries to think of a plan, and sees that this will not do for him, because the woods are not deep, and they must catch him as soon as it is light, and he would not wait for this if it could turn out this way. Now he goes down to the sea very quietly, so that they would not become aware of him. He goes this way along the tidal flats in to Haug in the darkness. He meets with the farmer there for a talk.

40. REF HIDES GISLI

The farmer who lived there was called Ref;[11] he was the son of Thorstein the Staffless.[12] It is told about him that he was a most cunning man. He greets Gisli well, and asks him the news. And he told him with haste all that had happened with Bork and the others. Ref was married to the woman who was called Alfdis — lovely in appearance and fiery of temper, and she was the greatest shrew; and there was an even match in this couple. And when Gisli has told him the news, then he calls on Ref for help and support — "They will soon be aware that I have gone away from the wood, and they will come here swiftly. Now plans are to be made quickly, if you want to give me some help."

Ref spoke: "I will make one condition for you, that I alone will handle things, however they shall go, and you will not meddle; otherwise, you handle things yourself, and I will not take part."

"This must be accepted," says Gisli, "what you offer."

"You go in now," says Ref. And so Gisli does.

Then Ref spoke with Alfdis: "Now I will change men in bed with you." Then Ref takes all the covers off the bed, and said that Gisli should lie down in the straw. He does this. After that Ref lays the bedclothes on top of him, and Alfdis lies down there on the bedclothes, and gets into her bed. Ref spoke: "Now both of you stay there in bed, whatever happens, and you let your behaviour be at its worst, Alfdis, and do not spare anything that is bad in your speech; and I will go to speak with them, when they come, and say what seems fit to me."

And after that he goes out and sees a company of many men, and there are Bork's companions, eight altogether, but he stayed behind at Forsa. Now Ref asks about the news when they come to the farm; and they tell him things that he already knew. They ask if he has seen any sight of Gisli. And he says both that he himself would not want to help Gisli and also he says Gisli has not come there — "And that is certain, that I would rather be a helper of Bork

---

[11]*Refr* means "fox."

[12]"The Staffless" is a literal translation of *vanstafr*. The significance of this nickname is not clear.

than a hinderer, however I can, because no one seems to me to be better in all ways than him, and I would be eager to be his friend; but you will not believe my story unless you search the household; and I am more than willing for that; and go in and look where you like."

And when Alfdis becomes aware of this, then she scolds them, and said whatever ill thing came into her head, and does not hold back any bad speech. And Ref is right next to them, and says she is no ordinary fool, and that she does not make a difference between them and other men — "And you are not a common fool." She speaks with him in the same way or worse than with them. And when they have searched the house as they please, then they go out, and do not suspect Ref at all, and wish him a good life.

Now they go away and meet Bork, and are unhappy with their expedition; they have got a great loss of a man's life and a great disgrace, as they see it. Bork now goes home with matters thus. And Spying-Helgi goes west into the Firths for a meeting with Eyjolf, and tells him what has happened.

Gisli stayed with Ref for two weeks, and after that he goes away, and they part good friends. Gisli gives him a knife and a belt, and those were good treasures; and he had no more such things. After that he goes into Geirthjofsfirth to his wife. Now his fame seemed to have grown again greatly, and much news of him goes about, and more than before. That was the talk of men, that there had never been a man more physically accomplished than Gisli. Nevertheless, he was not a lucky man, as it turned out.

41. THE SLAYING OF THORKEL WHEY-THORBJORNSSON

Now it is to be told about this, that Bork goes north to the Thing at Thorskafirth with a great crowd of men and intends to meet with his friends. Gest Oddleifsson went west from Bardastrand and also Thorkel Whey-Thorbjornsson, each on his own ship. And when Gest is ready to go, two very poor boys come to him; they were ill-clothed and had staffs in their hands; they asked Gest for a passage and spoke with him quietly for a while. He welcomed them and gives them the passage, and he takes them to Hallsteinsness. There they went ashore on the farm at Hallsteinsness, where it is called Nesgranatre; there Hallstein[13] sacrificed his son, so that sixty ells

---

[13]Hallstein Godi is Thorstein Codfish-catcher's brother, and the son of Thorolf Mostr-beard. He is Bork's uncle. This digression does not occur in the Shorter Version. This is also mentioned in *Landnámabók*, but it is not told there that it was his son that was sacrificed. *Íslendingabók Landnámabók: Íslenzk fornrit, I*, ed. Jakob Benediktsson

of wood drifted ashore, and the high pillars, which he had made out of the wood, are still there. The boys go up into Teigswood; they go along the woods until they come to the Thing at Thorskafirth.

A man was called Hallbjorn the Hooded;[14] he was a tramp, and he had ten other tramps with him, or more; he was used to roofing a booth for himself at the Thing,[15] and he is still doing this; now he has a great company of tramps with him. The boys go there to him and ask him for lodging in a booth there; and Hallbjorn was a good host, and says he has granted lodging in a booth to every man here who had asked him, he says he also would not deny them this — "I have also been here at the Thing many springs, and I know all the chieftains, those who have the rank of godi." The boys say they eagerly wish to have his help and to learn from him. Hallbjorn says he intends to go down to the shore, where the ships sail, and says he would tell them who was on the ships. They thank him for that, and say that seems a great sport.

Now they go to the shore where the ships are landing. Then the older boy begins to speak: "Who owns that ship that is sailing in here next?"

Hallbjorn says, "Bork the Stout."

The boy asks, "Who is sailing next to him?"

Hallbjorn says, "Gest the Wise is there, from Haga in Bardastrand."

The boy asks, "And who is sailing his ship out along the creek at the head of the firth?"

Hallbjorn answers, "That is Thorkel Whey-Thorbjornsson."

And now they see that he goes ashore and seats himself on a rock; and his companions carried their luggage from the ship, so that the tide would not reach it. Bork has a roof put over their booth, because both of the in-laws had one booth, and they were always on friendly terms. Thorkel had a Russian hat on his head and a grey cloak over himself with a gold clasp at the shoulder, and a sword in his hand. Then the boys and Hallbjorn the Hooded went with this group of men to where Thorkel sat.

Then the older boy began to speak: "Who is this very noble-looking man who sits here? And I have not seen such a handsome and lordly man."

"You speak well, boy," says Thorkel, "and I am called Thorkel."

(Reykjavík: hið Íslenzka Fornritafélag, 1968), 1: 163–64.

[14]*Hallbjörn húfa. Húfa* actually means "cap," but "the Hooded" keeps the alliteration.

[15]Booths "were shelters of turf and stone built around a framework of timber and roofed and decorated with homespun cloth. In the Old Icelandic literature many of the booths are identified by name." *A History of the Old Icelandic Commonwealth*, 43.

The boy spoke: "Will you allow me to look at that sword that you are holding, as great a treasure as it is?"

Thorkel says, "That is an unusual request; but certainly I shall allow you this, if you have such a great curiosity."

And now he receives the sword and undoes the peace-straps at once, then he draws the sword.

Thorkel spoke: "I did not give you leave to draw it."

"I did not ask you for your leave," says the boy. Then he brandishes the sword quickly and strikes Thorkel's head off.[16]

And when these things had happened, then Hallbjorn runs away as best he might, and will not let himself be taken, and the other tramps do likewise. And the boy throws down the bloody sword and took his staff, and then the boys run with the other tramps; and the tramps are nearly going mad with fear; they run up beside Bork's booth, where they were roofing the booth. And those who see Thorkel's death crowd around his body, and do not think they know who has done the deed.

Bork spoke: "What set off the uproar and the tearing about, which happened beside Thorkel's booth?"

And at this Hallbjorn the Hooded runs up beside them with his fifteen tramps; then the younger boy answers him (that one was called Helgi; and the other, who had done the slaying, was called Berg): "I do not know," he says, "what they are having a meeting about; but I do know this, what they are wrangling about."

"What, then?" says Bork.

"Whether Vestein would have left behind only daughters, or whether he would have left any sons."

Hallbjorn the Hooded runs to his booth. But the boys run into the woods that were near the booths, and are not to be found.

42. THE VESTEINSSONS VISIT AUD

And the men run to the tramps and ask what it means. And they say that two boys had come into their company, and say that this came entirely unawares, and said they knew nothing of them. They tell how the boys acted and what their appearance was like and also their speech. Now Bork thinks he knows

[16]In *Eyrbyggja saga* Ulfar also is killed with his own sword after he is flattered and asked to show it. See *Eyrbyggja saga; Islenzk fornrit*, 4, ed. Einar Sveinsson and Mattias Pordarson (Reykjavík: hið Íslenzka Fornritafélag, 1935), 88.

from the words that Helgi spoke, that Vestein's sons must have been there.

Bork and the others go to Gest's booth now, and consult with him about how things shall be handled; and now Bork wants to prepare a suit against the boys — "It should be up to me," he says, "to take up the suit for Thorkel, my brother-in-law; and it does not seem an unlikely thing to pursue, that Vestein's sons would have done the deed; and we do not think that it could be expected that other men would have something against Thorkel; but still they have got away for the time being; and I am most eager to make them outlaws here at the Thing. Advise us now, Gest," says Bork, "how to prosecute."

Gest said, "It would not seem hard to oppose; and I should know how to do that if I had done the slaying, to give my name differently than what I am called, and then the charge and suit that were brought against me would be void. Now it would seem to me that it also may be that the one who has done the deed thought the same" — and Gest lets it seem as if there were many hindrances about the suit. And some men were certain that Gest had rather been in league with the boys, because he was related to Vestein.

Now Bork and the others cease this talk; and the suit was not brought forward, and there at the Thing they bury Thorkel in a mound; the men go home when they are ready, and no more events took place there. Bork is again unhappy with his trip, as he had a right to be; now he goes home to the south and has great dishonour from this business.

Now the boys go on until they come to Geirthjofsfirth, and they have been sleeping out-of-doors for four and a half days without food. Gisli was staying there with his wife. They come there at night and knock on the door, and Aud goes to the door and greets them well and then asks the news. — It was often her custom that she would go out, but Gisli would lie in his bed-closet, since he had many enemies, and could not know exactly who would come and from where; and there was an underground passage beneath the bed-closet; she would raise her voice when he needed to be warned. — The boys tell her what they had been about and everything about their trip, and said they had been outside without food for four and a half days.

Aud spoke: "I will send you over the ridge to Mosdale, to Bjartmar's sons with tokens" — they were her mother's brothers — "and I shall give you food and the means to travel, and always give you shelter, such as I may; but I will not ask Gisli to help you henceforth."

Now they go away, and went into the woods, and hide themselves there, so that they can not be found; now they eat food, which they have done without for a long time; after this they lie down, and shortly fall asleep, since they were already weary and worn out from the travelling.

43. GISLI LEARNS OF THORKEL'S SLAYING

Now it is to be told of Aud that she goes in and sees Gisli, and says thus: "It is of much importance how you will take this, and now do me more honour than I am worthy of."

"I know," says Gisli, "that you will tell me of the slaying of Thorkel, my brother."

"It is as you guess," she says, "and Vestein's sons killed him, my brother's sons; and that was not without cause, if they wanted to avenge their father, whom Thorgrim and the others killed; and even though Thorgrim carried the weapon to him, that was mostly your brother Thorkel's doing. They have come here; and I would have liked you to all hide out together; and now they think that they have no one else to trust in."

Gisli says, "I cannot stand that, to be together with the slayers of my brother." He leaps up and wants to draw his sword. He spoke a verse:

Who knows but Gisli will draw sharp battle-ice from scabbards
— men will hear of what I will do with my chance — since victory-
trees tell the ring's polisher about the Thing, Thorkel slain; I shall do
daring deeds until death.[17]

Aud answers that he does not need to be so angry — "because they have both gone away; and I had my wits about me for this, not to let them come into your sight and thus endanger them."

"This is the best way," says Gisli.

And it is quiet for a while, and now two years are left of those that the dream woman said he had to live.

And now Gisli is in Geirthjofsfirth, and when summer draws to a close and autumn draws near, his dreams come back and his nightmares; the worse dream-woman comes to him now, but nevertheless, the other one does at times. On a certain night now he dreams that the better dream-woman comes to him, and it seemed to him as if she were riding a grey horse, and asks him to be with her and ride to her home, and it seems to him that he does that, and she comes to a certain house with him and shows him into the house, and it seems well-arrayed to him. She bid him to stay there and feel happy — "And you shall come here when you are dead, and enjoy riches here with me." And now he awakens, and he spoke a verse:

[17]Battle-ice = sword. Victory-trees = warriors: men. Ring's polisher = man: Gisli.

Seam-Hlokk asked praise-adorner to ride home with her on her grey
horse, then bride was friendly with hunter; bending-Sol of horn-flood said
she would heal me wholly; I recall words of prop of seagull's ground.[18]

And again he spoke:

Precious Dis of sea's fire has praise-poem's steerer shown where to
sleep, where lay a down bed; I forget little of this; the wise seam's Nauma
led me with her, skald got a soft bed: I saw not a hill in the bed.[19]

44. SPYING-HELGI AND HAVARD BUILD A CAIRN

The thing that is to be told next is that Eyjolf the Grey sends Spying-Helgi
into Geirthjofsfirth. Another man was also sent with him; he was called
Havard; he had newly come to Iceland, earlier in the summer; he was a
kinsman of Gest Oddleifsson. These men were sent into Geirthjofsfirth to hew
timber in the woods that are there, and to search for Gisli's dwelling, if they
might find his hiding-place. And the last evening, when they have been in
the woods three nights to look for Gisli, they see a fire burning up in the crags
in the woods south of the river, and that was around nightfall, and it was
pitch-black. Now Havard asks Helgi for a plan, how to deal with things so
that they would find their way to where the fire burned.

"There is only one thing to do," says Helgi, "to pile up a cairn of stones
where we are standing on the hill and mark with it where the fire burns; and
then the hiding-place will be found when it is daylight."

Now they do this, and when they have done this work Havard says he
needs to sleep — "And I cannot do another thing" — and so he does. And
Helgi heaped up the cairn and makes it very high. And when the night is
drawing to a close, then Havard wakens, and said that Helgi should sleep
— "And I will keep watch," he says. And when Helgi has slept for a while,
then Havard carries the cairn away, and scatters every stone. After that he
takes a large stone and flings it down onto a slab of rock, so that the ground
shakes, and it comes near the nape of his neck. Helgi springs up, and asks

[18]Hlokk, a valkyrie, seam-valkyrie = woman: the better dream-woman. Hunter = man: Gisli.
Sol, a goddess, horn-flood = ale, bending goddess of ale = woman: the better dream-woman.
Seagull's ground = sea, prop of sea = woman: the better dream-woman.
[19]Dis, guardian spirit, sea's fire = gold, guardian spirit of gold = woman: the better dream-
woman; praise-poem's steerer = skald: Gisli; Nauma, a goddess, seam's goddess = woman.

what the matter is, and becomes very afraid.

Havard says, "I think that a man is in the woods nearby us, because many such gifts have arrived in the night."

Helgi says, "Gisli must have come here and found out about us, and it will not be a good idea to wait here, and we will both be crushed if such a stone hits us."

Now Helgi runs as best he can, and bids Havard to go faster; but Havard says he feels faint, and asks him not to run away from him now. Now Helgi runs to their boat as fast as he can. Now they go home to Otradale and tell Eyjolf about their trip. But he says moreover that Helgi has not handled the spying as badly as he usually did, and says he now knows for sure what had become of Gisli.

After that Eyjolf goes with eleven men and Havard goes along on the trip, and Spying-Helgi. They go across the firth by boat, and come into Geirth-jofsfirth, and search far and wide during the day in the woods for the cairn that Helgi and his companion said they had piled up, and they do not find it, as was likely; and they do not find the hiding place either. Then Eyjolf asks Havard where they had piled the cairn. But he says he did not pile up the cairn himself — "and I was sleeping while Helgi was piling the cairn. But it seems to me that it may be, if Gisli became aware of us, that he broke apart the cairn when it was light, since we were gone." Now this seems most likely to Eyjolf; nevertheless, they search for a long time and find nothing.

Then Eyjolf spoke: "We are having bad luck in this business, and we will go back for the time being." And so they do.

45. EYJOLF OFFERS AUD SILVER

Now they turn home toward Aud's farm, and Eyjolf says he wants to visit her. They go to the door, and into the dwelling; Eyjolf sits down for a talk with Aud, and spoke thus: "I will make a deal with you, that you tell me about Gisli, and I will give you for this these sixty ounces of silver, which I have taken for a bounty on his head; and you shall not be at his slaying, because it is understandable that that would be trying to you; I will get a marriage for you not worse than this one, because you will have little delight from Gisli from now on."

"It does not seem certain to me," says Aud, "whether we will agree on that; it may be that a man in place of my husband Gisli seems poor payment to me, but what they say is true, 'money is best for bereavement,' and let me see what is offered to me, whether the silver is as good as you say."

"Yes," says Eyjolf, "it must seem so." Now he pours the silver into the lap of her cloak, and shows it to her.

And Gudrid, Gisli's foster-daughter, began to cry when she became aware of this, and she runs out into the woods to see Gisli, and tells him how matters stand — "Now my foster-mother has gone mad, and she intends to tell about you and betray you."

Gisli spoke: "Be calm; something else will be the cause of my death, rather than Aud being the conspirator." And now he spoke a verse:

> Men of firth's elk say mead-Hlin has hidden wrong ship-field's
> heart from her man; but I know stone-fish's floor-meadow sits
> tearfully; I do not think glory-slope of wave-flame proves thus.[20]

And now the girl goes home, and goes walking in, and does not tell her errand to Aud or where she has been. And now Aud has counted the money, and says that in no way is it worse than he has said — "Now you will think I have a right to handle the money," she says, "however I wish to do."

"Yes," he says; "that is surely so."

She put the money into her purse then, and after that flings it at his nose, so that blood lay on the ground at once — "Have this now," she says, "for your falseness first of all; or did you have some hope that I would give my husband up to the axe, into the hands of trash like you; now have these," she says: "shame and dishonour, but not what you wanted."

Then Eyjolf spoke: "Seize the dog now, and kill it, even if it is a bitch."

Then Havard spoke: "Yet this trip of ours has gone very badly, even if we do not do this coward's work; and we have got enough shame already; but this is a long way from that; for no worthy man would have had this done; and let those stand up who wish to help me, and let us not let this be done; the old saying is quite true, that 'ill-luck is home-bred'."

And after this Eyjolf goes home with great disgrace and dishonour.

And before Havard went out, Aud spoke: "It would not be proper that you would not collect your debt that Gisli and I have to pay you for goods that we bought from you in the fall; here is a gold ring that I want you to have, because I do not have any goods to repay you with."

"That is not such a great debt," Havard says, "and I would not have claimed it, unless you wanted to repay it."

---

[20]Firth's elk = ship. Hlin, a goddess, mead-Hlin = woman: Aud. Ship-field's heart = deep spirits. Stone-fish = serpent, serpent's floor = gold, gold meadow = woman: Aud. Wave-flame = gold, slope of gold =woman: Aud.

And she really gave the gold ring for his help, and he accepts the ring. And after this they go home. And a little later Havard gets himself a horse and rides away from Otradale with all his belongings and south to Bardastrand to Gest the Wise, and does not want to be with Eyjolf the Grey any longer. Eyjolf is not very happy with all of this.

46. THE DREAMS GROW WORSE

Gisli is on his guard now, and most of the time he is in his hiding-places. Now the winter passes this way until the summer comes, and now he does not intend to move away from there, because now he thinks all his hiding places are blocked; he thinks that he shall wait here now for better or for worse; and now all of the years foretold in the dreams have passed. And now Gisli dreams often during the summer, so that it does not leave off.

He is restless in his sleep one night; and when he awakes, Aud asks what he has dreamt. He says that the worse dream-woman came to him and spoke thus: "I shall turn around everything that the better dream-woman told you, and I shall fix things so that no protection or help will be of use to you that she promised you." Then he spoke a verse:

> "You two shall not be together," said prop of drink-vessel; "thus has poison of good-love led you two to grief; all-ruler of men has sent you from your house alone into a foreign land to know another home."[21]

"And I dreamt again," says Gisli, "that the woman came to me and tied a bloody cap on my head, and first she washed my head in blood and splattered blood all over me." And now he spoke a verse:

> I thought Thrud of wealth washed my hair red with Odin's fire's foam from blade's pole's well; and hand of the goddess of hawk's trail's blaze was blood-red in storm of wounds of fire graspers' wrists.[22]

And he spoke again:

[21]Prop of drink-vessel = woman: the worse dream-woman. All-ruler of men = God.
[22]Thrud, Thor's daughter, a goddess, goddess of wealth = woman: the worse dream-woman. Odin's fire = sword, sword's foam = blood. Blade's pole = sword, sword's well = wound. Hawk's trail = hand, hand's blaze = gold, goddess of gold = woman: the worse dream-woman. Fire = gold, gold-graspers' wrists = men.

I thought watcher-Gondul of battle-flames wrapped my bushy crisp-cropped parted hair in a gory cap; her hands were washed in sword-rain; thus seam's Saga woke me from my dream.[23]

And now the dreams let up at first, but even so the fall has not passed before he dreams often. And now such a great run of them takes place that he becomes so afraid of the dark from the dreams, that he cannot be alone in his hiding-places, and he needs to be where Aud and Gudrid were all the time. Every time when he has been acting most strangely, Aud asks what he dreams; and he always tells her.

Now it happens one night that his dreams are hard; and now Aud asks again, when he awoke, what had appeared to him. And he says that he dreamt "that men came here to us, and Eyjolf the Grey was there on a trip with many men. And we met, and I knew that something happened between us. Then it seems I hew one of their men in half; and on the man there seemed to me to be a wolf's head, and first he came howling at me, and there seemed to be many against me alone; but I seemed to have a shield in my hand and to defend myself against them so long that they did not overcome me." And then he spoke a verse:

> I knew foes attacked me in battle; I got less help from within, though I was not quickly dead; I gave raven's mouth slain-sacrifice; but your fair breast was reddened in my bright blood.

And again he spoke:

> They could not hurt skald's shield with shrieking swords; I had courage; shield helped me against cutter, until they who will cause my death got victory with overwhelming strength; sword's din was loud to hear.[24]

And again he spoke:

> I overcame one before early-flier's comforters wounded me; I gave to carrion-stream's hawk Munin's mouthful; of its own accord

---

[23]Gondul, a valkyrie, battle-flames = blood, watcher-valkyrie of blood = woman: the worse dream-woman. Sword-rain = blood. Saga, a goddess, goddess of seam = woman: the worse dream-woman.

[24]Cutter = sword.

sword's edge sheared leg in two; necklaces' wrecker lost his footing; that was an honour.[25]

Now the fall passes and his dreams do not leave off, but come rather more often. Now it happens one night that he sleeps even more badly than before. Aud asked him then, when he awakes, what appeared to him. And he answered and said:

I thought blood ran down both my sides; I had to endure distress of wound-sea; I dream such things when I sleep, bearing-Lofn of riches, I am somewhat outlawed by men; I wait for shafts' storm.[26]

Ring-Hlin, I thought carrion-net's god made blood stream down both my sturdy shoulders with sharp sword; and my hopes of life were grey, Vor of leeks, because of great harm of hawk-nourishers; I undergo such things.[27]

I thought ogress's shield's shakers lopped off both my arms with a mail-coat's switch; I got great wounds; Syn of twine, again I thought my helmet-stem was cloven down by sword's mouth, sword gaped over my head.[28]

I thought in my sleep silver-band's Sjofn stood over me crying; that belt's Gerth had wet eyelids, and the glorious wave's fire-Njorun very quickly bound my wounds; what do you think it boded for me?[29]

---

[25]Early-flier = raven, comforters = feeders, raven's feeders = warriors. Carrion-stream = blood, blood's hawk = raven. Munin, one of Odin's two ravens, raven's mouthful = carrion. Necklaces' wrecker = warrior.

[26]Wound-sea = blood, distress of blood = loss of blood. Lofn, a goddess, bearing-goddess of riches = woman: Aud, who is being addressed here.

[27]Hlin, a goddess, ring-goddess = woman: Aud, who is being addressed here. Carrion-net = shield, shield's god = warrior. Vor, a goddess, goddess of leeks = woman: Aud, addressed here. Hawk-nourishers = warriors.

[28]Ogress's shield = axe, axe's shakers = warriors. Mail-coat's switch = sword. Syn, a goddess who sits at defence in trials, goddess of twine = woman: Aud, who is being addressed here. Helmet-stem = head. Sword's mouth = edge.

[29]Sjofn, a goddess, silver-band's goddess = woman, the better dream-woman. Gerth, a goddess, a belt's goddess = woman: the better dream-woman. Njorun, a goddess, wave's fire = gold, gold goddess = woman: the better dream-woman.

47. EYJOLF AND HIS MEN FIND GISLI

Now Gisli is quiet at home afterwards that summer, until the last night of summer comes. Then it is told that he cannot sleep, and none of them could. And the weather has gone calm, with a slight frost. Then he says he wants to go away from the farm to his hiding-place south under the cliffs, and try to see if he might sleep there. Now they all go there; they wear long cloaks, and the cloaks drag and leave a trail where they go, and Gisli has a stick, and he cuts runes in it, and the chips fall down along the way. Now they come to the hiding-place. He lies down and intends to sleep; and they keep watch over him, and sleep comes upon him, and straightaway he dreams that two birds come into the house and attack one another like looms;[30] they were a little bigger than cock-ptarmigans, and screeched rather horribly, they were all coated with nothing but blood. He awakes after that; and Aud asks if he dreamt anything — "And now your dreams are not good," she says.

And he spoke a verse:

> In blood's house's home noise came to my ears, linen-Bil, when we two parted; I pour dwarf's drink; tree of sword-clash listened to looms' slaughter of two cock-ptarmigans; bow's dew will fall on a man.[31]

And next they hear men's voices outside, and Eyjolf has come with fourteen men, and has already come home to their house, and they see the

---

[30]The Icelandic is *í læmingi*. Some have thought this was the word for "lemming." George Webbe Dasent writes, "There is little doubt that it really means the 'Loom', or Great Arctic Diver, whose shrieking, heard in these vast solitudes at night, is most weird and doleful." *The Story of Gisli the Outlaw* (Edinburgh: Edmonston and Douglas, 1866), xxix. No bird is known that has this form as its name; however, G. Turville-Petre agrees with Dasent: "The diminutive suffixes -*ing*-, -*ung*- are particularly common in bird-names; *titlingr* and *fýlungr* may be cited.... In Icelandic the word *lómr* (cf. English *loom*, Danish *lom*) is applied to the red-throated diver. This bird is much larger than a cock ptarmigan; on his throat he has a patch of dull red, the colour of gore. His conduct is unpleasing, for he utters 'eerie wails, growls, hoots, goose-notes, screams and howls'." *Nine Norse Studies* (London: Viking Society for Northern Research, 1972), 151–52.

[31]Blood's house = heart, heart's home = breast. Bil, a goddess, linen-goddess = woman: Aud, who is being addressed. Dwarf's drink = poetry; sword-clash = battle, tree of battle = man: Gisli. Looms' slaughter = attack; bow's dew = shower of arrows.

trail in the dew where they had gone, and then it was as if the way was shown to them. And when they become aware of the men, then they go up onto the cliffs where it seemed the best vantage point to them, and each of the women has a club in her hand. Eyjolf and the others go up to the cliffs.

Then Eyjolf spoke: "It is advisable now, Gisli, not to run away and not to let yourself be chased, since you are called a great champion. We have had meetings for a long time; and I wish that this would be the last one."

Gisli says, "Have at me like a man, since I shall not run away any longer; and you come at me bravely, since you think you have a case against me."

Eyjolf spoke: "Now I will not put matters in your hands, and I shall take advantage of the odds and the brave men that I have with me."

Then Eyjolf spoke with Spying-Helgi: "It would be manly now," he says, "for you to decide to go up the cliffs at Gisli first, and this would be talked of for a long time, if you become his slayer; we always have faith in you when it comes to manliness."

Helgi answers, "You have always shown that you liked to have others in front of you, when there was mortal danger in it; but, nevertheless, I shall surely go up, since you egg me on so much; but then follow me well, and go right next to me, if you dare to do that."

After that Helgi sets off for where it seemed to him best for getting up the cliffs. He had an axe in his hand. Gisli also had an axe, was girt with a sword, and in a grey-striped cowl tied round him with a cord. And when he goes up the cliffs, then Gisli springs at him, and hews him apart at the middle with his sword, and both parts fell down the cliffside.

Eyjolf is then the next man to start up the cliffs, and Aud turns upon him, and smashes him with her club, so that she loses the strength in both her arms. Then the women are seized, and Eyjolf got two men to hold them.

And now the twelve attack Gisli and they come up the cliffs at him now; but he defends himself both with stones and weapons. Eyjolf strikes him with a spear; but Gisli cuts the shaft off the spear so that it falls on the rock ledges, and the blow is so great that he breaks the tip of the blade off the axe. And now he protects himself with his shield, and fights with his sword. Now they come at him hard; and they say he killed another two men. Eyjolf eggs them on fiercely now, to come hard at him — "And we are getting the worst of it from him," he says, "but still that does not matter, since the reward for our pains is good, if we overcome him."

Now Gisli runs down along the cliffs, and onto the crag that is called Einhamar; that is a good vantage point. Now he defends himself from there for a time. This takes them quite unawares, and their plight seems to be becoming hard again. Eyjolf eggs them on anew — "And it is very much because," he says, "this cowardice will be heard of everywhere," when they could not overcome Gisli, since they were fifteen, and he was alone. Eyjolf promises them great honours now, if they get to overcome him. He has hand-picked men with him, moreover.

48. GISLI'S DEATH

There is a man named Svein, who now started first up onto the crag at him. And Gisli strikes at him, and kills him at once, and he falls down dead in front of the crag. Now Eyjolf and the others do not know what place will do to fight against this man, and still do not want at all to turn away before they have beaten him.

Now they attack him from two sides and these followed Eyjolf foremost, one named Thorir, and another named Thord, near kinsmen of Eyjolf; now their onslaught is very hard; they get to wound him sorely with their spear-thrusts, but he defends himself none the worse, so that all who attack him become wounded. But it is to be told about the outcome, that they wound him internally, so that his bowels fall out. He wraps up his bowels with his shirt, and binds them to himself underneath with a cord. And then Gisli said, that they should wait a little bit — "And you will have the end of the business which you want." He now said this verse:

> Fair-faced Fulla of hall of spear-socket's rain who gladdens me
> shall hear of her friend's bold feats; I am happy, even if fair-hammered
> edges should bite; my father gave a sword's temper to his son.[32]

This was his last verse. And right after he had spoken the verse, he leaps down a rift in the crag, and thrusts his sword at the breast of Thord, Eyjolf's kinsman, and he dies at once. And now Gisli gives up his life there with great prowess and courage, and injured with many wounds, so that it was a strange thing; and it seemed unheard of to them, what a defence he made. Eyjolf and the others all were wounded, those who were still alive, and very worn out. — And there ends the life of Gisli Whey-Thorbjornsson; and it is right to say that he had been the most valiant of men.

Afterwards, they dragged him down to level ground, and took his sword from him, and bury him in a green spot. Later on they went down to the sea, and to their boat; and now the sixth man died beside the ship. Eyjolf asked

---

[32]Fulla, a goddess, hall of spear-socket = hand, hand's rain = gold, goddess of gold = woman: Aud.

Aud to go with him to his house, and her foster-daughter; but she would not accept that. Now Eyjolf and the others go home to Otradale; and the same night the seventh man died from his wounds; and the eighth man lies wounded for a year, and then dies. And the other men are healed of their wounds, so to speak, and yet get great maiming and much mutilation.

49. THORDIS'S REVENGE

As soon as Eyjolf thinks himself able, he goes away with eleven men, and south over Breidafirth to a meeting with Bork, and he tells him these events and all the details about this business, and thinks he has got nothing good from it. Bork is very glad about this report, and now bids Thordis, that she receive Eyjolf well and welcome him — "because he has driven shame and dishonour away from us; and let the love come into your heart that you had for my brother Thorgrim, and now receive them well, and treat them kindly."

Thordis says, "I must grieve for my brother Gisli; but I am glad about his death."

And in the evening the table was set before Eyjolf and Bork. They talk over many things during the evening and were very jolly. Afterwards, the tables were set up, and Thordis carries food to the table. Eyjolf had the sword in his hand that Gisli, her brother, had owned. Then she throws down the spoons, which she had meant to give to the men before, from the box[33] that she held, and she bends down, and acts as if she wants to gather the spoons together; she grasps the haft of the sword and draws it quickly; then she puts it under the table, and means to thrust it down into Eyjolf's belly; but the sword-guard was on the sword, and she did not heed this, and the point of the guard caught against the table, and the thrust came lower down than she had meant, and pierces the thigh, and that was a very large and deep wound.

Eyjolf and his men leap up, and shove away the table, and all the food tumbles down. Bork seizes Thordis, and takes the sword from her, and said she was witless, and gives her a box on the ear. Bork asks Eyjolf to be the sole judge of this event; at once Eyjolf fixes the amount at full payment for a man's life for the wound; and says he would claim much more, if Bork had not acted so well.[34]

[33]The Icelandic is *keraldr*, and there is no equivalent in English. This is a small, round, wooden container.

[34]This scene also occurs in Eyrbyggja saga: *Íslenzk fornrit* 4: 23–24.

After this Thordis named witnesses, and calls herself divorced from her husband Bork, and says she would not get into the same bed with him again; and she did just that. Then she went out to Eyr, to Thordis's Steading, and she lived there for several years afterwards.

And Bork stayed at Helgafell thereafter, until Snorri Godi got him out of there; and then he went to live in Glerarskog in Hvammsfirth.[35]

Eyjolf went home west to Otradale, and was not happy with his trip.

50. AUD AND THE VESTEINSSONS LEAVE ICELAND

After that, Vestein's sons went out to meet with Gest in Hagi; and they call on him to get them out of Iceland by his arrangements, and Gunnhild their mother and Aud their father's sister, who had been the wife of Gisli Whey-Thorbjornsson, and Gudrid, Ingjald's daughter, and her brother Geirmund. And all these people were brought from Iceland by Gest Oddleifsson, from Hvita with Sigurd the White, and they were at sea for a little while, and came to the north of Norway.

And one day Berg Vesteinsson goes down the road, and wants to find lodging for them, and there were two Norwegians with him. They meet two men in front of them, and one was in a scarlet tunic, a young man with a big build. He asked Berg his name. And he tells the truth about his name and kin; and he thought that this would happen in more places, that he would benefit from this, rather than suffer on account of his father, because Vestein was the most well-liked man on the trade routes. But as soon as Berg had said this, the man drew his sword and deals him a death-blow. And that was Ari Whey-Thorbjornsson, brother of Gisli and of Thorkel.

And when this had come about, then those who had come ashore with Berg ran to the ship, and tell this news that had come about. And Sigurd the captain got those who survived away and got a passage to Greenland for them, and Helgi makes a steading for himself there, and was thought to be a most good-hearted fellow; and men were sent after his head, but this was not the way it was to turn out, that they should slay him; he died later on a fishing trip in Greenland, and this was thought to be a great loss.

And Aud and Gunnhild went to Denmark to Hedeby, and became Christians there; later they went south to Rome, and neither came back.

Geirmund went to Greenland, and married there, and became quite

---

[35]In *Eyrbyggja saga* the divorce is not immediate. It is announced two years later when Snorri manages to get his patrimony, Helgafell, from Bork (24–26).

wealthy. His sister Gudrid was given in marriage to a man, and she was thought to be a clever woman. And many men in Greenland are descended from the brother and sister.

Ari made ready to go to Iceland, and he owned a trading ship then, and he came into Hvita with his ship; then he sold the ship; and he buys land at Hamar in Borgarfirth outside Borg, and he lived there for a few years, and he lived in various places in Myrar, and there are men descended from him; there is nothing more to be told about him in this story.

And here ends the story of Gisli Whey-Thorbjornsson.

Cattle die, and kinsmen die,
thyself eke soon wilt die;
one thing, I wot, will wither never;
the doom over each one dead.

Edith Pahlke
Icelandic Edda
(Edda, Hávamál)
linocut 12 x 8 inches

Sean Kane

HANDY IN AWKWARD CIRCUMSTANCES

"TREES ARE WOMEN, they bear God's earthy weight." It is the beginning of ENG 290 Anglo-Saxon and Professor Johnston is reciting a poem he has just written on his walk to the university. The poem became "The Siberian Olive Tree" (*Endeared by Dark: The Collected Poems*, page 99):

> Walking upwind under Bronson Bridge
> In winter time, thinking wintry thoughts,
> I look at a Siberian olive tree
> That has been planted alongside the canal.

Sixteen second-year students hear a poet out; then the class turns to Anglo-Saxon prefixes and suffixes. Professor Johnston is an odd one all right, almost as wacky as Gordon Wood, whose lecture on *Paradise Lost* the period before has turned on a distinction made by the Sufi mystics. Or Michael Hornyansky, who in order to instil an appreciation of the economy of the rhyming couplet has made us all squeeze a page of eighteenth-century epistemology into two clean lines ("Which swings the heavier ball and chain: / The eyeball, or the enfettered brain?" was our best effort). Yes, George was an odd one, but this was Carleton in the sixties, and ever since then I have thanked my gods that I didn't go to U. of T.

Without compromising intellectual integrity one iota, George taught from a whimsy that was captivating. One day, for no reason, he was teaching Old Norse instead of Anglo-Saxon. Another day, he took us into the world of the sagas. "What is the time getting to be?" he'd ask, his only concession to a world of timetables and scheduling. One day, in answer to a nervous question about grade standing at mid-year, he gazed at each of our faces in turn and intuited our probable final marks.

Then one day, suddenly, inexplicably, he made each of us memorize a hundred and fifty lines of Anglo-Saxon poetry. Any hundred and fifty lines will do. He didn't explain why it was important to do this irrational thing — we just did it, participating with an uneven grace in another of the teacher's whims. Outside, the snow fell on the Siberian olive tree by the canal, as each of us recited our one hundred and fifty lines from memory.

Something about the heft of the old language in one's blood maybe, perhaps some Arnoldian touchstone — whatever George's intention, the last cadences of *The Battle of Maldon* have served me well over the years. They have been my talisman, my wise counsellor, my guide. They have come in handy in awkward circumstances — in the dentist's chair, for instance, or during the dean's report on the use of performance indicators in academic restructuring, or on a Christmas flight delayed by snow. Luckily, the lines were there when I needed them when my unbelieving eyes fell on the first question of the Ph.D. comprehensives (Anglo-Saxon and medieval period): "Discuss the qualities of Anglo-Saxon heroic poetry." *Hige sceall þe heardra, heorte þe kenre.* Years later, during one of his visits to Trent with William Blissett, I was able to recite the lines again for George at a party. I can't decline an Anglo-Saxon irregular verb anymore, but I can, whenever I wish, step into a world where deeds are clean and carry an obligation to remember.

Ian Pringle

THE IMPLAUSIBLE SUCCESS OF *HARMSÓL*

IN THE HISTORY of Icelandic literature, *Harmsól* has been regarded as one of the four great masterpieces of medieval Christian poetry, and historically it is important for a great many reasons. The author of the poem was a man called Gamli, a canon in the Augustinian monastery at Thykkvabær, founded in 1168. What Canon Gamli did was to take over a traditional Icelandic literary form used for the praise of a hero or leader, and adapt it to totally new purposes: the penitential themes of guilt, confession, lament for sins, repentance, consolation, and atonement. His poem is one of the first long poems in the North to have dealt with these topics. Consequently, much of his diction is also non-traditional. In addition, he is believed to have been the first Icelandic poet to use direct speech in this particular form, and his poem is the first in the North to show signs of the shift toward the more inward, subjective kind of poetry stimulated by the Cluniac movement (Cf. de Vries 53–54; Lange 143–49; *Kindlers Literatur Lexicon, Bd. III*, 1482–83; Paasche 143, 150–51).

The country in which Gamli composed his poem was exceptional in many respects, as was its poetic tradition. From the time of its settlement Iceland was unique in Europe in that it was a kind of aristocratic or oligarchical republic. In effect, power was concentrated in the hands of a number of district chieftains, the *goðar*, but the only central authority in the country was the national assembly, which met once a year.

Christianity had come very late to Northern Europe. Even Denmark, which was in touch with both Germany and England, did not have a Christian ruler until Harald Gormsson was converted in 965 A.D. The Icelanders had been in touch with Christianity in Ireland, England, France, and Iceland itself, and during the tenth century a number of them were converted, especially abroad. However, until the end of the century, all attempts at missionary activity within Iceland were brought to a halt by the national assembly, and the missionaries were exiled. They persisted nonetheless, and returned; and by the year 1000 nine of the district leaders had become Christian. As such, they were excluded from the organization of the state, because under the governmental system the *goðar* were both district chieftains and pagan priests. With nine of these powerful men excluded from the system of government, and numbers of people being attracted into allegiance with them out of their own districts, a kind of separatist movement began: the Christian *goðar* felt strong enough to threaten to set up a state organization of their own. Partly to avoid this threat, in the year 1000 the national assembly was persuaded to accept Christianity as the national religion of Iceland. It was decreed by the assembly that all those who had not already been converted should receive the sign of the cross and be baptized. (For many, these two acts alone constituted conversion.) Since Iceland was a republic, the form of Christianity that came into existence as a result of this decree was very different from Christianity elsewhere in Europe. The essential difference was that there was no monarchy by means of which Christianity could be enforced. Elsewhere, the monarch was anointed by the Church; the secular power was considered to be countenanced by the spiritual power. In Iceland, the national assembly could only decree whatever kinds of compromises would be acceptable to most of its members. So, for example, it was decreed that it should be a punishable offence to worship the heathen gods openly, but secret or private worship was permitted. So were such heathen customs as exposing infants, and the sacred rite of eating horseflesh. The legal toleration of such heathen practices was gradually eroded over the century following the establishment of Christianity; nonetheless, many peculiarities persisted. For example, just as in heathen times the district leaders had been both political authorities and pagan priests, with an obligation to provide a temple on their estates, so too for the most part in the early Christian period the only churches were those built and owned by the *goðar*. Some of the *goðar*, moreover, took orders, in order to be able to combine under Christianity the offices of political authority and priest, just as they had done in the past, despite the fact that they often had no training as priests. Others hired, as priests, young men who were willing to be ordained for the sake of the small living that the chieftain would allow them. In either case, the priesthood became an office of secondary importance; the hired priests had approximately the same rank and rights as slaves. Again, almost until the period of the reformation, the Icelandic clergy continued to marry, and throughout most of the Middle Ages it was not uncommon for a priest not only to be married, but also to have several concubines — not that this did not happen elsewhere in Europe (as the history of the Church in such cities as Florence and Rome repeatedly reveals), but elsewhere no one regarded such a situation as canonically sanctioned, whereas in Iceland it seems to have been accepted by everyone without question.

Since the conversion of Iceland was so late, the pre-Christian Germanic tradition had time to develop there into a fuller and more elaborated religion than we have any evidence for in England or on the continent, and this fact by itself would probably have accounted for the survival of pre-Christian ideas in Iceland. But the effect of the lateness was to enhance the effects of the political organization that existed at the time of the conversion. The results included *pro forma* conversion, private ownership of churches, the complete subservience of the Church to secular authority, and the incompetence of the priesthood. It is thus not surprising that the character of Icelandic Christianity in the Middle Ages was strikingly different from what could be found elsewhere in Europe. As late as the thirteenth century it was possible for an Icelandic scholar to write a detailed account of the beliefs of the old religion, and even in the fourteenth century the Icelanders were less orthodox than the English had been in the eighth century. This unique form of Christianity was the cultural context in which *Harmsól* was written; some of its pecularities as a Christian poem can be attributed directly to that context.

More immediately, its uniqueness is due to the poetic tradition within which it was composed: the tradition of skaldic poetry. This development of the common Germanic poetic tradition was peculiar to Norway and Iceland. It has been characterized as a poetic tradition with "a greater formal artificiality" than any other in the literature of the world (Hollander 636). There were over 100 different stanza forms in use in skaldic poetry, but *Harmsól* is written in what was by far the commonest of them, the *dróttkvætt* stanza. The formal properties of this stanza, its metre, alliteration, and rhyme, are summarized and characterized by Johnston with the artistry and authority that one could only find in a practising poet who is also an authority on Icelandic literature (Johnston 4–6).

The exigencies of the tradition apply not only to metre, alliteration, and rhyme, but also to syntax. Within a stanza, the syntax is characterized by the traditional intercalation or intertwining of two or three independent syntactic structures in each half of the stanza, as for example in stanza 55:

> Brigðr es heimr, sás hugðak
> — hann døkkvir sið manna;
> opt verðr lýðr á láði
> lastauðigr — vinfastan.
> Eykr, sás eigi rœkir
> orð þín, friðar tínir,
> hjǫrva þollr, enn hylli
> hans leitar, sér vansa.

Literally:

> A Unstable is the world, which I thought
> B it darkens the conduct of men;
>   often become people on earth
>   sin-rich   A stable
> A Increases   B he who heeds not
>   thy words   C Lord of peace
> A sword's fir-tree   but seeks
>   his favour   his shame.

(Unstable is the world, which I thought stable. It darkens the conduct of men: often people on earth become rich in sins. Lord of peace, a man who does not heed thy words, but seeks his own favour, increases his shame.)[1]

The accessibility of skaldic poetry to modern readers is greatly limited, not only because of its intercalated syntax and its enormously complicated metrical requirements, but also by its diction. Canon Gamli uses traditional *heiti* (that is, the appellations, traditional fossilized metaphors) such as *gautr* for "man" (a *gautr* was a member of the tribe of *Gautar* of south-west Sweden, famed in heroic legend; *gautr* thus means "hero," and thus, in a poetic context, "man, person") and *jöfurr* (literally "wild boar," and thus "warlike [and therefore successful] chieftain") for a meaning like "excellent ruler" (applied in this poem to Christ). He uses the common Germanic technique of the *kenning*, such as *fold ölna* ("land of eels") for "sea." In their simplest forms, kennings are compressed similes; at their best, their effect is imagistic. Like other skaldic poets, Gamli exploits this technique in doubled kennings, such as *börvar hljóms lögðis* ("trees of the song of the sword") for "men" (the song of the sword is the noise associated with swords, that is, battle; trees of battle are those things that are upright, but associated with warfare, that is, men). Sometimes a doubled kenning includes *heiti* and traditional compound nouns, as in *geymi-runn grá-linns und-gjalfrs* ("watching-tree of the grey serpent of

---

[1]All references to the Icelandic text of *Harmsól* are to the version in Kock, Vol. 1, 266–74. The English translations are my own. I make no attempt to recreate in English the poetic effect of the Icelandic: no poet, I am one of those translators who "[give] the best prose version they [can], in the belief that this is the honest thing to do" (Johnston 2). The best English recreations of skaldic poetry are undoubtedly Johnston's translations of Gisli's, discussed in the same article.

the wound-roaring") for "man" (that which roars is the sea; that which is like
the sea but is associated with wounds is blood; the grey serpent associated
with blood is the spear; "watching-tree" is something upright but endowed
with vision, that is, "man"; the man of the spear is a warrior, and since all
men are potentially warriors in this poetry, in its denotation, this extremely
elaborate expression simply means "person"). But if, in this traditional poetic
vocabulary, the denotation is usually simple, the connotative effect can be
rich and complex. Much of the implausible success of *Harmsól*, as we shall
see, is due to Canon Gamli's ability to exploit the connotative potential of
the traditional poetic vocabulary, and to create a new Christian poetic
vocabulary that opposes those connotations.

Using all these devices, Gamli builds a poem that superficially has the
form of a traditional *drápa*, a stanzaic poem of at least 20 stanzas (*Harmsól*
has 65), with three formal divisions, the *upphaf* (introduction), the *stefjamál*
(middle part, marked by the use of refrains), and the *slæmr* (conclusion). In
this very elaborate 65-stanza example of the traditional form, the *upphaf* takes
up the first 19 stanzas; the *stefjamál* occupies stanzas 20 to 45, and is
distinguished by having two refrains (the first in stanzas 20, 25, and 30; the
second in stanzas 35, 40, and 45); the *slæmr* occupies stanzas 46–65.

Whereas the metre, syntax, and form of the poem (and to some extent its
diction) are all traditional, the content is very different from the content of the
traditional *drápa*: instead of an encomium, the poem is a penitential meditation.
The *upphaf* moves from an opening invocation and prayer for inspiration through
a confession of sins to a summary of the incarnation. The first half of the
stefjamál summarizes the crucifixion, the resurrection and ascension, the second
coming, and the Last Judgement. The second half moves from the separation
of the damned and the elect and the horrors of hell to a restatement of the need
for penitence, expiation, and atonement, and the uncertainty of the time of
death. The *slæmr* gives examples of notorious sinners who were saved, and then
moves through a series of prayers of intercession to a final prayer for mercy
for all. The poem is a very tightly organized work. Typical of the best skaldic
poetry, it is a poem in which *nothing* happens by accident. It is extremely self-
conscious. And the first reaction of a modern reader, well aware that "artifice
has not at any time been a favoured word in English poetry or poetic theory"
(Johnston 1), can be very like the reaction of the Benedictines of St. Maur to
the poetry of Matthew of Vendôme: "artifice stérile, et même ridicule, qui
suffirait pour déprécier le poème entier, s'il avait d'ailleurs le moindre prix."

But difficult, self-conscious, and mannered though their poetry is, there
is plenty of evidence that the skalds created for themselves an audience

capable of appreciating it even as they listened to it. The Icelanders provided a fit audience, apparently capable of understanding even the most subtle allusions, sorting out all the complexities of the syntax, appreciating the skill with which metrical requirements were satisfied, and criticizing poets who produced imperfect rhymes while they extemporized stanzas in this metre. One famous piece of evidence may be found in the *Hallfreðar Saga*. The skald Hallfreð had agreed to be baptized only if King Olaf Tryggvason (one of the most ruthless missionaries of all time) would agree to be his sponsor. In the presence of the king, the poet recited an ambiguous poem that could be taken to mean either that in the olden days, good luck came from Odin, but now better luck comes from the Christian God — or that in the good old days men worshipped Odin, and had good luck, but now there has been a change for the worse in men's luck. There follows a passage in which the skald is commanded by the king to produce a better, more acceptable verse, but three times in succession Hallfreð taunts the king by producing an ambiguous stanza, or producing a stanza that is nominally Christian in the last line but lists the powers of five pagan gods in the first lines (all this at the risk of his life: Olaf had killed people for less) — until he finally produces a stanza that saves his life and the king's honour. It is an ingenious stanza that is ambiguous throughout, but seems to be leading up to an emphatic statement of loyalty to the old gods, until the syntax of the last line resolves the ambiguity and reveals the whole stanza to have been Christian throughout (Wood 65–72).

Another famous demonstration is described in the *Flateyjarbók*. King Harald Sigurðsson, himself a poet of considerable repute, challenges another poet, Thjódólf, to match him in verses.[2] The king criticizes Thjódólf's second stanza because of a faulty rhyme of *skömm* (with a long consonant sound at the end) with *gröm* (with a single short consonant sound at the end). There is a suggestion that Thjódólf committed this fault deliberately: in the next stanza he commits the same fault twice more, thus tactfully revealing the king to be a more skilful poet (Hollander 204).

Judged by the standards of such critics as King Harald, *Harmsól* presumably deserved its tremendous reputation in medieval Iceland. Modern readers, including most of my own students who have studied it, have found

---

[2]Prisoners as we are of the habits of our entrenched literacy, modern readers find it astonishing that the earlier skalds (at least) composed in their heads, preparing a complete poem for oral delivery. My own discovery that George Johnston does the same helped to convince me that this is in fact possible.

it difficult to appreciate. Ultimately the difficulty is not only that its technical brilliance (by the criteria of the poetic context of which it is part) makes it intrinsically inaccessible. Partly as a result of the cultural context of medieval Icelandic Christianity (of which it is also part), the poem is trying to do three things that are ultimately incompatible with each other within the constraints of a form that cannot easily be adapted to any of them. As a result, for all the enormous technical skill, and the equally striking originality, the poem keeps evoking reactions that are inappropriate to the intention, and thus get in the way of the effectiveness of the poem.

The first aim of the poem is a homiletic one; the poet's stance is that of the preacher. There is evidence that Christian knowledge was spread in Iceland to some extent by skaldic poetry (cf. Olrik 143–47), and Attwood (223) notes that *Harmsól* could be characterized as a versified sermon. This intention is clear in stanzas such as stanza 6:

> Oss verðr ey, nema þessum
> aldr várn boðum haldim
> (menn búisk mǫrgu sinni)
> meiri ógn (við þeiri).
> Hver þvít hætt rǫ́ð bǫrva
> hljóms á øfsta dómi
> upp fyr allri skepnu
> ósǫgð koma lǫgðis.

(For us there shall never be a greater horror unless we keep these commandments during our lives. Let men prepare themselves many a time against these eventualities, because at the Last Judgement every unspoken dangerous thought of men will come forth before all creation.)

The tone and manner of the preacher is apparent in the account of the crucifixion in the middle section, and in the passage warning of the inevitability of judgement in stanzas 31–33:

> Enn mun ǫðru sinni
> ǫðlingr koma hingat
> mána tjalds enn mildi
> meðr til dóms at kveðja.

Geisar eldr, ok œsisk
ǫlna fold. Ór moldu
ferð vaknar þá fyrða
flest við ugg enn mesta.

Engr mun alls á þingi
ísheims vesa þvísa
jóskreytandi ítrum
óttalauss fyr dróttni.
Éla vangs þvít englar
jǫfurs skjalfa þá sjalfir
— ógn tekr mǫttug magnask —
mæts við ugg ok hræzlu.

Hǫrð munat hógligt verða
hjalmstýranda ens dýra
sunnu synðgum mǫnnum
sekðarorð at forðask,
systkin mín, þvít sýnask
sǫr ok kross fyr ossu
dróttins várs með dreyra
dyggs augliti hryggu.

(However, the merciful Lord of heaven will come here a second
time, in order to summon men to judgement. Fire shall rage, and
the sea shall boil. A vast multitude of men shall then awaken out
of the ground in the greatest terror. No man shall be without fear
at this trial before the glorious Lord, for the very angels of God
shall tremble with fear and dread; the sway of terror shall be increased. The harsh judgement of the dear Lord of the sun will not
be easy for any sinful man to escape, my brothers, for the wounds
of our faithful Lord, his bloody countenance afflicted, and his cross
will appear before us.)

Especially is this the voice of the preacher because of the "my brothers,"
systkin mín, (my siblings, my brothers and sisters), which is one of the basic
forms of address in the Icelandic homilies, like *góð systkin*, good brothers and
sisters, or *góðir brœðr*, good brothers (Paasche 145). The brothers can be
anyone, but there is at least a possibility that Gamli intended his poem to

be used in his own monastery, not as part of the liturgy but as something to be read or recited before the assembled brethren.

The second thing that the poet seems to want to do is to write a penitential poem of a much more typical medieval kind, a kind familiar in many English and German lyrics of the middle ages, German hymns of the Reformation, and some of the great Latin hymns. What such a poem must provide is a versified meditation that other Christians may use to organize their thoughts and emotions, so that they can heighten their own sense of the need for penitence in preparation for the sacrament of penance.

Stanza 57 will serve as a representative example of this stance in the poem; it deals with a stock idea in language that is as general and as commonplace as it is possible for medieval Icelandic poetic language to be:

> Heldr dœmðu mik, hǫlda
> happvinnandi, þinni
> meir af miskunn dýrri,
> mætastr, an réttlæti!
> Lít ok virð, sem vættik,
> valdr blásinna tjalda
> hreggs, at hjǫlp of þiggi,
> hár, óstyrkðir várar!

(Judge me, most excellent Winner of good for mankind, more according to Your dear mercy than according to justice. Look upon our weaknesses, high Ruler of the wind-blown tents of heaven, so that, as I hope, I might receive mercy thereby.)

Any penitent can use such a stanza as a focus for his own thoughts and feelings, or rather as a vessel into which his own thoughts and feelings will fit. Clearly it is as much this aim as it is the aim of the preacher that determines the overall structure of the poem, as it moves from confession to consideration of the pathos of the crucifixion as a means of evoking sorrow for sin, to the threat of doomsday as a means of inciting a desire for amendment, to the closing prayers for intercession. The stanzas praying for Mary's intercession (58–61) provide another good example:

Where then may we hope for shelter for ourselves, O God, from the guilt of our painful sin, unless You Yourself will show mercy, blessed Creator, to Your sinful thrall, whose sins make him tremble? Blessed

Mary, you can win for us each part of the grace of the Lord of heaven. Be always a previous help to me, kind Mother of the Lord, so that I may never lack your goodness. In fear I hope for mercy from you, pure mother of the Lord, because your sweet virtues console my mind, though my life is distressing. No evil man, gentle Lady, shall be ill-used who prays reverentially to you, as I trust, because, wise Mother of the Monarch of the sky, swiftest in glory, you desire, and are able, to grant to men all good.

Now clearly, insofar as this second stance is successful in its aim it is successful in the way that Rosemary Woolf, writing about English medieval lyrics, argues that all such poetry must be: the author is not concerned with his own "personal moods and emotions ... but only with what kind of response his subject should properly arouse in Everyman" (6).

Such a stance, however, does not consort very well with the first one: the poet of the second voice has to be able to think and speak like an ordinary member of an ordinary congregation, whereas the poet of the first voice, speaking as a preacher, automatically assumes a position of authority; he is himself a sinner, of course, and he must recognize that his subject applies to him as it does to all men. But he speaks as a man who, because of his position, is more knowledgeable than the congregation, with a responsibility for guiding them. Because both stances are there, the poem seems to move back and forth from one to the other, without ever being able to integrate them into a coherent whole.

Thirdly, however, the poet is himself caught up in the application of his subject matter to himself, and thus there is a third stance in the poem: the poet himself as meditator.

One example of this voice in Gamli's poem is provided by the anticlimax of the second four lines of stanza 6:

> Hver þvít hætt róð borva
> hljóms á øfsta dómi
> upp fyr allri skepnu
> ósogð koma logðis.

(At the Last Judgement, every unspoken dangerous thought of men will come forth before all creation.)

This is the first of the stanzas touching on the theme of the Last Judgement, but there is something of a discrepancy between the extreme terror of the day and the greatest horror that the poet can think of, which is that secret thoughts will be revealed. When Gamli is speaking in the second mode, he can be quite intense. Stanza 54 is a particularly good example of this:

Sólu veittak, sættir,
— sárr's minn tregi — várri
banahættligar benjar,
bragna kyns, fyr synðir.
Nú beiðum þik, þjóðar
þrekfœðandi, grœða
andar sór, þaus óru
ósvífr glata lífi.

(Reconciler of the race of men, I have given mortally dangerous wounds to my soul. Now, Supplier of strength to men, I beg you to heal my spirit's injuries, which, in their filth, are destroying my life.)

As an individual meditator, however, Gamli is a rather bashful penitent. The parts of the poem devoted primarily to confession are much less intense, and the reason seems to be that Gamli did not care to imply that he himself was particularly sinful. Typical passages in the stanzas of confession go like this:

Often did I make myself guilty of uncouth behaviour, Lord, when I saw another evil man doing the same thing. Little did I endure travail and danger for myself when I cheerfully passed judgement on other evil men. (Stanza 11)

I brought into the light before men several good deeds, but nevertheless concealed my faults as much as I could, so that my impulses might seem to mankind a little better than they were, merciful Lord; and I was well satisfied with that. (Stanza 13)

It is far from the case, my Lord, that I might enumerate each sin that I have committed, since I do not see you. (Stanza 16)

Of course, this is credible enough as a picture of the poet (although it does not make him very attractive). But it is disastrous for the public mode of confession, which is supposed to enable ordinary penitents to recognize their own sinfulness. And it is even more disastrous for the voice of the preacher, because, since it makes him look rather ridiculous, it undercuts his authority.

The problem is intensified by the extreme self-consciousness of the tradition of skaldic poetry. Again and again throughout the poem, Gamli adopts the stance of the skald, acutely conscious of his own skill. Whenever he draws attention to himself as a poet he weakens whatever effectiveness he has had in any of the three modes he has adopted. The poem is thus an extreme example of the common problem of highly artificial religious verse (cf. Woolf, Eliot, Johnson).

The problem begins with the opening stanzas. As Attwood points out (230–31), the conventional invocation to the patron in pre-Christian *drápur* was adapted to the new Christian context in ways that were typically Icelandic. Gamli starts with a prayer for Divine assistance:

> Mighty Lord, open up successfully for me the gate of the poem castle,
> so that the eloquent diction of my intercalary sentences might
> augment the atonement of sins, through your help.

Thus he alerts his audience to watch out for the skill with which he constructs his stanzas at the same time as he asks God to help him find appropriate ornaments for his poetry. In the second stanza he continues with an adaptation of the humility topos:

> No man (that is quite certain) can find fit words of praise for you,
> my Lord, since, wise King, you are more precious than anything that
> men may think of.

The third stanza asks the Holy Ghost for inspiration. Now, if the kind of faith in God's help that he implies in the first and third stanzas is justified, then, despite what he says in his humble second stanza, the words of his poem will be fit words of praise for God. And that is what makes the fourth stanza so outrageous:

> Mér vil ek *ok eirar*,
> — oss byrjar þat — hnossa
> himins stillandi, hollrar,
> hæstr, miskunnar æsta.

> (For myself do I wish, highest Stiller of heaven, to request the
> ornaments of mercy and gracious peace, albeit in unworthy words.)

He has already said that he does not expect to be able to find fit ornaments for his verse, but in saying that, he has found them. It seems that God has answered his prayers. And so, with full confidence in his Creator, he asks for some more ornaments, not for his poem, but ornaments with which he himself can be decorated: God's mercy, and the peace that passes all understanding. There is an implicit comparison of the poet to God. The poet decorates his creation with poetic ornaments, and God (Gamli's fellow Creator) decorates His creations with ornaments of grace. The problem is the same in stanza 17, the climax of the passage of general confession:

> Hverr es greppr, sás gerra,
> grunnúðigr, þér unna,
> — slíkr hǫfumk synðar auki
> sótt — heimstǫðu dróttinn.

(Every man is perverse [Every poet is incompetent] who is not ready to love [praise] Thee, Lord of the course of the earth; such a one, I have sought for myself an increase of sins.)

The word *gleppr* literally means "poet," but it was used as a *heiti* for any man. If it is taken to mean "man," then the intention of the stanza is to express the perverse folly of men who disobey God's law. But if it is taken to mean "poet," then the meaning is that only incompetent poets do not praise God as they should. The stanza is genuinely ambiguous, but the self-consciousness of the verse insists that you consider the second meaning, and its implication that since this poet is very competent (and knows it) he must be all right: God will save him. In the same way, there is something astonishing in the choice of examples of famous sinners with which he consoles himself: King David and Saint Peter and Mary Magdalene. This is the class of people to which he thinks he belongs, spiritually. Conversely, he condemns the impenitent thief for his pride, without seeing that his pleasure in his own cleverness is itself an example of pride. The poem is thus an extreme case of the problem discussed by Helen Gardner in the introduction to her edition of John Donne's *Divine Poems*:

> In all poetry which attempts to represent the intercourse between
> an individual soul and its Maker, there is a conflict between the
> ostensible emotion — ... penitence overwhelmed by the sense of
> personal unworthiness — and the artist's actual absorption in the

creation of his poem and his satisfaction in achieving perfect
expression. (xv–xvi)

Consequently some of my students have reacted to the poem with disgust:
it is too much like the Pharisee standing apart in the temple, thanking God
that he is not like other men, or the medieval German bishop who is reported
to have said, "Humility is the rarest of the virtues; praise be to God, I have
it." The point that I want to make, however, is that this obtrusiveness on the
part of the poet is a consequence of the Icelandic skaldic tradition. If it is true
that this can never work as a Christian poem, then the reason is that it is an
Icelandic Christian poem, a Christian *drápa*.

But I think that it does work. What saves it, despite the problems forced
upon it by the self-consciousness of the poetic tradition, is also a product of
the tradition: its kennings.

I count a total of 111 kennings in the poem, an average of nearly two
per stanza. Of these one is the "gate of the poem-castle" kenning of the first
stanza, another is the "land of eels" kenning for the sea cited above, and three
of them deal with the Virgin Mary. All the others are kennings either for men
or for God (34 of the former to 69 of the latter).

The kennings for men draw extensively on the traditional lexicon of the
traditional *drápa*. Men are always involved in battle, "trees of the strong gale
of the serpent of battle" (stanza 2), "trees of the song of the sword" (stanza
6), "setters in motion of the flame of thunder" (i.e. of the sword, stanza 39),
"trees of the din of the fire of shields" (stanza 43), "stout-hearted hardeners
[i.e. temperers, by plunging into liquid] of the storm of shoulder-strap wheels"
(i.e. of shields, stanza 64), etc. The world evoked in such kennings is the pre-
Christian world of endless fighting and feuding.

Men are avaricious, preoccupied with gold and silver: "bearing-trees of
the serpent of the land" (i.e. upright trees [= men] carrying the bed of the
serpent of the land [i.e. snake], i.e. carrying gold, stanza 18), "down-trees
of the fish of the valley" (i.e. trees of the down [= bed] of the snake, stanza
44), "measurers of shoulder-ice" (= silver, stanza 47), "trees of arm-fire" (=
gold rings, stanza 27). Again the evocation is of a pre-Christian world of
perilously distorted values.

Above all, men are unregenerate, fittingly characterized by references
to the pre-Christian religious traditions of the North: "slingers of the flame
of [the valkyrie] Mist" (i.e. slingers of spears, stanza 2), "the Thrótt (i.e. Odin)
of the storm" (stanza 11), "trees of the plank of [the shrieking valkyrie] Hlökk"
(i.e. trees [=men] of the shield, stanza 14), "messengers of the (female troll)

Gifr of the war-tent" (i.e. messengers of the destroyer of the shield, stanza 42), "wishing-Odin of the sea-glory" (i.e. the Thor-like being who wishes for gold), and so on.

Such kennings are indeed traditional, but in this context they are serving a very untraditional purpose. They weave throughout the whole length of the poem an insistence that men are sinful: always involved in battle, feuding and murdering, or hungry for gold and silver, avaricious and rapacious, or (worst of all) totally unregenerate, but desperately in need of regeneration, because still in touch with the old gods and the old religion. The traditional vocabulary has become an agent of the medieval Christian assertion that unregenerate man is the old Adam.

Conversely, the kennings dealing with God are predominantly original, if not with Gamli himself, then at least with him and a small number of other authors with whom he must have been closely associated (cf. Attwood *passim*). The vast majority of them describe God as Lord of creation. In general terms, God is "sole Creator of the nations" (stanza 3), "high Guide of the setting of the sun" (stanza 13), "Creator of the kingdom of earth" (stanza 24), "excellent Lord of the hall of the mountains" (stanza 30). Above all He is characterized as Lord of the sky (representing Heaven). You have to bear in mind the sky of Iceland: a northern sky and an island sky, so a sky often clouded over, subject to sudden changes of mood, and to violent storms. It is in the sky that Gamli finds evidence of both the power and the love of God.

The power is suggested by the threatening, stormy aspects of the sky: "energy strong Lord of the roof of storm and rain" (stanza 9), "Ruler of the swiftly moving flame of the highest storm-tent" (stanza 28), "Lord of the realm of the flame of the roof of lightning" (stanza 53), "Boar (i.e. fierce Lord) of the high castle of storm and rain" (stanza 45), "high Ruler of the tents, blown about by the wind, of storm and rain" (stanza 57).

The love of God is suggested in kennings that evoke a more peaceful, benevolent sky: "kind-hearted Boar (= Lord) of the launching-roller (= support) of the gentle breeze" (stanza 15), "King of the realm of the thawing wind" (stanza 15), "extremely powerful Lord of the flying sea of the earth" (= Lord of the sky with its scudding clouds, stanza 56), "dear Ruler of the vault of the sun" (stanza 33), "King of the wheel of the helmet of the sun" (stanza 36), "Guardian of heaven's lights" (stanza 37), "Prince of the pavilions of the heath-fire" (= of the vault of the starry heaven, stanza 14), "deed-renowned Boar (Lord) of the flame of the flight-land of swans" (stanza 44).

It is the kennings that save the poem. Despite Canon Gamli's all too obvious intentions, despite the apparent insincerity (by our standards) to which they testify, despite the impossibility of responding simultaneously to Gamli's authorial smugness and to his calls to penitence, *Harmsól* does succeed as a penitential poem. It succeeds because the effect communicated, imagistically, almost subliminally, by the kennings, is an emotionally persuasive sense of man as an unregenerate creature totally in the power of a God who, as His creation itself testifies, is omnipotent, but merciful.

Hence the significance of the kenning *Harmsól*, "Grief-sun," used as title to the poem in stanza 64: just as the sun breaks through the storm clouds, bringing light and warmth and brightness, so also does Christ drive away the storm of grief and bring the peace that passes all understanding. So Christ is the *Harmsól*.[3]

[3]I wish to acknowledge with gratitude the patience and help of Tracey Poirier, who entered the original text of this paper onto a disk not once, but twice. I also wish to acknowledge the help of Pat Bethel with proofreading, with the bibliography, corrections of mistranslations, and many discrete words of advice. She has made the paper more scholarly than it would otherwise have been. All its inadequacies are mine.

WORKS CITED

Attwood, Katrina. "Intertextual Aspects of the Twelfth-Century Christian Drapur." *Saga-Book* 24.4 (1996): 221–39.

de Vries, Jan. *Altnordische Literaturgeschichte*. Berlin: de Gruyter, 1941.

Eliot, T.S. "Religion and Literature." *Essays Ancient and Modern*. New York: Harcourt, 1936.

Gardner, Helen. Introduction. *The Divine Poems*. By John Donne. Oxford: Clarendon, 1952.

Hollander, Lee M. "The Parenthetic Sentence in Scaldic Poetry." *JEGP* 64 (1965): 636.

Johnson, Samuel. "Life of Waller." *Lives of the English Poets*. Ed. G.B. Hill. Oxford: Oxford UP, 1950.

Johnston, George. "What Do the Scalds Tell Us?" *University of Toronto Quarterly* 52.1 (1982): 1–8.

Kindlers Literatur Lexikon. Ed. Wolfgang von Einsiedel and Gert Woerner. Zurich: Kindler, 1965–72. 7 vols.

Kock, Ernst A. *Den norsk-isländska skaldediktningen*. Lund: Gleerup, 1946–49. 2 vols.

Lange, Wolfgang. *Studien zur christlichen Dichtung der Nordgermanen 1000–1200*. Palaestra, Band 222. Gottingen: Vandenhoeck and Ruprecht, 1958.

Olrik, Axel. *Viking Civilization*. New York: The American Scandinavian Foundation, 1930.

Paasche, Fredrik. *Heldenskap og Kristendom: Studier i norrøn middelalder*. Ed. Philip Houm. Oslo: H. Aschehoug & Co. (W. Nygaard), 1970.

Wood, Cecil. "The Reluctant Christian and the King of Norway." *Scandinavian Studies* 31 (1959): 65–72.

Woolf, Rosemary. *The English Religious Lyric in the Middle Ages*. Oxford: Clarendon, 1968.

A little lake hath but little sand
but small the mind of man;
not all men are equally wise,
each wight wanteth somewhat.

Edith Pahlke
Icelandic Edda
(*Edda, Hávamál*)
linocut 13 x 8.25 inches

Richard Outram

FOUR NORTHUMBRIAN POEMS
[for George Johnston]

LINDISFARNE PRIORY
(*Holy Island October 1994*)

It is the long dark waves and their serpentine ways of cresting,
collapsing at last into cobalt slather; and the unthinkable rage
of late sun catching the chip of some glittered distant vessel,
making for somewhere for some reason, that brings the page

to mind: the meanders of faded azure, and gold, and delicate rose;
and the intricate margins with beaked creatures entwined, exact;
and the aureoled wingèd man, lion, calf and the wing that is eagle,
each bearing a book. Only the one rainbow arch is intact

where, as from The Beginning and all uncomprehended beginnings,
to the four or however-many-reckoned quarters of the unknown
and meantime irreconciled teeming world the intransigent Word,
we are told, has gone forth forever parlous, the winds have blown

harum-scarum over the coney-riddled, marram-tufted dunes,
over the staggered wracklines where, at present, one must walk
through the fierce pink, raw orange, garish yellow, unnatural green
and once-white plastic trashed on oil-blackened rock.

GERTRUDE JEKYLL'S
LINDISFARNE CASTLE GARDEN

So patterned it looks from above, as a migrant bird
might view it, or Icarus, or latterly man aloft,
like a skewed micro-chip fallen on ochre baize
dotted with placid sheep. It may be, that a soft

answer turneth wrath: when the terrible Danes
came the Christians fled. On three sides, high
limestone walls ward off the levelling gales;
Hudson lowered the south wall, to descry,

framed from the garden bench, his Castle's heights.
On the crazed stone I watch one October day
the ' ... thin as a curve, a muscled ribbon,' uncoiled
and recoiled spring of a tawny weasel at play,

time and again in spasmodic savage attack
slashing a hollyhock head. One never knows:
plagued by a larval worm that may fatten deep
in the skull, sometimes a stoat or stricken weasel goes

berserk, indiscriminate mad, all incarnate rage.
The western rose border, after some sixty years,
suffered a soil sickness; the new roses did not
prosper, and couch grass took hold. Terror's arrears

will be paid in full, we are warned by those who recall
another implicate Garden; who reckon that God is just.
The whole show is owned now, and has been of course
managed since 'sixty-eight, by The National Trust.

' ... TWITCH AND CRY LOVE.'

Considering that it was
a farmhouse B. & B.,
and in the Cheviots,
it came as no surprise
when on arrival we
were greeted by a mask,
a vulpine, wry grimace
set with gemstone eyes,
beside the lintel, placed
to face the paying guest.

But neither of us saw,
or not until the next
morning, as we left
after our night's rest,
opposite the door,
an otter's snarling head
and under it two webbed
paws, the rear and fore,
spiked together, crossed.

And, curious, we asked:
'Oh, dear me, no, oh dear,
not at Otterburn; oh no,
there are no otters now
at Otterburn. Long gone.'
the Wooler baker said,
' ... a military base, and
nowadays, well, Sir,
you wouldn't want to know
the place; not nowadays.'

And there was a text
on our bedroom wall
in glazed lusterware;
it was mounted next
the mirror. I recall
what it said here:

But man dieth,
and wasteth away:
yea, man giveth
up the Ghost, and
where is he?

There must have been,
in former times,
a thriving taxidermy
trade: that stocked
wholesale supplies
in crafted glass
of otters' eyes
and graded them
by colour, size,
and one would pay,
back then as now,
for quality, excess
somehow ...

God knows,
the river otter
put to rout
the salmon and
incorrigibly ate
the rose-mole-
stippled trout
and sorely tried
the syndicate;
that wasn't on.

Long gone, long
gone. But once,
one gathers by
the evidence
of things unseen
here nowadays,
it was you see,
and must be still,
in many ways
a coveted and rare
delight to be
in at the kill.

RELICT

The
icy sea's
salted deeps
did not divide
nor sustain Saint
Cuthbert up but
a loving pair
of otters came
to warm his feet
where he stood
as he prayed
in the chill
sea.

Nor
did the dread
tempest slacken
but held them fast
on bleak Farne Isle
those heedless monks
for seven days
since they would not
cook and eat Saint
Cuthbert's eider
he gave those
friars what
for!

And
as Bishop
Eardulf bore
unto Ireland
Cuthbert's relics
out of nowhere
three mazèd waves
washed overboard
our Lord's Gospels
till Hunred dreamt
them unharmed
found on dry
land.

When
eleven
years after
Eadbert came to
unearth Cuthbert's
cleansed corruption
and no decay
nor taint had claimed
this Saint's remains
his Virtue hence
was surety
to pious
men.

No
otters knotted
storms snarled
waves woven
not even the carnal
body found untainted
not
even the sumptuous
incorruption proffered
no,
not any not one for all are
in childbirth God's commonplace.
No,
her riven vision did not follow
hard on hearing Eadfrith preaching
' ... yea, four things say not, It is enough':
the which she knew,

but when she had suffered
alone more long nights
of the canker's agony.

A wench's words let no wise man trust,
nor trust the troth of a woman;
for on whirling wheel their hearts are shaped
and fickle and fitful their minds.

Edith Pahlke
Icedlandic Edda
(Edda, Hávamál)
linocut 13 x 8.25 inches

Patricia Bethel

WIDER THAN WIDSITH: CROSS-CULTURAL AWARENESS IN ANGLO-SAXON ENGLAND[1]

IT WAS RECENTLY suggested that for its courtly Anglo-Saxon audience *Beowulf* was not a *liber monstrorum*, but an exotic tale, that its Scandinavian story and context were as foreign to its listeners as a tale about India, and that Heorot was in effect part of the same genre as *Wonders of the East*. This argument was advanced as the result of an orthographic study that had led to the proposal of a new manuscript stemma for the Nowell Codex. But this codicological approach may engender a somewhat blinkered view of the literature of the period. It runs the danger of completely overlooking indications of a network of international contacts evident in the material culture, the history, and the literature, such as the voyages of Othere and Wulfstan, for example, or the negotiations that Harun al-Rashid (reg. 786–809) carried on with Charlemagne on the one hand, and with the Chinese on the other. This paper is a short overview of historical and archaeological indications that Anglo-Saxon England and, indeed, Western Europe had extensive contacts with foreign lands; the evidence appears cumulatively to argue against an easy presumption that the subject matter of the vernacular literature of medieval courts was perceived as exotic.

It is clear that the great majority of Western Europeans in the early Middle Ages travelled very little[2] and that readers at the time might read the letters of Alexander to Aristotle as bald fact. To overlook indications of foreign trade, however, especially in luxury goods, can have the effect of minimizing those links that Europeans made, often at several removes, with the rest of the world. It can also have the effect of treating a discipline such as Anglo-Saxon history as if it were entirely circumscribed by the boundaries of a subsequent nation state.

This paper seeks to isolate some of the links that have been identified, especially as they apply to the British Isles. It deliberately excludes probably the most important, those attributable to pilgrimage routes,[3] in favour of those resulting from trade. Because evidence for contacts is very sparse in some periods,[4] and easily destroyed,[5] the paper does not attempt to be more than a superficial survey, moving from better-known trading links, particularly between the courtly milieus of various countries, to those for which there is less archaeological and historical evidence, and for which Scandinavia was likely pivotal.

1. EARLY ARCHAEOLOGICAL CONTEXTS

In a period in which overland transport in north-western Europe was difficult, some substantial contact between the countries of the Western European littorals is to be expected, and it is therefore not surprising that the character of grave goods from the sixth and seventh centuries attests to close connections between Merovingian Franks and Kent,[6] as do Merovingian claims to suzerainty over southern England from the 550s until the mid-seventh century, claims that appear in context to be more optative than descriptive.[7]

While Kent is probably the Franks' best-known overseas dependency, Fredegar, the seventh-century Franco-Burgundian chronicler, records (in Book 4) that the Saxons (either continental or insular) also acknowledged Frankish overlordship, in their case by paying a tribute of 500 cows (Charles-Edwards 30). The archaeological record also shows close early links between Aquitaine and Bordeaux on the one hand, and Cornwall, Devon, and Somerset on the other, but not between either and Wessex (Hinton, *Archaeology* 40, 56). Excavations of early Anglo-Saxon sites have also yielded less widespread but still abundant material from Byzantium (*solidi*), Gaul (*trientes* or *tremisses*,[8] both real and, as at Yeavering, forged[9]), and Egypt,[10] as well as some from the Indian Ocean.[11] Such imports were not entirely restricted to royal circles: an excavation at Puddlehill, Bedfordshire, yielded a cowrie shell from the Persian Gulf or the Red Sea (Hinton, *Archaeology* 26). From about 600, however, there was a sudden restriction in the flow of gold moving north, with the result that the gold content of both coinage and jewellery in England and northern France dropped from about 80 percent at the beginning of the century to between 18 and 30 percent by about 660. The provenance of the coins, regardless of the degree to which they were debased, can be equally significant. Coin finds in urban or pre-ninth-century[12] burial sites, such as Anglo-Saxon *sceattas* in the old Danish capital of Ribe, can arguably identify specific commercial links, examples of which may be those between Ipswich and the Frisian ports of Domburg (on the Frisian island of Walcheren) and Dorestad (on the old course of the Rhine, south of Utrecht on the Frisian-Austrasian border). Other probable ties between the littoral states witnessed by coin finds are also unexceptionable, especially between such adjacent coastal areas as Frisia and East Anglia, and Wessex and North France. The Sutton Hoo ship burials famously attest to wider early East-Anglian, Merovingian,[13] and Swedish[14] links; not only are some of the grave-goods from the Sutton Hoo ship burial Byzantine or Coptic[15] in origin, but Martin Carver, the most recent excavator of the site, has reported a blue glass vase from Mound 2, though he has not stated its provenance.

Other foreign contacts were more literary. If the information available to Fredegar about the Byzantine and Persian world[16] was typical of that current in contemporary courts in France, it is clear that Franks and

Burgundians were well informed about international gossip, certainly well enough to be aware that the Persian emperor Chosroes I (531–79) was named something like Anosharwan (Fredegar's Anaulf), that his favourite wife, Shirin or Sira (Caesara), was a Christian, and that he had made remarkable concessions to his Christian subjects; well enough, too, to report in chapter 9 a mass conversion in about the year 587.[17] It has even been suggested (Hellmann 44) that the Persian *akus* (knife, chisel) lay behind the weapon *(uxus)* with which, according to Fredegar,[18] the Byzantine emperor Heraclius was armed in single combat, rather than the arrow (τοξόν), with which, according to Theophanes, Anosharwan was killed. Furthermore, Fredegar seems to have had access to at least one native speaker of a Slavic language, perhaps through the Frankish emissary Sicharius, to have been notably well informed about early Czechoslovakia, and possibly to have tried in chapter 48 to latinize the Wendish word for herders of buffalo.[19]

In Old English literature, much of which is preserved in manuscripts datable no earlier than the beginning of the eleventh century, traders and sailors seem archetypically and perhaps somewhat anachronistically associated with Frisia, whose commercial heyday seems to have been the century following 750 (Unger 60–64, 76–80.) From the seventh century the Frisians appear to have been responsible for much of the international seaborne commerce of northern Europe, even from the mid-seventh century supplying Sweden with both Rhenish wine and Rhineland glasses from which to drink it.

Frisia's absorption into the Carolingian state resulted in a still greater expansion of its trade network, with Frisian colonies developing in London and York, in Hedeby,[20] near Sleswig, and in Birka,[21] Worms, Mainz, and Rome, where the Frisian quarter had its own church. Indeed, the B version of *The Anglo-Saxon Chronicle* listed Frisian sailors among the notable casualties of Alfred the Great's first large-scale naval encounter with the Vikings, in the year 987:

> ða het Ælfred cing timbran lange scipu ongen þa æscas; þa wæron fulneah twa swa lange swa ða oþre, sume hæfdon .lx. arena, sume ma; þa wæron ægþer ge swiftran ge unwealtran ge eac hearran þonne þa oþre; *næron hie naþor ne on Frysisc gesceapen ne on Denisc* buton swa him sylfum þuhte þæt hie nytweorðoste beon mihton.... Þær wearð ofslegen Lucuman cinges gerefa, & *Wulfheard Frysa, & Æbbe frysa, & Æþelhere Frysa, & Æþelferð cinges geneat, & ealra manna frysicscra & engliscra .lxii.*[22] (45; emphasis added)

In another famous passage, the poet of *Maxims I* clearly assumes that a typical contemporary merchant will have a Frisian wife:

> Scip sceal genægled, scyld gebunden,
> leoht linden bord, leof wilcuma
> Frysan wife, þonne flota stondeð
> bið his ceol cumen ond hyre ceorl to ham,
> agen ætgeofa, ond heo hine in lædaþ,
> wæsceð his warig hrægl ond him syleþ wæde niwe,
> liþ him on londe þas his lufu bædeð.[23] (*Exeter Book* 160, 93–99)

Still, despite these references to close ties between Frisia and Anglo-Saxon England, it is clear both from the archaeological record, which indicates that it was a shortage of merchants rather than a lack of demand that limited imports, and from the Anglo-Norse law that describes the circumstances (the successful completion of three foreign journeys) under which merchants could be granted the status of *thegn*, that relatively few people must have made repeated foreign journeys.

2. FOREIGN SETTLEMENTS AND TRADE IN PRE-CONQUEST ENGLAND

It is, however, equally clear, if the onomastics of late Anglo-Saxon charters are to be taken at face value, that there was a substantial foreign population not only in London, where a number of High-German names are attested, but also in such places as Abingdon, where a priest named Godesscealc is one of the signatories of a document dated 931 (Kemble 1104, 1106; Birch 680, 681).[24] Furthermore, Theodred, one of the bishops of London, and some of his relatives and legatees, Gosebricht, Odgar, and Gundwine, have German or West-Frankish elements in their names (Whitelock 2–5: 99–103). Other continental non-Scandinavian tenth-century names in assorted charters are Gundlaf, Waltere Reginwald dux (dated 924–941; Birch 648), Irdwold (dated 955; Kemble 436), Aðulf, and Theodred (dated 975; Birch), and, in the eleventh century, Grimbold and Fulcheric (Whitelock 211, note 1 to 96). London in the tenth century also contained a German merchant community influential enough to allow those of its members from Magdeburg, Quedlinburg, Goslar, and Halberstadt to enjoy the same taxation status in the city as Anglo-Saxons did (Drögereit 61).

Moneyers, by far the best-documented occupational group in pre-Conquest England, represented a distinct wealthy urban stratum apparently without significant landholdings,[25] and therefore possibly of atypical mobility; in contrast, the Scandinavian influx beyond the Danelaw during Canute's reign seems to have been limited to landholders (Smart 179). In the first half of the tenth century especially, there is a high proportion of moneyers in Anglo-Saxon England who have West-Frankish names, in addition to those who have the Scandinavian, Hiberno-Norse, Celtic, Old-English, and occasional Biblical ones that might also be expected.[26]

Other foreign contacts, as indicated by literary and historical sources, were somewhat rarer. They included the travels of missionaries to Germany, the training of later German and Old-Saxon clergy in England, and the journeys, of which there are traces toward the beginning of the period, by Hadrian, Theodore of Tarsus, Bishop Wilfrid, and several members of the West-Saxon royal house. Contacts were made in later episcopal trips to Rome for *pallia*,[27] the stoles that confirmed episcopal appointments, in the international recruitment of scholars by Charlemagne, in the clerical appointments of Edward the Confessor, and in the town of York, which the *Vita Oswaldi* describes as a locus for merchants, especially from Denmark. E.A. Lowe has suggested that the scribe Erkanfrit, who left his name on Würzburg Universität-Bibliothek Hs. M.P. Th. F. 47 (Lowe 9:1414), was active in the Canterbury scriptorium, and in the tenth century St. Dunstan spent two years as the guest of Abbot Womar of Ghent. Priebsch suggests that the visit may have been returned (39). On stylistic grounds, Pauli identifies the anonymous author of the *Vita Sancti Oswaldi* as probably Frankish. Sir Frank Stenton observes that the community at Abingdon was sufficiently informed about continental news to record the death of Otto, duke of Swabia, in 982, in their copy of *The Anglo-Saxon Chronicle*, and to describe the duke's descent from Æthelstan's sister Edith,[28] while Æthelweard translated the *Chronicle* into Latin for Matilda, Abbess of Essen, a distant cousin of his through Edith. Peter Sawyer notes that evidence for English participation in Baltic, Danish, and Norwegian commerce from the eleventh to the thirteenth centuries seems to describe a trade already well established at the earlier date ("Trade").

Several indications combine to argue the presence of a substantial Scandinavian, rather than necessarily Danelaw, colony in England; these include saga accounts of the esteem in which skalds were held in Anglo-Saxon courts, Æthelred's massacre of Danes in England,[29] the presence of six churches dedicated to St. Olaf (ob. 1030) in London,[30] a church of St. Olaf in York by 1051, a church incorporating the personal name Haakon (St. Nicholas Acon), and the traditional association of St. Clement Dane with the Danes, despite its use by the German community by the thirteenth century. The existence of a Scandinavian community is consonant with indications of a substantial export trade with Scandinavia, quite apart from the levy of repeated Danegelds: excavations in the Scandinavian ports of Bryggen and Gamla Lödöse show late Anglo-Saxon and Anglo-Norman pottery, and those at Kaupang, eighth- and ninth-century insular bronze jewellery. Of the more than 50,000 English coins of the late Anglo-Saxon period found in Scandinavia and the lands south and east of the Baltic, those minted at Lincoln predominate at the end of the Anglo-Saxon period (Sawyer, "Trade" 192–97), and, not having been restruck at London, were probably not wholly *heregeld*. An identification of a significant commercial component in the Scandinavian coin hoards is supported by the discovery that Lincoln had expanded enormously in the late ninth and tenth centuries, presumably under the impetus of trade between the Danelaw and Scandinavia.

Onomastics is admittedly an exceedingly problematic field, especially concerning the advanced forms of names found on eleventh-century coinage, but our argument from onomastics is supported by evidence for further widespread international contacts, particularly in circles about the Court, in both the historical and the archaeological record. Hence, in 1054 it was possible for Edward the Confessor to locate and summon from Hungary his chosen successor, Edward the Exile,[31] a member of the West-Saxon line that had gone into exile when Canute seized the English throne in 1016. It is likely that in this search the Anglo-Saxon court used as intermediaries the Danish court and Vladimir of Kiev.

The Biddles' excavation of the old royal palace and two pre-Conquest minsters at Winchester yielded in the palace itself an Arab *dirham* (one of a number found in late Anglo-Saxon England)[32] and a fragment of a large Fatimid-period alabaster vase, the nearest analogue of which they eventually located in Egypt (Biddle).

Arab coinage reached the West, especially Scandinavia, from a relatively early date: almost 80,000 Cufic coins, mainly from Samarkand (in Sogdania, just north of modern Afghanistan) and Tashkent, have been found in Sweden, about 5,000 in Denmark and 400 in Norway, although the number drops after about 970 (Roesdahl 200), when Anglo-Saxon *heregeld* increases. That it could also have occurred in quantity in the Heptarchy is supported first by the fact that it impressed Offa of Mercia enough to make him strike his own dinar,[33] complete with an announcement in Arabic that there is no God but Allah, and secondly by a change in the composition of the silver alloy used in coinage in later Anglo-Saxon England, which argues a very high component of remelted oriental coin silver.[34]

Since Peter Sawyer has argued that the coins even from the Arab world were the product of raiding rather than commerce (*Kings* 124–29), and since a good many of the imports that have survived, save (Norwegian) walrus ivory,[35] cannot be nailed to a single source, even the presence of coins of various sources without hacksilver peckmarks is difficult to reconcile definitively with trade. Some trade can, nonetheless, be adduced. An eighth-century silver denier found in Repton issued by Pepin the Short at a mint in Verdun, a major slave-trading centre, might be taken to corroborate literary records of a substantial export of slaves.[36] There are also indications of the breeding of and possibly a commerce in large hunting dogs, and of a cloth trade, but it has been suggested that the Heptarchy generally ran a deficit in trade with Merovingian and Carolingian France, and that as a result there was relatively little spare coin. Danish archaeology shows, moreover, that imports could include destructible goods as well as such luxury goods as beads of amethyst, rock crystal, and carnelian: a quantity of high-quality rye from the Fyrkat fortress was probably from Poland, and pollen grains in Denmark seem to indicate the introduction of several plants in the early Viking Age (Roesdahl 200).

3. THE RUS: INSULAR, BYZANTINE, AND SOGDANIAN LINKS

Scandinavian contacts eastward are undeniable, but they are often viewed as specifically Swedish, and those with the west as Norwegian or Danish. Yet the presence of some of Æthelred's Danegeld in hoards in the eastern Baltic, a number of dynastic marriages, particularly with the Rurikan Kievan Rus dynasty, and direct links between the insular West and Byzantium, especially in the decades after the Norman conquest, all attest to closer contacts that are easily overlooked.

One such link was Ingigerd, the wife of Yaroslav the Great of Kiev. The half-sister of Ealdgyth, the wife of Edmund Ironside, she is probably best known as the mother-in-law of Henri I of France. Another of her children, a son, Vsevelod, married a daughter of the emperor Constantine IX Monomachos, possibly Maria or Anastasia; their son, Vladimir Monomakh (d. 1126), married Gytha, the daughter of Harold Godwinson. According to Saxo Grammaticus (*Gesta Danorum*, 11, 6, 3; cited by Shepard 57), King Swein, who had received her and two of her brothers at the Danish court after the Battle of Hastings, arranged this marriage to Vladimir before his death in 1074; it is perhaps noteworthy in this context that the Scandinavian name adopted by Gytha's oldest son Mistislav was Haraldr.

It is also possible that a raiding expedition from Uppsala to Serkland ("the land of the Saracens" or, alternatively, "the land of silk") commanded by Yngvar passed through Yaroslav's Kiev, as *Yngvars saga víðforla* has it. But given that the Serkland for which it was bound and, according to a large number of memorial stones, in which it was destroyed in 1042, could have been anywhere east of Kiev, Sir David Wilson has suggested that the expedition might simply have consisted of an attempt to reopen an old trade route down the Volga to the Caspian Sea after the collapse of the Khazars and their stronghold, Sarkel, at the mouth of the Don.

According to the tenth-century chronicler al-Mas'udi, the Rus had in 912–13 managed to penetrate and raid the coast of the Caspian as far as Azerbaijan and Baku, three days' march from the sea. Liutprand of Cremona, whose stepfather was in Byzantium at the time, recorded a similar attack in 941,[37] this time on Byzantium itself, by a large fleet of *Nordmanni* that had first devastated the lands round the Black Sea. This expedition is also referred to in the Russian *Primary Chronicle* or *Povest Vremennykh Let* ("Chronicle of Past Years"), where it was said to have been commanded by one Igor (ON Ingvarr; cf. the name Inger, given by Liutprand) (Ellis Davidson 130).

In addition, as Sir David Wilson observes, the Volga river, one of the two major routes used by the Varangians, could not be controlled by Rus-founded or Rus-dominated centres in the way the Dnieper was, because cities on the Volga had already been established by the Bulgars and the Khazars to control the fur trade. He continues:

> From the Bulgar bend it was possible for traders to strike out across the desert to reach the silk route to Baghdad and China somewhere near the Aral Sea. Though the documentation is scanty, Arab sources and archaeological finds encourage the belief that it was of some importance, and it was probably along this route, rather than through Byzantium, that many of the Arab coins found in Scandinavia had travelled. (106)

4. NORSE, ENGLISH, AND NORMAN VARANGIANS

It is clear that Scandinavia is vital to any consideration of relations with the East, simply because of the Rurican dynasty's ties with much of Europe, and because of the routes to Byzantium and points east that Novgarod and Kiev controlled. Indeed, the Varangian Guard, the personal guard of the

Emperor, seems at one point to have been Scandinavian, though the ethnicity of the Guard, like that of the Rus, is a subject of constant nationalistic wrangling.[38] Its most notable member was Haraldr Harðráði Sigurðarsson[39] (fl. 1045–66), whose fall at the Battle of Stamford Bridge is described in *Haralds Saga* and *Fagrskinna*. Even so, however, *Haralds Saga* in *Heimskringla*, which has a great deal to say about the Varangian Guard, tends to trade on a widespread ignorance of detail about Byzantium in its domestic Scandinavian audience. Thus, Harald's attempt to explain his wealth by stating that on the death of an Emperor the Varangian Guard had a right to whatever it could carry (*polutasvarf*) seems a desperate rationalization.[40]

Haraldr and the Varangians under him, despite the corps's origin as an imperial bodyguard, spent much of their service, under George Maniaces and his Patricios, Basil Theodorokanos, attempting to reconquer Sicily from the Normans; this attempt was aborted by their premature recall by members of the anti-military faction (Vasiliev 313, 323, 329). During the period of the growth of feudalism, at about the time of Constantine Porphyrogenitus, the great armies of Asia Minor, which had originally shared with the navy responsibility for the safety of the Emperor whenever he was outside the city of Byzantium,[41] tended to attach their loyalties to the great provincial magnates, such as the Phokas, Skleroi, Maleinoi, and Comnenoi. The Emperor as a result needed a bodyguard whose loyalties were less likely to be subverted than those of troops from within the Empire. According to Deno John Geanakopolos, the bodyguard was successively composed of Germanic troops, Turks from Ferghana, east of Samarkand in West Turkestan, Sogdanians,[42] Varangians, Normans, and Germans, though it is unclear whether this was the same corps throughout. After the Norman Conquest there was a strong Anglo-Saxon and Norman element. Christine Fell, Krijnie N. Ciggaar, and Jonathan Shepard have suggested that this increase in the guard may have been due to a large emigration from Anglo-Saxon England between 1071[43] and 1081, including disaffected sons of dispossessed landowners, and possibly even led, as the *Saga Jatvárðar Konungs Hins Helga* states, by an individual variously identified as the Earl Sigurðr of Gloucester (Siweard in Old English) and as *Stanardus, comes cladicestrie*. This emigration, first to Byzantium via Gibraltar, is largely overlooked by historians, or treated as fiction, despite its having been mentioned by Odericus Vitalis (2: 171–72 and 3: 169, 490) and by the hagiographer Goscelin,[44] and in detail in two manuscripts of the early thirteenth century, *Chronicon universale anonymi Laudunensis*, written by an English Premonstratensian at Laon.[45] According to the *Chronicon* there was a second emigration, to a territory six days' sail north of Byzantium.

It has been argued, too (Shepard 70, 92–93), that the English element in the guard was earlier and more important than it was thought to have been, that the *Chronicon Laudunensis* and *Jatvarðar Saga* record a genuine second emigration to a New England and the foundation of towns named London and York in the Crimea, then threatened by Pecheneg tribesmen, and that some of the Varangian place names mentioned in this tradition survived into the late Middle Ages. Even if the size and importance of such an emigration may be questioned, there remains a mention, albeit in a somewhat untrustworthy source, of an embassy to the court of Henry I from the Byzantine Emperor Alexius. The leader of this legation from Constantinople, Wulfric of Lincoln, is identified in passing as the source of a relic.[46]

There are other scattered traces of a possible pre-Conquest Anglo-Saxon presence in Byzantium. Ciggaar cites a monk from Canterbury who describes a church of St. Nicholas and St. Augustine (315)[47] that served the English community and used the Latin rite.[48] And there is even a stray observation that evokes the image of the use of English in court ceremonies: Pseudo-Codinus writes that the Varangian Guard attended the Emperor during the Coronation ceremony, and during the feast at Christmas (VII Περὶ τῆσ τοῦ Βασιλέως τραπέζης [Codinus col. 76]) the various corps wished the Emperor long life in their own languages — the Vardariotes in Persian, the Genoese and Pisans in Latin, and the Varangians in English.

Whether the Greek writer was actually able to identify the various barbarian languages as precisely as he might seem to be is open to question. An identification of the Island of Thule, too, may reflect some contemporary confusion between the vernaculars of, on the one hand, such indisputably Scandinavian Varangians as Haraldr Harðráði and, on the other, an English cohort in the Varangian Guard that drew a significant proportion of its numbers from the Danelaw or from the descendants of Canute's Danish followers granted property in England, and thus — as Anna Comnena describes Thule — from an island formerly part of the Roman Empire.

The idea that the Varangians were from the Island of Thule and therefore either Icelanders or British (proposed among others by Shepard [56] and by B.S. Benedikz in his revision of Blöndal's *Væringa Saga*) is perhaps over-literal and does not by itself necessarily exclude a Scandinavian Guard. The historian Anna Comnena, in a famous passage in the *Alexiad*, book 2, about her father's plans to induce the Imperial bodyguard to revolt, describes the Varangian Guard as being from Thule:

> He learnt that in one place the "Immortals" were on guard (this is the most select regiment of the Roman army) and in another the Varangians from Thule (by these I mean the axe-bearing barbarians) and in another the Nemitzi (these too are a barbarian tribe who have been subjects of the Roman Empire of old); and he thereupon advised Alexius not to make an offer to the Varangians or the Immortals. (63–64)

The Island of Thule need not actually have been an island: Ptolemaic geography described *Scanza* (Scandinavia) as an island, and it would therefore be reasonable for a Greek historian to describe Norway and Sweden as νῆσος θύλη (the Island of Thule). Certainly Procopius described Britain and Thule as separate places, Thule as recognizably Scandinavian, approximately ten times the size of Britain, and inhabited by several pagan tribes, including the Gautoi.[49]

Despite the complimentary remarks Anna Comnena made about the Varangians, they appear to have had mixed reviews. Ioannes Curopalata, who described events roughly contemporaneous with the reign of Comnenus, mentions the Varangian component of a highly multicultural and ill-equipped army, and does so in an extravagant lament about the nadir to which the Empire had sunk (667–69).

By the twelfth century, Byzantium contained a large number of nationalities, including a considerable Latin Christian community, mostly from the Mediterranean. The Venetian district, apparently the oldest, had been conceded in 991 and had its own church (St. Acindyrus) by 1070 at the latest; this church owned among other unlikely items four taverns (Janin, "Les sanctuaires" 163). Most of the Europeans, particularly the Germans, the French (from the French kingdoms of the Levant), and the Genoese, were kept in the area of the Golden Horn, on the northern side of the European city, and there are records of the massacre of 6,000 during an anti-Latin riot there in 1182. Although one would ordinarily expect the Scandinavians and the Rus to have been there too, they were not, nor were they on the Asian side with the other districts, which were carefully checker-boarded with Greeks to avoid a possible anti-Greek coalition; it has been speculated that they were trusted sufficiently to have had a district elsewhere in the European part of the city (Janin, "Les sanctuaires"

163). According to a disputed reading of a Turkish district name (Langabostani, the garden of the Vlanga) they could have been centred on the south coast, about the harbour of the districts of Eleutherios and Theodosius. No site of the Varangian Church St. Mary Varangiotissa has been identified,[50] though as there were at least 118 churches in the city dedicated to the Virgin Mary (Janin, "Les églises" 153) this failure is not entirely surprising.

Again, however, possible links with the east become apparent. Sogdanian troops from an area greatly influenced by the Chinese, Indian, and Iranian civilizations preceded the Varangians as Imperial bodyguards, for example, and Chinese records speak of embassies from Byzantium (Fu-lin) that were received in China in the years 643, 667, 719, and 720 (Needham 1: 186, 205). Thus, in spite of the greater difficulty of direct contact between Europe and the Far East after the Arab conquest of Persia in 652, but before the closing of the overland route to the Byzantines following the Battle of the River Talas in 751, there is evidence of continued relations between the peoples of the east and the peoples to the west. Even after the loss to the Chinese of the nominally tributary kingdoms in Afghanistan in 751, dealings, particularly with Persia, seem to have continued. Needham observes that in 798 Chinese chroniclers mention a mission from Harun al-Rashid to Xian to arrange for a co-ordinated strategy against the Tibetans (Needham 1: 215–16). It is possible that the embassy Charlemagne sent to Harun al-Rashid in 797, which returned in 801, was aware of that other mission, although the Chinese chroniclers understandably supply the date of its return to China rather than that of its dispatch.

The lockstep debasing of gold and silver in early seventh-century France and Anglo-Saxon England suggests that routes between Western Europe and the Near East existed via the Mediterranean before the first appearance of the Varangians in the records. It is quite possible, then, that the sixth- or early seventh-century Byzantine or early Islamic blue glass vase that was found in the Finsbury area of London[51] came along a separate route from the south, notwithstanding the fact that the quantity of similarly deep blue glasswork, this time with gilded patterns that was deposited a century or two later in the Muscovy area was so large that it has prompted speculation concerning a native ornamental glass industry (Kennesson).

The importation of Cufic coins from Samarkand and Tashkent into the West, the presence of Sogdanians in Byzantium, Fredegar's knowledge of gossip about the Sassanids, and archaeological indications, even in the early Middle Ages, of at least occasional links with the Eastern Mediterranean, show an awareness of the Near and Middle East at the level of the courts. So, indeed, does contemporary male jewellery.

5. GARNET CLOISONNÉ JEWELLERY

i. *Eastern Origins*

The grave goods found in the late fifth-century burial of Childeric at Tournai are a concrete illustration of such an awareness of the eastern Mediterranean and Near East. The large number of Byzantine coins in Childeric's grave suggests that he was sponsored in his struggle against Aegidius by the Emperor. It seems also to be accepted now that the inlaid gold and garnet decoration that one finds on early medieval ornament, including, for example, that at Sutton Hoo, that of Childeric's regalia, that produced by the Merovingian workshops at Toulouse, and that of Langobardic design, was originally of Byzantine or Sassanid inspiration. Indeed, it has been suggested that because Childeric's son Clovis had been made a consul by the Emperor Anastasius, and, according to Gregory of Tours (38), was thereafter called Consul or Augustus, Childeric's contemporaries might have considered him to have been buried in Roman consular regalia,[52] and the splendour of the Sutton Hoo hoard to have been imperial, not barbaric.[53]

The garnets used in this regalia were from India, some possibly cut part-way along their journey, at Alabanda in Asia Minor, where they were mass-produced (hence almandine garnet). It is generally agreed that the use of garnets in this style was Sassanid or Byzantine, and that it was introduced to the West by the Huns, who brought a number of Iranian, Pontic, and Hunnish artifacts into central Europe. An example is the sword-belt buckle buried near Wolfsheim in the Rhineland, but inscribed with the name of the Persian king Ardashir I (reg. 224–41). Although cloisonné garnet work was rapidly naturalized, and manufactured for example among the Alemanii and the Ostrogoths, and, pre-eminently, in the Merovingian royal workshops at Tournai, its eastern origin was clearly remembered: the cover of the Gospel Book of Theodelinda, presented in 603 by Gregory the Great to the sovereigns of Monza, seems to be the item described in a contemporary list as "Theca Persica" (Persian container).

It is therefore not surprising that Bruce-Mitford identified as the closest analogue to the purse at Sutton Hoo one found in a fifth-century Ostrogothic grave in Romania,[54] or that a suggestion explaining the suspension apparatus of the Sutton Hoo sword should be modelled on Iranian exemplars. There is, therefore, some evidence of a wide-ranging raiding and trading network extending into central Asia and as far south as India.

ii. *Eastern Dissemination*

In his monumental six-volume work, *Science and Civilisation in China*, the sinologist Joseph Needham of Cambridge, working with Wang Ling, has made some sensational and perhaps sometimes over-enthusiastic claims about the movement of technology, mostly from East to West,[55] during the Middle Ages. Some of his examples of oriental influence on the West and his enthusiastically *post hoc, ergo propter hoc* attitude to scientific innovations have been questioned.

The first caravans from China to Persia began in 106 B.C., eventually extending via either Samarkand or Bactria[56] to Iraq, Antioch, and Egypt, and the retinue of a Chinese embassy settled in Persia in about 100 B.C. In the first three centuries A.D. a sea route between Greece and India was established through the Persian Gulf and the Red Sea. By the fifth century, Chinese ships appear to have reached Yemen and the mouth of the Euphrates.[57] After the Battle of the River Talus in 751, contact with the Gulf appears to have been maintained; on his return by sea eleven years later, a Chinese prisoner described the settlement of Chinese captives in Kufah in Iraq, the capital of the Abbasid Caliphate.[58] It is thus possible that the silk presented to Charlemagne by Harun al-Rashid[59] was the product of a newly-naturalized Abbasid technology acquired from Chinese prisoners taken at that battle. Not only Notker's revealing description of the tepid reception given Charlemagne's return gifts (apart from the hunting dogs), but the *Annales regni francorum* (*Annales laurissenses* [Lorsch] *maiores*) indicate that there were contacts between the two courts. The compilers of the Lorsch *Annals* had sources close enough to the court to be able to furnish the names of members of two embassies to Harun al-Rashid and of one embassy to Charlemagne,[60] to record the Arabic title Amir al-Mumminin (*Annales* 114),[61] and twice to supply the information that Frankish embassies made the return journey in four years.

Probably the most spectacular example of the range of trade is provided by what can only be described as the archaeological equivalent of a glacial erratic. It is a cloisonné almandine garnet ($Fe_3(Al_2(SiO_4)_3)$) and gold sword-decoration with pelta spirals and granulation that, although not dissimilar to the gold and garnet decoration of contemporary Western Europe, was uncovered in 1972 in a Silla-period (57 B.C.–A.D. 935) tomb, probably of the sixth century, in Kyongju, south-eastern Korea. The reputation of the Silla period among Korean art historians as the most isolated and artistically conservative of the Three Kingdoms of the peninsula[62] makes the discovery of the Kerim-Lo sword doubly surprising: the kingdom's location in south-eastern Korea inhibited contact with China either by land or sea. As Wakoh Anazawa and Jun-Ichi Manome, the authors of the only study of the sword, note, "Anyone familiar with the history of art will notice that the decoration on this dagger is very similar to the polychrome style of decoration often seen on relics of the European early medieval period." This is the only example of its kind in the Far East, and its closest analogue is a fifth- to seventh-century cloisonné sword decoration found in 1928 in Borovje, Khazakstan, now in the Hermitage Museum. Very similar daggers are depicted on wall paintings in Iran, Tadjikistan (including one in the city of Samarkand), Uzbekistan, and Afghanistan, as well as on a Sassanian silver plate, now in the Bibliothèque nationale in Paris, with a portrait of an emperor, considered to be either Hoslo II (590–628 A.D.) or Yasdugald III (632–51 A.D.).

But the suspension fittings, one P-shaped and one D-shaped, testify to a very wide and very rapid technological transmission, distinguishing the decoration of the Kerim-Lo sword from such other nearly contemporary erratics as the miniature fifth-century Buddha discovered in the fifth- and sixth-century settlement at Helgö, Sweden,[63] or the Chinese silk in the ninth- and tenth-century settlement at Birka. The fittings on the Kerim-Lo sword seem to have been rapidly naturalized: Drs. Anazawa and Manome state that Japanese archaeologists consider the P-shaped suspension fittings, often seen in Sassanid art, to be the prototype of mound-shaped metal fittings found on Japanese swords and daggers of the Nara period and later. They also point out that in Europe the P-shaped fitting is usually attributed to the invasion of the Avars in the late sixth century, and that apart from the Kerim-Lo sword the earliest example known is a late sixth-century dagger with exactly the same P- and D-shaped suspension fittings as those at Kerim-Lo but discovered in a Langobardic cemetery in Castel Torino, Italy. It is quite clear that weaponry from Persian and central Asia, and a fashion for garnet work, spread rapidly both east and west; it is an object lesson in the reach of trade routes.

Though this paper does not seek to suggest that any of these routes were widely travelled from end to end after the fashion of Frans Bengtsson's rollicking saga travesty *Röde Orm*, translated into English as *The Long Ships*, there remain indisputable traces throughout the early Middle Ages of very wide-ranging trade networks. Hence, the possibility of some awareness of and perhaps acquaintance with a wider world on the part of the courtly audiences of such vernacular epics as *Beowulf* is too easily discounted when we seek to project upon them pet theories about their attitudes and their milieus.

NOTES

[1] A shorter version of this paper was delivered at the Second Annual Conference at the Arizona Center for Medieval and Renaissance Studies, Phoenix, Arizona, 17 February 1996. A greatly enlarged version of the part of this paper dealing with the Varangian Guard was also delivered at the graduate Scandinavian Studies seminar, University College, London, in January 1976. I am indebted to Peter Foote, the late Christine Fell, D.M. Wilson, and B.S. Benedikz for their comments on that occasion, but any mistakes remain my own.

[2] It is possible to localize, for example, epigraphical decorative schools within a very few miles by analyzing closely such variables as the size and ratio of grids on which interlace decorations were superimposed. See Bailey, and Bailey and Cramp.

[3] Hence I have not treated the hoard of ninth- and tenth-century Carolingian and Anglo-Saxon coins unearthed at Rome in 1830 (lost), that found at the Vatican in 1928 and sold over the next two years (517 Anglo-Saxon coins from the first quarter of the tenth century and six Continental deniers and three silver ingots), that found near Catania, Sicily, before 1914 (a lump of fused Anglo-Saxon coins from the first half of the tenth century), the Forum hoard of 1883 (over 800 Anglo-Saxon coins, four Continental deniers, and a gold solidus of Theophilus from the second quarter of the ninth century), coins bought from a dealer in Rome in 1846 (94 coins c. 950), a small hoard at the Hospital of Sancto Spirito in Rome sold between 1957 and 1980, and a possible eleventh-century Anglo-Saxon coin in a hoard of 213 late tenth-century coins, mostly German, found south of Rome in 1885

[4] Because no hoards of coins from any of Offa's mints, for example, have been unearthed since the eighteenth century, it is difficult to conduct much analysis of their discovery, their distribution, the dates of moneyers, the mints, and the debasement of silver. Even the famous dinar, a fortuitous find in Rome, can be traced no further than a dealer some time before 1841, when a description was first published (de Longpérier). See also Blunt; Stewart.

[5] A second ship burial (Mount 2) at Sutton Hoo has yielded a number of fittings very similar to those from the articles of the first, including a heavily gilded silver terminal for a drinking horn in the form of the head of a bird with a strongly curling beak, indistinguishable from one of the bird-headed terminals found in the first Sutton Hoo ship-burial (Evans). As the mound was dug up either in the Middle Ages or in an 1860 expedition that is recorded to have found several bushels of iron rivets, and as the burial chamber was unexpectedly located under the ship, very little undisturbed material remained. The excavator, Martin Carver, estimates that it could have been contained in one bucket. He gives the inventory for the grave as follows:

Mount 2 (Burial 2) inhumation W-E in chamber under ship; originally with sword, shield, belt-buckle (?), silver buckle, drinking-horns, tub (?), iron-bound bucket, cauldron (?), bronze bowl, blue glass jar, silver-mounted box, silver-mounted cup, 5 knives in sheathes, textiles.

ROBBED OR EXCAVATED without record, possibly in 1860 (INT 1).

Excavated 1938 (INT 3 Bruce-Mitford 1975). Excavated 1986–1989 (INT 26–41)

DATED Late sixth/early seventh century (grave goods). (Carver 367).

[6]Frankish jewellery is found on bodies in Kentish graveyards in locations in which it does not seem to have been worn among the Franks (Hinton, *Archaeology* 21).

[7]The first is Procopius's sceptical report of the Franks' pretensions to rule Britain and efforts to have Justinian recognize their lordship:

οἱ δὲ αὐτοὺς ἐνοικίζουσιν ἐς γῆς τῆς σφετέρας τὴν ἐρημοτέραν δοκοῦσαν εἶναι, καὶ ἀπ' αὐτοῦ τὴν νῆσον προσποιεῖσθαί φασιν. ὥστε ἀμέλει οὐ πολλῷ πρότερον ὁ Φράγγων βασιλεὺς ἐπὶ πρεσβείᾳ τῶν οἱ ἐπιτηδείων τινὰς παρὰ βασιλέα Ἰουστινιανὸν ἐς Βυζάντιον στείλας ἄνδρας αὐτοῖς ἐκ τῶν Ἀγγίλων ξυνέπεμψε, φιλοτιμούμενος ὡς καὶ ἡ νῆσος ἥδε πρὸς αὐτοῦ ἄρχεται. (*Wars* 8: 20, 9–10)

(And they [the Franks] settle [the many migrants] in the lands they consider rather desolate and say that by this means they are gaining the island. Consequently recently the king of the Franks, on sending some friends in an embassy to Byzantium to the Emperor Justinian, sent some Angles with them, with the ambition also of ruling the island itself.)

Ian Wood (Frankish 235) notes that Venantius Fortunatus records grandiloquent claims by Sigibert I and Chilperic I to hegemony over the Britons and the Saxons as well as, among others, over the Danes, the Basques, and the Estonians. The Fortunatus text reads

Quem Geta, Wasco tremunt, Danus, Estio, Saxo, Britannus,

cum patre quos acie te domitasse patet

terror et extremis Frisonibus, atque Sueuis,

Qui neque bella parant, sed tua frena rogant. (carmen IX 1, 73–76)

Wood notes too that Gregory the Great seems to have taken Theuderic II and Theudebert II's superiority to Æthelberht of Kent for granted in an otherwise unintelligible logical swerve in the preface to a letter to them (Epistola LVIII, PL 77, cols. 841–42), and that Theudebert I claimed that Eucii (probably Jutes of Kent or the Isle of Wight) were dependent peoples. Elsewhere, he points out that Eadbald, the son of Æthelberht of Kent (and possibly of Bertha, daughter of Charibert I), seems to have married a Neustrian noblewoman, Emma, the daughter of Erchinoald, and that both his son, Eadbald, and granddaughter, Earcongota, have Frankish names (*Kingdoms* 176-177).

[8]These are very rare outside Kent except in elite graves (Hinton, *Archaeology* 22).

[9]A forgery made of copper with a gold wash and imitating a *triens* of the second

quarter of the seventh century from Huy (Belgium) of the moneyer Bertoaldus was found against the inner edge of the wall near the north doorway into the middle room of Building A3 at Yeavering (Hope-Taylor 182–83).

[10]Copper-alloy "Coptic" bowls (Hinton, *Archaeology* 21).

[11]Paste, cuttle fish shell, or shell from the Indian Ocean was used for whites in coloured jewellery such as composite disc brooches (Hinton, *Archaeology* 21).

[12]"The custom of burial with a coin seems not to have outlasted the eighth century" (Hinton, "Coins" 17).

[13]For example, the 40 coins and blanks in the purse.

[14]The bird, which contains three of the five pieces of garnet inlay on the Sutton Hoo shield, seems to be Gotlandic. The five pieces of garnet cloisonné inlay on the shield, for example, have close parallels with Vendel work, and the inlays are similar in technique and cell form to those of the Åker burial of Hedmark, Norway (Bruce-Mitford 2: 58–59, 79).

[15]The Coptic bowl at Sutton Hoo is one of twenty found in Anglo-Saxon England, and of four in East Anglia, three from south-east Suffolk near Sutton Hoo (Wickham Market, Suffolk; Badley, near Needham Market, Suffolk; Chilton Hall, Sudbury, near Stowmarket, Suffolk; and Caistor-by-Norwich, Norfolk) (Bruce-Mitford 3: 732–41).

[16]See the discussions in Wallace-Hadrill.

[17]Wallace-Hadrill notes in his edition that Paul the Lombard was also familiar with the tale of Anosharwan.

[18]Chapter 64:

> Patricius ille girans capud conspecere qui postergum eius uenerit, Aeraglius aecum calcaneum uehementer urgens, extrahens uxum capud patriciae Persarum truncauit.

[19]Wallace-Hadrill discusses the linguistic evidence briefly in the apparatus to his edition of the *Chronicon,* citing a Polish article by Gerard Labuda, *Pierwsze państwo słowiańskie. Państwo Samona,* summarized by Chaloupecky.

> buffalo (*byvolð), buffalo tenders (byvolci), Latinized to *befulci* or *befulti* and used in
>> ideo belfulci uocabantur a Chunis (chapter 48).
> Labuda, however, suggests that *befulci* was actually a German-Latin hybrid (bis + folc), i.e. "double regiment" (Chaloupecky 227).
> Fredegar also uses the Slavic titles *gagano* (Khan) and *walluc* in
>> Sclaui iam contra Auaris coinomento Chunis et regem eorum gagano ceperant (chapter 48).
>> post haec cum Wallucem ducem Winedorum annis plurimis uixit cum suis (chapter 72).

See also Chaloupecky 225:

À l'opposé du scepticisme que Frédégaire a inspiré à certains historiens, Labuda attribue à sa chronique (surtout en ce qui concerne les renseignements sur les Slaves) une considérable valeur historique. Il base son opinion sur le fait que la dite partie de la chronique avait été écrite dans un milieu où l'intérêt porté à l'orient slave était particulièrement vif et que, datant d'environ 660, la chronique provient d'un contemporain des événements décrits.

[20]Dubbed by Rudolf Poertner "Babylon on the Baltic" (183).

[21]A trading centre, possibly an offshoot of Helgö, founded about 800 on Lake Mälar near Stockholm and rediscovered in 1687.

[22](Then King Alfred ordered long ships to be built to counter the Viking ships; they were very nearly twice as long as the others. Some had 60 oars and some more; they were both swifter and more stable and also higher than the others. *They were constructed neither in the Frisian nor Danish fashion* but as it seemed to him they could be most useful.... Lucuman the King's reeve was killed there, as were *Wulfheard the Frisian and Abbe the Frisian and Athelhere the Frisian and Æthelferth the king's companion, and a total of 62 Frisians and English.*)

[23](A ship is nail-fastened, the bulwark bound, bright lind-wood board; a dear and welcome arrival to the Frisian wife when the ship is beached; his keel and her man, her own provider, have come home. And she invites him in, washes his weary garb and gives him fresh clothes, grants him ashore what his love requires.)

[24]Stenton argues that the decree is based on a genuine document containing the name "Godesscealc sacerdos minister," otherwise attested in Old English only as that of a Wendish prince who entered the service of Canute (*Early History* 38).

[25]At least in the Winchester area (Smart 180).

[26]These were not limited to the period. Smart notes the goldsmith Eusebius at Canterbury in the early seventh century as well as Ludoman, a moneyer for Offa (757–96), Odilo, a moneyer in Northumbria, and Reghelm and Rernher for Æthelstan I of East Anglia (825–45). She further identifies (176) the continental non-Scandinavian names Chrestien, Samson, Simon, Stephan, Iudelbard, Abenel/Abonel, and Winiger, all on the later coinage of Alfred the Great (d. 899) (178 ff.), Gunni, Irfari, Thurlac, and Ellaf under Edward the Elder (899–924), as well as Ergimbalt, who was active in the reign of Edmund (939–46). Surprisingly, in the Norse kingdom of York she finds a number of non-Scandinavian continental Germanic names among the moneyers; these include Sibrant, Odeler, Baciager, Bleseret, Nothe, Rodbert, Sigar, Ascolv, Rathulf, Radulf, Ingelgar, Ulfelm, and Wadter, and possibly Adel..d(md), Arnulf, Hildulf, and Farman.

[27]Mentioned in his will, for example, by Bishop Theodred of London.

[28]And Otto, the son of Henry the Fowler. Sixteen years after Edith's death, and five years after the death of her son, he became Emperor of the Romans (*Anglo-Saxon England* 346–47).

[29]13 November 1002, St. Brice's Day. Among the casualties was Gunnhild, the sister of Sven Forkbeard.

[30]The cult was widespread: an eleventh-century Uppland runestone memorializing four men mentions a church dedicated to St. Olaf, this time in Novgarod (Wilson 108).

[31]The son of Edmund Ironside, and grandson of Æthelred the Unready. In 1057 he, his wife, and his son Edgar (later known as the Ætheling) travelled to London, where within 48 hours he suddenly died.

[32]The Viking Age Croyden Hoard, presumably buried by a member of the Danish Great Army between 865 and late 872 and found in 1862, contained in addition to hacksilver and 157 ninth-century Anglo-Saxon coins of various kingdoms, seven Carolingian deniers (814–77) and three Cufic coins in the form of Abbasid dirhems, two of Harun al-Rashid (786–809) and one of Al-Wathik (842–47). It has been argued partly on the grounds that since no Cufic coins were found in English hoards before the end of the ninth century — barring the dirham in the small hoard in Talnotrie (Kirkcudbrightshire) — whereas there are over 100 known from the same period in Scandinavia, Estonia, Latvia, and European Russia (Brooks and Graham-Campbell 99 ff.), these coins cannot reflect commercial links with the British Isles. See, however, note 34.

[33]Found in Italy and now in the British Museum. It imitates a gold coin of Caliph Al-Mansur (774 A.D.).

[34]Analysis of the traces of gold and bismuth in English coinage in the second half of the tenth century suggests, however, that enough oriental silver was reminted as English coinage, particularly in London, to change the make-up of the stock radically (McKerrell and Stevenson, cited in Metcalf).

[35]Though the presence in Gao (Mali) of Spanish marble stelae as well as pottery and glass from the ivory-working areas of Spain, Ifriqiya, and Egypt argues that subsahelian hippopotamus ivory may have been used in Al-Andalus, in the Christian kingdoms of Northern Spain, and in parts of the Near East (Insoll 332–35).

[36]In connection with the burgeoning Viking slave trade in the ninth century, see Smyth 154 ff., and in the eleventh century Wulfstan's threnody in the *Sermo Lupi ad Anglos, passim*.

[37]Gens quaedam est sub aquilonis parte constituta, quam a qualitate corporis Graeci vocant Ρουσιος, Rúsios, nos vero a positione loci nominamus Nordmannos.... Huius denique gentis rex vocabulo Inger erat, qui collectis mille et eo amplius navibus Constantinopolim venit.... Cumque cogitationibus non paucis insomnes noctes duceret et Inger cuncta mari vicina deriperet, nuntiatum est Romano XV semifracta se habere chelándia quae populus ob vetustatem sola reliquerat.... Russorum etenim naves ob parvitatem sui, ubi aquae minimum est, transeunt, quod Grecorum chelándia ob profunditatem sui facere nequeunt. Inger ingenti cum confusione postmodum ad propria est reversus, Greci vero victoria potiti vivos secum multos ducentes Constantinopolim regressi sunt laeti. Quos omnes Romanós in praesentia

regis Hugonis nuntii, vitrici scilicet mei, decollare praecepit. (Liutprand, *Antapodosis* 5: 15: 137–39)

(There is a certain people living in a part of the north, which the Greeks call Rousios from the type of their body, but which we call Northmen from their geographical location.... And the king of this people, Inger by name, assembled a thousand and more ships and came to Constantinople.... And while [the Emperor Romanos] passed sleepless nights making many plans and Inger plundered all the coastal areas, Romanos was advised that he had fifteen broken-down chelandia [ships] only, which the people had left because of their age.... [There follows a naval battle, in which the chelandia, using Greek fire, completely defeat the raiders.] for the ships of the Rus, because of their small size, sail through shallows that the Greek Chelandia cannot navigate on account of their deeper draught. Inger shortly thereafter returned to his own land in great disarray and the victorious Greeks joyfully returned to Constantinople, bringing many prisoners. Romanos had all the captives executed in the presence of my stepfather, the envoy of King Hugo.)

[38]The term Varangian (in Russian варяг, Greek βάρραγγοι, Arabic *varank*, and Turkish *varmak*) may have been derived from ON *vārar* or *var*, but seems to have been adopted early into Russian and an unumlauted Slavic **var,egū*, and borrowed into Greek and Arabic (Stender-Petersen).

Even the word "Varangian" seems to be encountered quite late. Although possibly originally used of circum-Baltic populations, it is first found with reference to Russia in 972–88, when Vladimir of Kiev sent 6,000 men to the aid of Basil II Bulgaroctonus against Bardas Phokas. In the eleventh-century Kiev Chronicle, however, they are described in unequivocally Scandinavian terms, and, according to A.D. Stender-Petersen, are clearly distinct from the Rus (31–32).

Certainly the English component, whatever its size, would have been very late. [39]He is described in the nearly contemporary *Λόγος νουθετητικὸς πρὸς βασιλέα,* "Advice for the Emperor" (attributed to Cecaumenos, c. 1080):

᾽Αράλτης βασιλέως μὲν βαραγγίας ἦν υἱός, ἔχων δὲ ἀδελφὸν τὸν
᾽Ιούλαβον, ὃς καὶ μετα θάνατον τοῦ πατρὸς αὐτοῦ κατέσχε τὴν βασιλείαν
προβαλόμενος ᾽Αράλτην τὸν ἀδελφὸν αὐτοῦ δεύτερον μετ᾽ αὐτοῦ εἰς τὴν
Βασιλείαν. ὃς δὴ καὶ νέος ὢν ἠθέλησεν εἰσελθειν καὶ προσκυνῆσαι τῷ
μακαριωτάτῳ βασιλεῖ κῦρ Μιχαὴλ τῷ Παφλάγονι.

(Haraltes was the son of the king of Varangia. He had a brother Ioulavos, who, following the death of his father, took the throne, advancing his brother second to him in the monarchy. But being young, he wished to go and do obeisance to the most blessed Lord Emperor Michael the Paphlagonian.)

[40]   Haraldr hæfði þrim sinnum komit í pólútasvarf, meðan hann var í Miklagarði. Þat eru þar lög, at hvert sinn, er Grikkjakonungr deyr, þá skulu Væringjar hafa

pólútasvarf. Þeir skulu þá ganga um allar pólútir konungs, þar sem féhirzlur
hans eru, ok skal hverr þá eignask at frjálsu, er höndum kømr á. (Snorri
Sturluson 90)
(Harald had participated three times in polutasvarf [a pillage of the palace]
when he was in Constantinople. There the law is that the Varangians must
have a polutasvarf on the death of the king of the Greeks. They then must go
about the entire palace of the king, where his treasury is, and each one then
shall own without restraint whatever falls into his possession.)

Similarly, the famous Spes episode of *Grettis Saga* (chapter 88), with its trapdoor
introduced as abruptly as a fabliau element and its epic underwater getaway,
presumably across the Golden Horn, was transposed over the years in the Færoese
"Grettis Kvæði" to Russia:

> Nú er sagt frá Gretti sterka
> fáir finnast slíkir.
> Hansara deyði hevndur varð
> eysturi í Garðaríki.

(Now it is said about Grettir the Strong that there are few men like him. His
death was avenged in the east in Russia.)

[41]According to Deno John Geanakopolos, officers known as the *domestici* were
responsible for troops about the Imperial palace and the Hippodrome. The second
division of the cavalry troops, *candidati* (so named for their white trappings over gilded
armour), known as *excubitores*, were responsible for the safety of the Emperor, the
arithmus, commanded by a *drungarius* or admiral, were in charge of marine security,
and the *hikanatoi* were responsible for the Emperor in the city. In the reign of Alexius
Comnenus, the Varangians replaced the excubitores as palace guard, though, as B.S.
Benedikz has remarked, the emperor had been attended by foreign guards since 989.

[42]From the areas of modern Samarkand and Bokhara.

[43]The year of the Battle of Lake Van. In this encounter with the Seleucid Turks, the
army of Asia Minor was destroyed and the emperor Romanus Diogenes captured. He
was returned unharmed, but discovered that during his absence an ascendant anti-
military faction had installed Michael VII Ducas as emperor. Romanus Diogenes was
shortly thereafter killed. Under Michael Ducas Asia Minor fell, and in the reign of
Michael VII Parapinakis Constantinople itself was besieged. The Comnenid dynasty,
which delayed the break-up of the Empire, relied on and used Latin troops, possibly
partly because at Lake Van the light cavalry, who felt a closer affinity to the Turks
than to their employers, deserted.

[44]Primo ex Normannis regnatore Angliae Willelmo Angliam captante, vir honorifi-
cus de curia et nutritura B. Augustini, cum multis Optimatibus patriae profugis,
Constantinopolim transmigravit; tantamque gratiam apud Imperatorem et Im-

peratricem ceterosque potentes obtinuit, ut super sapientes Milites multamque partem sociorum Ducatum acciperet, nec quisquam advenarum ante plurimos annos tali honore profecerit. Duxit uxorem nobilem et opulentam, memorque beneficiorum Dei, in honorem B. Nicolai sanctique Patroni sui Augustini construxit Basilicam domui suae contiguam, et utriusque Sancti, id est B. Augustini ab Australi et B. Nicolai ab Aquilonali latere, quam formose depingi fecit iconiam. Addidit et luminaria, cereos vel lampades flagrante oleo perspicuas, coram sacra imagine domestici Protectoris sui noctibus accendere, quae etiam diem suum referrent in nocte, quoties placida aura concederet sub sereno aethere. Haec ibi videlicet splendida consuetudo est patriae. Haec itaque Augustianiae memoriae Basilica et iconia Anglis exulibus erat patriae suae consolatrix matertera; hic orationes frequentare; hic dulcem Parentem, velut advenae orphani, repetere dulce habebant. (Goscelin 406)

(When William the first Norman ruler of England was in the process of subduing England, a man honoured by the court and devoted to St. Augustine emigrated to Constantinople with many aristocrats fleeing their native land. He was so greatly favoured by the Emperor and Empress and the other authorities that he received the governorship over the sapientes soldiers and over a large part of his companions and no foreigner had for many years attained such an honour. He married a noble and wealthy woman and, mindful of the blessings of God, built a church dedicated to St. Nicholas and his patron Saint Augustine and attached to his house. He caused the images of both saints to be painted splendidly on the sides, Saint Augustine on the south and Saint Nicholas on the north. And he added lighting, wax candles or lamps gleaming with burning oil, which even produced its own daylight at night whenever the gentleness of the breeze under a calm sky permitted. This is of course a splendid custom of his homeland. This basilica to Saint Augustine was as it were a maternal comforter to the English exiles for (the loss of) their native country; here they delighted in holding frequent services and in seeking out a sweet parent, as if they were foreign orphans.)

[45]Phillipps Ms 1880, now at the Deutsche Staatsbibliothek, Berlin, and Paris, BN Lat. 5011.

[46]   Qualiter autem et illud sacratissimum brachium [Sancti Iohannis Chrysostomi] habuerit, operae pretium est breui recitare. Constantinopolitanus Imperator Alexius litteras et dona Henrico regi et Mathildae reginae per hos dies Angliam direxit. Ipsa legatione Wlfricus, genere Anglus, Lincoliae urbis natiuus, (ut tantae dignitatis directorem decuerat,) magna cum pompa functus est. Is plurimum familiaritatis ausum circa eundem imperatorem habens, praedictas Beati Iohannis reliquias ob suae patriae subleuationem petens, et ab ipso accipiens, Abbendoniam commendaturus se fratrum orationibus venit. (*Chronicon* 46–47)

(It is, moreover, worthwhile relating briefly how it obtained that very holy arm [of St. John Chrysostom]. The Emperor Alexius of Constantinople at this time sent letters and gifts to England for King Henry and Queen Matilda. Wilfric, English by race, a native of the city of Lincoln, discharged the office of ambassador with great ceremony, as befitted a supervisor of such high rank. He, presuming greatly on his position in the household attending the Emperor, seeking the above-mentioned relics of St. John because of the distinction it would be for his native land, and on receiving them from him, he came to Abingdon in order to commend himself to the prayers of the brothers.)

It is quite possible that the use of an English rather than a Greek name testifies to a genuine legation, though the paragraph is clearly intended to explain the presence at Abingdon of an exotic relic.

[47]The church, owned by a holy man named Coleman, is very tentatively identified by Dawkins with the Bogdan Sarai near the Adrianople Gate, near which was found an inscription ΙΝΓΒΑΡϜ, possibly an abbreviation of ᾽Ινγ[λίνου] βαρ[έγγου], "English Varangian." Though there is no known location, Dawkins points out that in about 1865, in response to an attempt to seek permission to remove to the English cemetery at Scutari a large number of funeral inscriptions pertaining to the Varangians between the Adrianople Gate and the site called Top Kapou, the Turkish government used the stones for building.

[48]See also note 44 above. After the schism between Latin and Orthodox churches in 1054, there appear to have been in Byzantium at least nine Latin churches, one convent, and eight Latin monasteries. Janin, *La géographie.*

[49]Βριττία δὲ ἡ νῆσος ἐπὶ τούτου μὲν ᾽Ωκεανοῦ κεῖται, τῆς ἠιόνος οὐ πολλῷ ἄποθεν, ᾽αλλ᾽ ὅσον ἀπὸ σταδίων διακοσίων καταντικρὺ τῶν τοῦ ᾽Ρήνου ἐκβολῶν μάλιστα, βρεττανίας δὲ καὶ Θούλης τῆς νήσου μεταξύ ἐστιν. ἐπεὶ Βρεττανία μὲν πρὸς δύοντά που κεῖται ἥλιον κατὰ τῆς ᾽Ισπανῶν τὰ ἔσχατα χώρας, ἀμφὶ σταδίους οὐχ ἧσσον ἢ ἐς τετρακισχιλίους τῆς ἠπείρου διέχουσα, Βριττία δὲ ἐς τῆς Γαλλίας τὰ ὄπισθεν, ἃ δὴ πρὸς ᾽Ωκεανὸν τετραμμένα, ᾽Ισπανίας δηλονότι καὶ Βρεττανίας πρὸς βορρᾶν ἄνενον. Θούλη δὲ, ὅσα γε ἀνθρώπους εἰδέναι, ἐς ᾽Ωκεανοῦ τοῦ πρὸς τῇ ἄρκτῳ τὰ ἔσχατα κεῖται. ἀλλὰ τὰ μὲν ἀμφὶ Βρεττανίᾳ καὶ Θούλῃ [ἐν] τοῖς ἔμπροσθέν μοι λόγοις ἐρρήθη. (Procopius, *Wars* 8: 20, 4–6)

(The island of Brittia is located in the Ocean, not far from the shore being about 200 stades [23 miles] out and about opposite the mouth of the Rhine, between Britain and the island of Thule. Britain lies toward the west at the longitude of the furthest reaches of Spain, approximately 4,000 stades out and Brittia is past the part of Gaul turning toward the Ocean: it is north of Spain and Britain. And Thule, as far as people know, lies in the Ocean to the north. But I have made a description about Britain and Thule in my own words above [i.e., *Wars* 6: 15, 4–26].)

[50]Schlumberger suggests that a Church of the English, either the Church of St. Nicholas

and St. Augustine or a Varangian church Panagia Varangiotissa, was situated near St. Sophia, possibly between the wall of Byzas and the west wall of the Seraglio.

[51]The Finsbury vase has been given about the same date as the blue glass jar found in Sutton Hoo Mound 2 and described in note 2.

[52]The regalia need not have been specifically pagan. One of the items recorded before the theft of the huge treasure in 1831 was a gold cross-bow fibula of the type worn by Roman officials in the late Roman period; another was a seal ring inscribed CHILDERICI REGIS.

Patrick Périn draws attention to the parallels with the grave of the indisputably Christian King Childebert II (ob. 674), furnished with a sword, a belt, and a gold ornament from a sword harness, discovered during the seventeenth century in the Saint-Vincent and Holy Cross basilica in Paris (today Saint-Germain-des-Prés). Other sarcophagi, found intact in 1645, were reopened in 1656 and found to have been plundered. The monk who confessed in the 1660s to the grave robbery was found in 1664 still to have 13,000 livres from the clandestine sale (261–62).

[53]The helmet, for example, while exhibiting clear affinities with the Valsgärde 7 helmet, also shows in its characteristic late Roman crest or comb and neck-guard with a flange at the top its derivation from a group of fourth- to fifth-century Roman helmets from the Constantinian workshops (Bruce-Mitford 2: 214–25).

In addition, the shoulder-clasps appear to be related to those found on Imperial Roman cavalry dress and parade armour (Bruce-Mitford: 532–35).

[54]Apahida, Romania, in 1968, and now in the museum at Cluj (Bruce-Mitford 2: 517). The treatment of garnets in the scabbard bosses of the Sutton Hoo hoard, he notes, resembles that in the fifth-century Pietroassa (Romania) treasure and the Tressan (France) buckle (2: 602).

[55]The screw and possibly the key (4: 2: 236–43, cf. Riddle 44 in *The Exeter Book* 204) might have been early exceptions.

[56]Shortly after Chang Chhien's expedition west to Greek Bactria, chronicled in two lost books named *Record of Chang Chhien's Expeditions Beyond the Passes* and *Record of the Strange Things of Countries Overseas*, and about a century after an unsuccessful Bactrian attempt to reach the Seres by a route north of the Thien Shan mountains, possibly mentioned by Pliny the Elder (ultra montes Hermodos Seras quoque ab ipsis aspici, notos etiam commercio [*Historia Nat.* 6: 88]) and thence to Iraq, Antioch, and Egypt (Needham 1: 176).

[57]Ammianus Marcellinus xiv, 3, cited in Needham 1: 179. Certainly the Chinese knew about Parthia and Mesopotamia in some detail from the late second century B.C. The first caravans direct from China to Persia, the inhabitants of which were described as writing horizontally on pieces of leather instead of paper and possessing a silver coinage with portraits of their current rulers thereon, began in 106 B.C. The Chinese

may also have been aware of the Baltic shortly thereafter, though amber found in Canton could have come from either the Baltic or the Yunnan-Burma border.

[58][A]fter the Battle of the Talas River (+751), Chinese paper-makers were captured and induced to continue their craft at Samarqand. This is known to have been the earliest passage of paper-making from East to West, and it occurred no less than six hundred years after the first invention. There does not seem to be any record of the names of these men, but by a fortunate chance certain details have been preserved of other technicians captured in the same battle. One of the prisoners taken was an officer, Tu Huan, and when he returned to China eleven years after he told his family about the Chinese artisans who had settled at the Abbasid capital (Kufah) [in Iraq]. It so happened that his brother was the great scholar Tu Yu and the information was thus written down. In Tu Yu's *Thung Tien*, we find:

> "As for the weavers who make light silks (in the Arab capital), the goldsmiths (who work) gold and silver (there), and the painters; (the arts which they practice) were started by Chinese technicians. For example — for painting Fan Shu and Liu Tzhu from the capital (Sian [Xian]), and for silk throwing and weaving (chi lo) Yüeh Huan and Lü Li from Shensi." (Needham 1: 236)

Needham also suggests that this eventual transmission to the West was not unique, and that the Arab population of Sicily could have been a source of further information into the later Middle Ages. As a possible illustration, he cites the Sicilian geographer Abu 'Abdallah al-Idrisi, writing about 1154 for Roger II of Sicily, who, Needham surmises, mentioned the rebellion of Huang Chao in 875–84, when the Arab quarter of Canton was destroyed (4: 2: 496).

[59]Radbertus missus imperatoris, qui de Oriente revertebatur, defunctus est; et legatus regis Persarum nomine Abdella cum monachis de Hierusalem ... ad imperatorem pervenerunt munera deferentes, quae praedictus rex imperatori miserat.... Fuerunt praeterea munera praefati regis pallia sirica [serica].... (*Annales* 123)

(Radbertus, the envoy of the Emperor, died while he was returning from the East, and the legate of the King of the Persians, Abdulla by name, came with monks from Jerusalem ... bearing gifts which the aforementioned king had sent to the Emperor.... There were in addition gifts of mantles of silk from the king mentioned above.)

[60]Qui Isaac Iudeum, quem imperator ante quadriennium ad regem Persarum cum Lantfrido et Sigimundo miserat, reversum cum magnis muneribus nuntiaverunt, nam Lantfridus ac Sigimundus ambo defuncti erant. (*Annales* 116, for the year 801)

et legati, qui dudum ante quattuor fere annos ad regem Persarum missi sunt, per ipsas Grecarum navium stationes transvecti ad Tarvisiani portus receptaculum nullo adversariorum sentiente regressi sunt. (*Annales* 122, for the year 806)

(They announced that Isaac the Jew, whom, with Lantfrid and Sigimund, the Emperor had send almost four years before to the King of the Persians, had returned with great gifts, for Lantfrid and Sigimund had both died.)

(And the envoys, who had been sent to the king of the Persians almost four years earlier, travelled by way of those stations of the Greek ships to the shelter of the port of Tarvisianus and returned, with none of the enemy realizing it.)

[61]Even the name of the war elephant presented to Charlemagne, Abul Abaz, is given (117).

[62]The Koguryo Kingdom lasted from 37 B.C. to A.D. 668 and that of the Paekche from 18 B.C. to A.D. 660; the two kingdoms were eventually conquered by Silla, the capital of which was located at Kyongju (Kumsong).

[63]An island (now Ekerö) on Lake Mälar, about 30 km. west of Stockholm, an important trading centre during the early Middle Ages. The period of its greatest prosperity coincided with the Vendel and Uppsala dynasties commemorated in *Beowulf*.

WORKS CITED

Anazawa, Wakoh, and Jun-Ichi Manome. "Various Problems Concerning the Inlaid Gold Ornamental Dagger Among the Objects Excavated from Kerim-Lo Grave No. 14 in Kyongju, Korea, with an Appendix of Some Comments About the Kerim-Lo Dagger by One West German and Three Soviet Archaeologists." The Kyushu Association for Research into Ancient Cultures. *Reports on Ancient Cultures* 7 (1980–84): 251–78. In Japanese.

Annales Laurissenses majores. Annales regni Francorum, inde ab a. 741. usque ad a. 829., *qui dicuntur annales Laurissenses maiores et Einhardi.* Ed. Friedrich Kurze and Georg Heinrich Pertz. Monumenta germaniae historica. Scriptores rerum germanicarum. 1895; rpt. Hanover: Hahn, 1950.

TheAnglo-SaxonChronicle:A Collaborative Edition: Vol. 4, Ms. B: A Semi-diplomatic Edition with Introduction and Indices. Ed. Simon Taylor. Cambridge: D.S. Brewer, 1983.

Bailey, Richard N. *Viking Age Sculpture in Northern England.* London: Collins, 1980.

—, and Rosemary Cramp. *Corpus of Anglo-Saxon Stone Sculpture in England: Volume II: Cumberland, Westmorland and Lancashire North-of-the-Sands.* British Academy. London: Oxford UP, 1988.

Benedikz, B.S. "The Evolution of the Varangian Regiment in the Byzantine Army." *Byzantinische Zeitschrift* 62 (1969): 20–24.

Bengtsson, Frans. *The Long Ships: A Saga of the Viking Age.* Trans. Michael Meyer. Translation of *Röde Orm.* London: Collins, 1954.

Biddle, Martin. "Anglo-Saxon Winchester." Unpublished paper delivered at the sixth ISAS conference, Oxford, 3 August 1993.

Birch, W. de G. *Cartularium Saxonicum: A Collection of Charters Relating to Anglo-Saxon History.* 4 vols. London: Whiting and Co., 1885–93.

Blackburn, M.A.S., ed. *Anglo-Saxon Monetary History: Essays in Memory of Michael Dolley*. Leicester: Leicester UP, 1986.

Blöndal, Sigfús. *The Varangians of Byzantium: An Aspect of Byzantine Military History*. Trans. and rev. Benedikt S. Benedikz. Cambridge: Cambridge UP, 1978.

Blunt, C.E. "Anglo-Saxon Coins Found in Italy." Blackburn 159–69.

Brooks, N.P., and J.A. Graham-Campbell. "Reflections on the Viking Age Silver Hoard from Croyden, Surrey." Blackburn 99–110.

Bruce-Mitford, Rupert. *The Sutton Hoo Ship Burial*. 3 vols. London: British Museum P, 1975–83.

Carver, M.O.H., ed. *The Age of Sutton Hoo: The Seventh Century in North-western Europe*. Woodbridge, Suffolk: Boydell, 1992.

Cecaumenos (attributed to). *Logos Nouthetaïkos pros Basilea*. Ed. V.G. Vasilevskii and P. Jernstedt. St. Petersburg, 1896.

Chaloupecky, V. "Considérations sur Samon, le premier roi des Slaves." *Byzantinoslavica* 11 (1950): 223–39.

Charles-Edwards, Thomas. "Early Medieval Kingships in the British Isles." *The Origins of the Anglo-Saxon Kingdoms*. Ed. Steven Basset. Leicester: Leicester UP, 1989. 28–39.

Chronicon monasterii de Abingdon. Ed. Joseph Stevenson. 2 parts. Vol. 2 of In Rerum britannicarum medii aevi scriptores (The Rolls Series). London: Longman, Brown, Green, Longmans and Roberts, 1858.

Ciggaar, Krijnie N. "L'émigration anglaise à Byzance après 1066." *Revue des études byzantines* 32 (1974): 301–42.

Codinus, Georgios Curopalates (attributed to). *De officialibus palatii* XVII. Vol 157 of *Patrologia cursus completus, sive bibliotheca universalis ... omnium sanctorum, patrum, doctorum, scriptorumque ecclesiasticorum qui ab aevo apostolico ad usque Innocenti III. tempora floruerunt, Series Graeca*. Ed. Jacques Paul Migne. Paris: Garnier, 1857–1912.

Comnena, Anna. *The Alexiad of the Princess Anna Comnena: Being the History of the Reign of Her Father, Alexius I, Emperor of the Romans, 1081-1118 A.D.* Trans. Elizabeth A.S. Dawes. London: Routledge & Kegan Paul, 1967.

Ioannes Scylitza Curopalates. "Excerpta ex brevario historico." *Georgios Cedrenus, Ioannes Scylitza Curopalates Ope*. Ed. Immanuel Bekker. Corpus scriptorum byzantinae pars 24. Vol. 2. Bonn: Ed. Weber, 1839.

Dawkins, R.M. "The Later History of the Varangian Guard: Some Notes." *Journal of Roman Studies* 37 (1947): 39–46.

de Longpérier, A. "Remarkable Gold Coin of Offa." *Numismatic Chronicle* 4 (1841): 232–34.

Drögereit, Richard. *Niedersachsen und England bis zur Hansezeit*, in *Niedersächsisches Jahrbuch für Landesgeschichte*. Sonderdruck, 1938.

Ellis Davidson, Hilda. *The Viking Road to Byzantium*. London: Allen and Unwin, 1976.

Evans, A.C. "Finds from Mound 2 and Mound 5." *The Sutton Hoo Research Committee Bulletin* 6 (1989): 11.

The Exeter Book. Ed. George Philip Krapp and Elliott van Kirk Dobbie. Vol. 3 of *The Anglo-Saxon Poetic Records*. 6 vols. New York: Columbia UP, 1936.

Fell, Christine. "The Icelandic Saga of Edward the Confessor: Its Version of the Anglo-Saxon Emigration to Byzantium." *Anglo-Saxon England* 3 (1974): 179–96.

Fredegar. *The Chronicle*. Ed. Bruno Krusch. *Monumenta germaniae historica, Scriptores rerum merovingicarum*. Vol. 2. 1888.

Geanakoplos, Deno John. *The Emperor Michael Palaeologus and the West 1258–1282: A Study in Byzantine-Latin Relations*. Cambridge, MA: Harvard UP, 1959.

Goscelin. "Miracula Sancti Augustini Episcopi Cantuariensi in Anglia." In G. Henschenius and D. Papebrochius, ed., *Acta sanctorum quotquot tot orbe coluntur, vel a catholicis scriptoribus celebrantur ex Latinis et Graecis, aliarumque gentium antiquis monumentis collecta, digesta, illustrata*. Paris and Rome: Victor Palmé, 1863–1940. Vol. 19: May, Vol. 6.

Gregory of Tours. *Gregorii turonensis opera*. Ed. Wilhelm Ferdinand Arndt and Bruno Krusch. Monumenta germaniae historica. Scriptores rerum merovingicarum. Hanover: Hahn, 1884.

Gregory VII, Pope. *Das Register Gregors VII*. Ed. Erich L.E. Caspar. 2 vols. Monumenta germaniae historica. Epistolae selectae. Berlin: Weidmann, 1920–23.

"Grettis Kvæði." *Kvæðabókin*. Vol. 1. Ed. Sverri Egholm. Tórshavn: Landprentsmiðjan, 1960.

Hellmann, S. "Das Fredegarproblem." *Historische Vierteljahrschrift* 29 (1934): 44.

Hinton, David A. *Archaeology, Economy and Society: England from the Fifth to the Fifteenth Century*. London: Seaby, 1990.

—. "Coins and Commercial Centres in Anglo-Saxon England." Blackburn 11–26.

Hope-Taylor, Brian. *Yeavering: An Anglo-British Centre of Early Northumbria*. Department of the Environment Archaeological Reports no. 7. London: HMSO, 1977.

Insoll, Timothy. "A Cache of Hippopotamus Ivory at Gao, Mali; and a Hypothesis of Its Use." *Antiquity* 69 (1995): 327–36.

Janin, Raymond. *La géographie ecclésiastique de l'empire byzantin: le siège de Constantinople et le patriarcat oecumenique, les églises et les monastères*. Paris, 1953.

—. "Les églises et les monastères de Constantinople byzantine." *Revue des études byzantines* 9 (1951): 143–53.

—. "Les sanctuaires des colonies latines à Constantinople." *Revue des études byzantines* 4 (1946): 163–77.

Kemble, J.M. *Codex diplomaticus aevi saxonici*. London: English Historical Society, 1839–48.

Kenesson, Summer S. "From Hamah to Hälsingborg: The Migration and Location of Medieval Islamic Glass." Unpublished paper delivered at the International Medieval Congress, University of Leeds, 7 July 1994.

Liutprand. *Liudprandi opera*. Ed. Joseph Becker. *Monumenta germaniae historica, Scriptores rerum germanicarum in usum scholarum ex monumentis germaniciae historicis separatim editi*. Hanover and Leipzig: Hahn, 1915.

Lowe, E.A. *Codices latini antiquiores: A Palaeographical Guide to Latin Manuscripts Prior to the Ninth Century*. 11 vols. and supplement. Oxford: Clarendon, 1934–71.

McKerrell, H., and R.B.K. Stevenson. "Some Analyses of Anglo-Saxon and Associated Oriental Silver Coinage." *Methods of Chemical and Metallurgical Investigation of Ancient Coinage*. Ed. E.T. Hall and D.M. Metcalf. London: Royal Numismatical Society, 1972. 195–209.

Metcalf, D.M. "The Monetary History of England in the Tenth Century Viewed in the Perspective of the Eleventh Century." Blackburn 133–58.

Needham, Joseph, with Wang Ling et al. *Science and Civilisation in China*. 6 vols. to date. Cambridge: Cambridge UP, 1954–.

Odericus Vitalis. *Historica ecclesiastica*. Ed. Augustus le Prévost. Paris, 1838–55.

Pauli, Reinhold. "Deutsche Kirchenmänner im England im 10. und 11. Jahrhundert." *Nachrichten von der königlichen Gesellschaft der Wissenschaften und der Georg-Augusts-Universität zu Göttingen*. Göttingen, 1879. 317–31.

Périn, Patrick. "The Undiscovered Grave of King Clovis I (+511)." Carver 255–64.

C. Plinius Secundus. *Naturalis historiae libri XXXVII*. Ed. L. Ian and C. Mayhoff. 6 vols. Stuttgart: Teubner, 1967.

Poertner, Rudolf. *The Vikings: Rise and Fall of the Norse Sea Kings*. Trans. Sophie Wilkins. London: St. Martin's, 1975.

Priebsch, Richard. *The Heliand Manuscript, Cotton Caligula A VII, in the British Museum: A Study*. Oxford: Clarendon, 1925.

Procopius Caesariensis. *Opera omnia*. Ed. J. Havry and G. Wirth. Leipsig: B.G. Teubner, 1963.

Roesdahl, Else. *Viking Age Denmark*. London: British Museum Publications, 1982.

Sawyer, Peter. H. "Anglo-Scandinavian Trade in the Viking Age and After." Blackburn 185–99.

—. *Kings and Vikings: Scandinavia and Europe, A.D. 700–1100*. London: Methuen, 1982

Schlumberger, Gustave L. *L'Épopée byzantine à la fin du dixième siècle*. 3 vols. 2nd ed. 1896–1905. Rpt. Paris: Hachette, 1969.

Shepard, Jonathan. "The English and Byzantium: A Study of Their Role in the Byzantine Army in the Later Eleventh Century." *Traditio* 29 (1973): 53–92.

Smart, Veronica. "Scandinavians, Celts and Germans in Anglo-Saxon England: The Evidence of Moneyers' Names." Blackburn 171–84.

Smyth, Alfred P. *Scandinavian Kings in the British Isles: 850–880*. Oxford: Oxford UP, 1977.

Snorri Sturluson. *Heimskringla*. Ed. Bjarni Aðalbjarnarson. Reykjavík: Hið Íslenzka Fornritafélag, 1951. Vol. 3.

Stender-Petersen, A. "Zur Bedeutungsgeschichte des Wortes *Væringi*, Russ. *várag*." *Acta Philologica Scandinavica* 6 (1931): 26–38.

Stenton, Sir Frank M. *Anglo-Saxon England*. Oxford: Clarendon, 1943; 3rd ed. 1971.

—. *The Early History of the Abbey of Abingdon*. University College, Reading, Studies in Local History. Oxford: Oxford UP, 1913.

Stewart, Ian. "The London Mint and the Coinage of Offa." Blackburn 27–43.

Unger, Richard W. *The Ship in the Medieval Economy, 600–1600*. London: Croom Helm, 1980.

Vasiliev, Alexander A. *History of the Byzantine Empire, 324–1453*. 2nd English ed. Madison: U of Wisconsin P, 1952.

Venantius Fortunatus. *Carmina*. Vol. 88 of *Patrologia cursus completus, sive bibliotheca universalis ... omnium sanctorum, patrum, doctorum, scriptorumque ecclesiasticorum qui ab aevo apostolico ad usque Innocenti III tempora floruerunt, Series Latina*. Ed. Jacques Paul Migne. Paris: Garnier, 1857–1912.

Wallace-Hadrill, J.M., ed. and trans. *Fredegarii chronicorum liber quartus cum continuationibus*. London: Nelson, 1960.

Whitelock, Dorothy. *Anglo-Saxon Wills*. Cambridge: Cambridge UP, 1930.

Wilson, Sir David. *The Vikings and Their Origins: Scandinavia in the First Millennium*. London: Thames and Hudson, 1970.

Wood, Ian. "Frankish Hegemony in England." Carver 235–41.

—. *The Merovingian Kingdoms 450–751*. London: Longman, 1994.

Wulfstan. *Sermo lupi ad Anglos*. Ed. Dorothy Whitelock. London: Methuen, 1939.

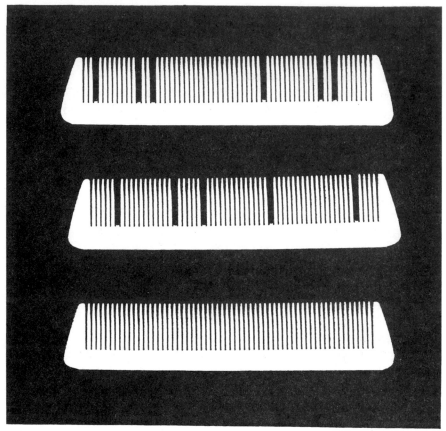

Runic Hair-combs / Childe Roland

This semiotic poem was inspired by the objects of everyday life mentioned in the direct and down-to-earth language of the Norse sagas that George Johnston captured so beautifully in his translations, where, for example, the word "comb" would be for me as much a Viking treasure trove as the whale-bone carved object of the time. I would like to believe that the finding of a haircomb at an archaeological site (like L'Anse-aux-Meadows in Newfoundland) would be evidence of a certain level of civilization or culture, and that the missing hair-comb teeth would not be seen as having been broken off by accident, but on purpose, as part of a secret runic code or a musical notation for a kazoo-like instrument. This is an interactive poem and the readers are invited to complete the message by blacking out a few additional teeth with a black ink pen if they wish to experience the magic of the runes.

Naomi Jackson Groves

A VIKING ON THE DOORSTEP

DO OTHER PEOPLE'S best memories — that is, their most clear-cut, vivid remembrance of special persons and of events connected with them — come to mind in brief visual flashes, as mine do? Or does mention of a certain name call forth a lengthy sequence of continuing thoughts, more a sort of brooding ... ? Maybe it depends on how close or how extended the relationship has been.

I have two special memory flashes of my good friend George Johnston, now emeritus professor at Carleton University. I first met George Johnston when I came to live here in Ottawa after retiring in 1958 from McMaster University in Hamilton, Ontario. George taught in Carleton's English Department here; I in Fine Arts down there. Both of us are well on in years — I, born in 1910, ahead of him by several! — so the term good "old" friends suits us well.

As I recall, it was a Nordic subject that first brought us together: a showing of prints on Icelandic themes (Edda, Old Norse) by a German-Canadian, Edith Pahlke, on view at the Goethe Institute, whose then head, Dr. Gertrud Baer, my neighbour on Highfield Crescent in Ottawa, invited me to attend. Edith Pahlke, graphic artist, North-German born, keen traveller in Iceland, became a good bridge to many aspects of Norse-related material and did a fine linocut for me in memory of my husband, J.W. Groves (1906–1970).

As for my northern interests ... they began in my teens. I was born in Montreal of an Irish (Murphy) grandma, a Scottish great-grandfather, Alexander Young, a teacher, father of Georgina, my paternal grandmother, and Henry Allan Jackson, eldest son of Henry Fletcher Joseph Jackson, who came to Canada in 1824 to sell gold watches. People only wanted their clocks mended, but he stayed on and fathered a goodly crop of four sons and daughters, mostly in the areas of Kitchener-Waterloo, Brockville, and Montreal.

As for me, I added to this good mix a warm friendship with a lovely family from Denmark, de la Cour, actually Cornonville de la Cour, who lived for a time in the 1920s across the street from us on Campbell Avenue in Montreal West. When I finished at Montreal West High School at age 17, the de la Cours invited me to stay with them in Denmark, and thus I became bonded with the Scandinavian north.

"Our Jackson compass always points north," said my uncle A.Y. Jackson (1882–1974), Montreal-born landscape painter of Quebec, Ontario, and the north. He reached the Canadian Arctic in 1927, travelling on the ship *The Beothic* in company with Dr. Frederick Banting. As if fated to emulate my favourite uncle, I got to Denmark in 1928, to Greenland in 1941 for several months, then to Finnish Lapland on post-war Quaker work from December 1945 to June 1947. By this time A.Y. referred to me as his "Viking niece."

My academic studies could not include Danish — alas, none was offered at McGill at that time — but rather German, with the greatly gifted, musically inclined, German-Swiss professor, Dr. Herman Walter.

Now back to George Johnston, who also became warmly connected with Northern culture. My first "flash" memory of George Johnston is linked to the Icelandic Saga Reading Circle. He was coming to the annual midwinter feast I put on just before Christmas every December for members and friends of the Reading Circle. This started as a choice small group, not only of university people (George taught Old English and Old Norse at Carleton), brought together by the two noted Padolsky brothers, Barry and Enoch, one of whom actually brought the saga-reading idea with him from California. Another early member, a judge who had a special interest in medieval law, was able to set us straight on such things as the complex legalities of inheritance — it was fascinating.

It is a December night in the early seventies, in the cold, clear winter here in Ottawa. There is a cheerful, loud knock at my front door, which I throw open in glad expectation. There, outside in the cold darkness, stands my friend George Johnston. He is two steps down outside, and his head is level with mine. He is wearing a two-horned hat of the kind worn by Hagar the Horrible and his wife Helga in the comics. We call it a Viking hat (though it is questionable whether true tenth-century Norsemen had horns as part of their battle gear). If not Viking, then, certainly Nordic, and George, with his full white gleaming beard and rosy face, looked a perfect Norseman.

Our group benefitted by George's great gifts as a translator of several northern languages, among them Old Norse (*Icelanders' Saga, Greenlanders' Saga*, the magnificent *Edda*, parts of which preserved our Old English *Beowulf*) and Faroese (*Rocky Shore*), and as the writer of several volumes of his own poetry.

Mention of his poetry brings on the second "flash": when George was given an honorary degree by Carleton University on June 4, 1979, Nan Griffith, the gifted architect from Carleton, invited me to join her in her loge's comfortable space with a full view of the stage and its gathering of notables, who were there for George and for Maureen Forrester, the pride of our singing world, as the other honouree. Maureen Forrester's induction came first, and, as her thanks, she sang Schubert's beautiful "Du holde Kunst," on the comfort of music to poor and lonely artists. These words, sung in Maureen's glorious mellow voice, were so moving that I sat there in the dark loge streaming with tears. The dignitaries down on the stage began hauling out handkerchiefs too, mopping and blowing. We all melted.

Then it was George's turn. After the brief warm presentation by Professor Robert McDougall at the lectern over on the right side of the big stage, we could see George head across, loping laboriously, head bent. Having arrived at the lectern, he laid down his speech, gripped both sides of the tall lectern, and said in a broken voice, "I don't think I can speak." Then, he, as he puts it, "took a grip" on himself and said, "Wasn't she wonderful?" In response there was a roar of applause from the audience that lasted long enough for George to pull himself together. He then read the sensitive, flowing poetry of his convocation address. This impressed me so much that I later on asked George for a photocopy, but instead he sent me his entire speech beautifully hand-written in medieval calligraphy. I find this address so distinctive that I am (with the permission of the editor) reproducing the entire speech, which was George's good-bye to Carleton and is my own farewell for this tribute.

* * *

CONVOCATION ADDRESS
CARLETON UNIVERSITY, JUNE 4, 1979

Fellow graduates,
not many of you
have taken so long
to get here;
thirty years ago,
take away a year,
my labours began
at Carleton.
Now what do I know?
Not much about me,
by what right lucky
and fearful-happy;

not much about us,
learned and perplexed;
nothing about what next.
Otherwise enough
to get on with.
I know that I learned;
do not know that I taught —
maybe, maybe not.
I think we only learn
what is already there
in the grain.
Let us say we all learned.
For instance, I found out
something I always knew
about grades —
recovered knowledge
feels hard-earned.
Thirty years ago,
take away one,
honour, pass or fail
seemed weighty matters.
No longer so.
That was then.
Outlived all that,
out of school again.

Some of you have sat
and cerebrated with me,
taken notes, yet;
now I wonder what
you may remember
when you have careers,
affairs, families,
fetters of that sort,
will our thought
and learning together
give comfort
or make strange?

What did we not do
in the years, that they
became history
in that headlong way,
gone before we knew?
Nothing gets begun
but finds its time
and its look
and gets done;
the dearest moments
touch and are gone,
leaving thumb-prints.

Now is a moment
of the dear kind;
long-winded you say,
but never mind,
it will not stay;
already, see, it
is turning away,
tired of us,
going for good.
We have felt its eye
upon us,
its print is in us;
we would not hold it
if we could.
Goodbye moment.
Goodbye thirty years,
take away one.
Goodbye.

The night is cold, the Northland
has disappeared, and he has no home.
(A man finds himself in the middle of sands
and deserts on his way to South Iceland.)

Edith Pahlke
Icelandic Poem
(by Kristjan Jonsson)
linocut 12 x 8 inches

Marianne Bluger

IMAGINARY PORTRAIT OF
THE REAL GEORGE JOHNSTON

The forehead — glacial
sweeps sheer
to snowsqualls of white hair

and when he speaks
the voice evokes northern summers
like a soft chinook

If arthritis had long since
icicled his fingers
still pursing lips hard time kissed blue
he would effect
the famous scrimshaw script

And though he shuddered an instant
harpooned by pain
he'll smile soon
aurora

and the *borealis* flashing
quick in him
be life itself
silver running
smelt in an icemelt stream

Out late in springtime's
Arctic night
you glimpse a fragile igloo
radiant from within

and think of him

(from *Summer Grass*
Brick Books, 1992)

Bob Hogg

THE POET TREE

ONCE THERE WAS a poet who climbed a tree. He was an old poet then, or so he seemed to the young poet who watched him climb. It was curious to watch him because he was very tall and distinguished, with grey beard and balding pate, the white fringe of his tonsure curling slightly at the ends in a kind of defiance of his obvious dignity. There was another betrayal, or maybe two: the first and most noticeable was a gold earring in one of his ears, a recent acquisition, we all knew, the product of a dare by his emboldened children, a little too much wine, perhaps, an awl and a door, the way it was always done. The other was a slight indelicacy of balance that made the precarious climb somewhat dramatic, and this was noticeable because it was not typical of his poetry, certainly, nor of his demeanor generally. Of course there was a backdrop to all this.

It was May Day 1972, if I recall accurately, and George had helped me plan for a wing ding of a party at the farm Leslie & I then rented in Ottawa's Greenbelt. George had given me the recipe for a May Wine, and I had diligently made up two five gallon jugs. I'd had to order something like a kilogram of woodruff for the seasoning, and it had come in from Europe in a box to Haberman's Chemists, the closest thing to a Natural Food store in Ottawa back then. So, maybe it was the curious potency of the herb, maybe it was the bacchanalian spirit still evident within our faculty back then, and most had turned out for the event. There were some other curious antics that occurred that May Day as well, best left unsaid. Maybe George, like the rest of us, had been emboldened by the noble spirits who had come to visit the party. There may be others who will remember this incident more clearly than I. In any case I am left with this indelible impression of a man in a tree, beautifully perched, and as if presiding over the festivities. Why does that somehow remind me of the poet and the friend and mentor I was always looking up to? And still do.

Well, precariously also, and a little abashed, I offer this recent, somewhat irreverent elegy to the late Roy Rogers for your enjoyment, George. It goes a little further out on a limb than I typically went when you saw a lot of my poems. I hope you can come with me joyfully, once more. Now that I too am grey haired going on white, and at least as old as you were when you climbed that Manitoba maple in my yard. Or about.

* * *

ROY ROGERS, A JAZZ ELEGY

Roy Rogers you come galloping across the silver screen of my mind tonight
just as you did fifty years ago in the Garneau Theatre on the South Side
my brother George & I wd ride to across the treacherous High Level Bridge
the trolley swaying dangerously or so it seemed summer or winter
always a Saturday afternoon our nickels clenched in sweaty palms
or mittened and fingered there in the endless ride that seemed to be
more in the sky than anywhere I remember the conductor would just sit back
nothing to do but stoke the coal fire once in a while and look round at
us kids hooked on the long thrill of the ravine below or pressed up against
the straw seats yellow as the day they were made to hold you up not
comfortable that was not the purpose then convenience maybe yes but
we didn't care we just wanted to get there get over that North Saskatchewan
menace that roiled tinily down below everything was down below the tram
ran on top of the bridge no side rails nothing out there but emptiness which I
misspell as em pitness the pit we all hover over whether Jonathan Edwards
and his Angry God or Roy and Trigger dashing to freedom across equal tracks
in time galloping full tilt guns ablazing the bad guys falling
like flies eventually though it takes time it takes time
but then the Bad Guy none of us can outrun gets off a lucky shot
and bang bang you're dead you have to play dead you can't get up
that's cheating that's not the way it is in the movie and no fair
shooting the horse out from under that's not fair either
especially Trigger a horse that could almost talk he was so
like his rider galloping galloping across that silver screen

Tonight they tell us on TV which was really your home for nearly
forty years that you died in your sleep last night eighty-six years old
and still hopeful still riding to that eventual horizon that forever recedes
like it does in the fade ins and fade outs of the movies Roy are you fading
now or are you sailing into some cowboy heaven the memory of Dale and Trigger
firmly planted in the brim of your ethereal Stetson that never falls off no matter
how precipitous the plunge over the cliff the leap to freedom across the chasm
whole Grand Canyons opening and closing beneath you as you hurtle on your
Palomino Pegasus to the other side

Roy Rogers why do I love you and mock you at the same time why
do I sing your praises and cringe at the corny simplicity of your impossible
war against evil and outlaws bandits tricksters cheaters of women and kids
why do I balk at the trivial facts of your life the stuffing and mounting of your
favorite horse — our favorite horse let's face it — the opening of endless chains
of fast food outlets in your name the perfect smile and mannered squint of the eyes
that every kid of my generation envied and emulated to the nth degree
the colorful black and white dazzle of your perfect horsemanship riding
full speed the reins wrapped around the horn those mother of pearl six guns
twirling round your index fingers and firing so perfectly the outlaws seemed
to fall and die but not really it was just like the make-believe we also played
Jesus Roy did you know all that when you practised your squint in the
        mirror and yodeled
all those songs on the radio nights we were too young to know any better
        and thought it was real romance?

You did and you didn't and that's the beauty of it I mean you were so much
        the myth
it just had to be played that way the old battle of good against evil white
        against black
no further consequences right it was just law and order and a little dusting
        up nobody really
gets hurt and America gallops half way through the century Tom Mix Gene
        Autry The Cisco Kid
Lash Larue and the rest of the rough and tumble heroes of the old Wild West
        made over into fun
and games and playing playing dead.

Various Hands

THE ENCHANTER AT WORK

THE CARLETON OF the late sixties was far smaller than it is now, and, despite a large contingent of Colombo Plan students, its population was considerably less diverse. The campus was still growing to accommodate a host of baby boomers surging into the Ontario university system. Study in the library was inevitably disrupted by construction noises that reached a crescendo at about the time of the final exams.

The student body had in the main recently graduated from an Ontario secondary system as yet unchanged by the Hall-Dennis reforms and had — even in the Sciences — studied Grade 12 Latin or a foreign language. Because most of the teaching staff were also very young there were only about four or five full professors in the English Department. Indeed, when in September 1966 Munro Beattie, then head of English, welcomed the first-year contingent with a short description of the staff, the most memorable detail, apart from the assurance that there were no duds in English, was that half the department had obtained a first degree within the past nine years. Those of us who were students then were exceptionally fortunate to have both a young and enthusiastic staff and a university prosperous enough to offer a large number of relatively esoteric courses. The atmosphere was far more relaxed and self-confident than is imaginable now.

One of the few full professors in the English Department was George Johnston. Very tall, with a striking white beard, he gave the impression of being somewhat shy. Most students in the department would have met him through his second-year course in Old English, at that time still compulsory for honours. It is chastening to notice that in those days the Yearbook staff could publish a travesty of the *Battle of Maldon* without feeling obliged to explain to the student body why the diction had suddenly become odd.

Professor Johnston was responsible until 1967-68 for most of the Old English and Old Norse taught in the department; the introductory course was large, and the enrolment for *Beowulf* and Old Norse healthy. I had no first-hand acquaintance with Professor Johnston's introductory Old-English course, but heard older contemporaries describe it with considerable affection, the memorization of parts of the verse canon excepted. Since a great many students still had a background of high-school Latin, Old English was not yet considered a particularly difficult subject. The course appeared, though, to have been something of a sink-or-swim matter, at least until one realized that Professor Johnston was there as a resource person, unwilling to spoon-feed, unfailingly gentle, and happily characterizing various manifestations of a violent period with the all-purpose adjective "ferocious."

It was not until I was planning to take Old Norse that I met Professor Johnston for the first time. His office on the top floor of the Paterson building was far larger than his later one in the new Arts Tower, though I can persuade myself that even then he had enlivened the standard academic decor with a very high-backed carved wooden chair that could quite as easily have come from a local or Scandinavian farmhouse. His seminar was unstructured, since he was essentially a facilitator rather than a lecturer, comfortable enough with the field to steer the group quietly through the departmental requirements of the seminar reports, papers, and examinations. His teaching communicated a deeply humanitarian enthusiasm for the literature and for the culture from which it had sprung. Old Norse could ignite a tremendous if haphazard excitement. Professor Johnston managed to indicate the range of material to be found even on the periphery, especially traditional, but still current, Faeroese folk songs in the pentatonic scale on saga themes. Other details remembered from that course, though not specifically Old Norse, include his descriptions of the long northern summer twilight that had played hob with night-flying training during the Second World War, his reminiscence of travels in the Faeroes, the family ordering everything in fives because "fimm" was the first number that was not declined, his meeting in Torshavn with an authority on the Faeroese language who turned out to be far younger than he had expected and who boasted a room called "the Snorri stofa." It was Professor Johnston, too, who illustrated the various changes of the word "stove" in several of the Germanic languages with the only sample of spoken Frisian I have ever heard.

Sometimes Professor Johnston's subject strayed to verse. I seem to recall his reminiscences of a famous poet of the sixties, his head in the Johnston family refrigerator, looking for ingredients to be assembled into a sandwich. I may have heard them in the Saga reading group that operated in the seventies. At that time Ottawa contained enough people with an interest in the language to make such a group feasible. Tenuously balancing translation, gossip, and dinner, it lasted until the early eighties, some years after the Johnstons' retirement to a farm on the American border near Athelstan, Quebec.

(Patricia Bethel)

I first met Professor Johnston in 1950 in his course on Anglo-Saxon literature. His first words to us were that he had never before taught this subject, and then he added that he had not yet studied it either. I am ashamed to say that my preparation, and that of the others, was often less than optimal, but he kindly ignored our failings, or at least his surface appearance was unruffled and forbearing. We studied in a small room up a winding staircase under the eaves on the fourth floor of the First Avenue campus, like so many gnomes in an ivory tower.

I was in classes he taught in nineteenth-century thought. I remember particularly having been assigned an essay on the economic ideas in Carlyle and J.S. Mill, and in preparation for the essay reading some of the classical economists. The preparation was very challenging — reading on economics, about which I knew nothing at all. The finished essay incorporated all my new knowledge, as I thought, especially the theories of Adam Smith, but not much about Carlyle nor about J.S. Mill, the writers whose works were on the course. Professor Johnson gave it a D. I was indignant, and wrote a hot letter to him explaining all the work I had gone to and how difficult it had all been. Then, like a coward, I pushed the envelope under the door of his office. He never mentioned it at all. Now, of course, I know that, considering the essay had no central theme, no connection between the parts, no comparison to the ideas of Carlyle nor to J. S. Mill, but was full of the paraphrased ideas of the economists I had read, the mark was extremely generous.

Professor Johnston recommended Yeats's "The Words upon the Windowpane" to the Sock 'n' Buskin Club, and I produced it. We presented it at Arnprior in a set of one-act plays, and it was chosen to represent Carleton College at the Inter-Varsity Festival held at Bishop's. The actors and backstage crew went down to Lennoxville, but, unfortunately, not the technical crew. The stage there, unlike Carleton's, had no dimmer switches on the stage lights, so the séance was quite difficult to play, especially as we had given the "voices" to students hidden in the wings, rather than to one actress on stage. During the séance, our make-up girl scurried past the window in the set like a ghost, giving the adjudicator a new and strange experience.

On the comprehensive exam at the end of our course I recognized the question that Professor Johnson had set immediately — to detail the hunting scenes in English literature. I thought of man-hunts in Jane Austen, and other kinds of hunts as well, and then decided against, because while I knew I could do a workmanlike job on the other topics, what might be required on that question? Would anything whimsical I might say match the master of whimsy? And how might it be marked?

Professor Johnston was attuned to a world view that pre-dated the advent of modern English, especially the ideas of persons born "lucky" and of the necessity of enduring your fate. "Gathering in your fate" he called it. He seemed a keen observer of persons unaware that they were about to be ambushed by fate, and this seemed to provide him with an anticipatory and joyous frisson.

(Alberta Aboud)

George Johnston was generous with his time when I was a student at Carleton. We sat together for countless hours while I translated *Beowulf*, preparing to do my honours essay. Later, he supervised my master's thesis on *Gísla saga*. For students like me and my future husband David McKercher the Saga Reading Club was not just an intellectual activity, but a social event we would look forward to, with wonderful Scandinavian-style "spreads."

As a teacher George Johnston would not let you get away with half-measures. If I asked where I should start translating (hoping for some concessions), he would reply, "Start at the beginning, carry through to the end, then stop."

But my favourite recollection about George is this: once, when the mass of research that loomed ahead seemed overwhelming, he amazingly advised me to start writing immediately — I could revise later. I have passed on this sage advice, and this anecdote, to many people. It was truly the most liberating piece of advice I've ever received.

(Rosalind Conway)

I first met George Johnston when I came to the English Department as the departmental secretary. In those far-off days it was a department of five faculty members doubled up in offices, with only the Chairman having the luxury of his own telephone. I was thrilled for everyone when the extension was built onto Paterson Hall: now faculty members had their own offices and, better still, their own telephones. I was therefore baffled to find Professor Johnston's telephone missing, and was even more astonished to find it hidden in a small room along the hall. Thinking we had a prankster in the office (which we did), I returned the wandering phone to Professor Johnston's office only to find that the following morning the telephone had gone walk-about again. This was one faculty member who did NOT want a telephone!

I should have realized that a man who did not want a telephone would not want a filing system. I was gently chided after I made an effort to tidy what I presumed to be a desk, the top of which was not visible under the piles of papers. From then on I ceased trying to play the efficient secretary (and succeeded) and became very glad of that untidy desk covered in never-filed papers, for I could always find, if I rooted deeply enough, many items that had gone astray in my own efficient filing system.

(Ismay Wand)

I was there on that bright Convocation Day in June of 1979 when George Johnston followed Maureen Forrester onto the stage to receive an honorary degree and share his thoughts about Carleton and things past. In his memorable poetic finale he said,

> The dearest moments
> touch and are gone,
> leaving thumb-prints.

George left his "thumb-prints" everywhere, including on the memories of this Carleton grad, who had the privilege of knowing him and, on that day, greeting him as a fellow graduate.

I put his photograph on my office wall, I kept a copy of the famous Convocation poem among my Carleton treasures, and best of all, I became the keeper of George's rickety old sawhorse. Years before, he had brought it from the country to hold his neatly-stacked piles of marked essay papers. It was a strange sight in a modern office environment and raised many an eyebrow.

George trusted that old sawhorse to my care on his last day at Carleton. He was ending his 29-year teaching career at the university as I was beginning my first job as a writer in the (then) Information Office. He saw this passing of the sawhorse as a kind of continuance. For the next twenty years that relic of another time had a place of honour by my desk. It was a curiosity to visitors, an object of art to a few, an eyesore to some, but for me it served as a constant reminder of a modest, gentle, wise man who inspired generations of Carleton students and who was, like that poet of another age, a man "who used to notice such things."

(Mary Huband)

As a newly minted professor fresh from the States, I arrived at my office on the nineteenth floor of the Arts Tower in 1971 without much notion of the

distinguished company in my immediate orbit. On one side there was Patrick
Cruttwell, on the other George Johnston. But I soon came to realize that they
were both very willing to have a chat from time to time, though a tart — but
quite polite — remark from George signalled its conclusion. Our windows
overlooked the Rideau Canal and the Central Experimental Farm, which provided
a pleasant distraction, especially when I was marking papers. One autumn
afternoon I noticed something that seemed to be swimming up and down the
Canal. Identifying George as my source on things Canadian, I went next door
and asked him what it might be. A muskrat? A beaver? But why was the animal swimming so obsessively, especially during the daytime? George puzzled
and thought and then, in a moment of uncharacteristic triumph, said, "Of
course! Today must be the day they drain the Canal. It's a beaver. It's looking
for the leak!"

(Faith Gildenhuys)

George didn't like the golf carts. But let me explain. Beneath Carleton University
a labyrinth of reinforced-concrete tunnels connects building to building,
passageways of convenience for a refrigerated clime. They are more than that,
though: for some, they are what the quad is to an Oxford scholar, for others
what the *Ramblas* are to a Spaniard, what interreticulated burrows are to prairie
gophers, or what the Decarie expressway is to a Montreal trucker. It was this
last association that may have troubled George. Or perhaps it was a simple
distaste for the intrusion of the mechanical into a space that, if not quite an
Oxford quad, should at least have been human. Not all the maintenance staff
employees who were commissioned to pilot Carleton's fleet of golf carts through
the tunnels shared his feelings. Understandably perhaps, because they often
had but little time to get from one end of the system to another. Understandable
too, perhaps, that their urgency might occasionally have become aggressive.

George didn't like those carts — for all the motives that one might expect
in a Quaker and a poet. And there may have been a deeper motive that lay
slumbering inside him too, like many another that slumbers in the mind of
a people who have filled their transcontinental spaces with compromise and
accommodation; given just the right circumstances to arouse it, it might turn
a declared pacifist into a combatant-with-a-cause.

For on a day, now many years ago, strolling westward in a pack through
the tunnels after drinks and dinner at the "ordinary" called The Oasis, we
were assaulted from the rear by a golf cart, piloted apparently by one of the
testosterone unchallenged, mighty in his unsleek honker-equipped chariot.

He sounded his horn. The message explicit was that those on foot should press themselves to the walls that the pharaoh of the commissariat might pass with provisions of wine and cheese for those at the front. George snapped, both within and without; he turned and, brandishing an imaginary sword, he levelled at the indignity an heroic harangue that, for all of me, might have been in tetrameters. But the caesura was observed only by those of us in the rabble. Tin-pot pharaoh passed, righteous in his misplaced indignation, and George subsided into murmured heroics.

Well that's as I choose to remember it: the man of infinitely human scale against the implacable machine. George had taken a stand for us all, our David, our hero of reflective spaces. It was a moment of miff from a man of unruffled calm — memorable in its exceptionalness. George has written many things that he will be remembered for remembering. He may never have thought the charge upon the golf cart something worthy of memorializing, but even for such memories as these we are grateful.

(Don Beecher)

When Munro Beattie, the founding chairman of Carleton's English Department, picked up my letter of application he thought it was from George Johnston. George and I both write an italic script but neither of us would have confused our hands: George's is angular, sparely elegant, mine curved and somewhat decorated. It seems to me that our hands reflect our literary allegiances.

George welcomed my arrival at Carleton because, as he told me at our first meeting, it meant that he would no longer have to teach Middle English. He could leave the ornamental landscapes of romance, the green forests and garden of the rose, and commit himself to the austere heroic world of saga and epic where narrow places were defended against insuperable odds and emotions crystallised in tightly packed lines and kennings.

The conversations with George that I remember best are the ones held as a group of us crunched our way home by the canal on winter evenings and caught the crisp phrases he launched into the icy air. His thought and its expression, like his poetry, seemed to be at one with winter's "clear anatomy" — with "what is pure and will survive."

(Maureen Gunn)

When I browse through the later sections of George Johnston's *Collected Poems* I find myself thinking of George as Court Poet to that rich and stately world that he seems always to have inhabited. He unfailingly finds the right tone for the ceremonial moment, whether the occasion be the birth of a grandchild, the retirement of a colleague, the death of a dear friend, or the acceptance of an Honorary Doctorate. I must have had his ceremonial tact in mind when, fairly early in my time at Carleton, I called upon him for a job of poetic work that I needed done.

It was the fall of 1972, and, as co-ordinator of extra-curricular theatre, I had decided to produce a selection from the Wakefield Mystery Plays, one of those great cycles of Bible stories that were produced outdoors during the feast of Corpus Christi to teach the mostly illiterate faithful of medieval England the essentials of Christian belief. In an effort to offer our audience at least the beginning, middle, and end of the story, I chose four plays, the Creation, the Second Shepherd's Play (a Nativity play), the Crucifixion, and the Last Judgement — a quick précis of the history of the universe.

I didn't want to lose entirely that wonderful sense of inclusiveness that the complete cycles provide, and so I asked George if he would write me two sets of choral verses to act as transitions between the plays, summarizing the narrative that leads first from the Creation to the Nativity, and then, after the intermission, from the Crucifixion to the Last Judgement.

As I recall, George didn't say much, he just mused a moment, and agreed to give it a try. A few days later I found three stanzas in my mailbox, written, of course, in George's beautiful script, stanzas that served my immediate theatrical purposes perfectly, but were also in themselves an unusually eloquent and reverent meditation on the meaning of the familiar stories.

As I look at these stanzas today I am struck by how vividly each of the two transitions calls to mind the long-past theatrical moment. At the end of the Creation play, with the voice of an angry God still echoing in the air, Adam and Eve fearfully make their way from the garden into the fallen world, through the space occupied by the audience, with the angel standing behind them, sword held high, guarding the gates of Eden. When the music that accompanies their sad journey into exile comes to an end, the Chorus, a single actress dressed in monastic robes, moves into the playing space and reads George's words from a scroll, acknowledging what has just happened and then turning to what is to come:

> Through Middle Earth from this day
> man betakes his toilsome way
>   self murderous and dark;

then God repents his rebel brood
and overwhelms them in the flood
    save Noah and his ark.

From Sinai Moses fetched the stone
on which the law was written down,
    the prophets raised their cry,
Mercy not sacrifice; now God
knows that to be his creature's good
    He will be born and die.

For the second transition, George again quietly affirms the significance of what we have just seen, and then turns to the inexorable future. We have lived through the horror of the Crucifixion, and Jesus is being carried slowly and tenderly by his loving friends through the audience to his place of burial. The space is empty of actors for a moment, then the Chorus steps forward once again:

Creation's lord has now endured
death's bitter pain upon the rood
    and scoured the pits of hell;
risen again He comes again
to bring His judgement among men
    when all things shall be well.

For many years I kept George's manuscript of these stanzas pinned to the corkboard above my desk, a reminder of George's contribution to my play, and of the Chorus's role as wise and compassionate guide, which was, according to George's students, something of the role he played in the classroom. When the great Producer in the Sky indulges me by letting me direct my plays over again, this time with all the earthly imperfections erased, there's one change I'll be sure to make when I get to this production: I'll cast George himself as the Chorus.

                                  (Douglas Campbell)

M.I. Cameron

AND WILD AND HIGH:
A MASQUE OF MASKS FOR GEORGE JOHNSTON

[*It is the banquet marking George Johnston's retirement from Carleton University. The head table is at one end of the hall, and a tiny, make-shift proscenium stage is at the other. A lute and other musical instruments rest on chairs beside the stage. The space between the head table and the stage is open, lined on each side with tables in two tiers, where the guests are seated. The main course of the dinner is over. Dessert and coffee are on the table. It is time for the speeches.*]

Host. Ladies and gentlemen, it falls to me to welcome you to the event we all hoped would never come. Though George Johnston is always the first to deny it, Carleton's English Department without him will no longer be the English Department it was. George, we'll have to manage without you, and we're not looking forward to it. I suppose we'll survive all right, but things won't ever be the same.

A number of us have put our heads together to try and decide what could be done on a state occasion like this that would somehow express your colleagues' regard for you and the regret they feel at your retirement. We know that nothing can do that adequately, but we've put together an entertainment for you and we hope that it will serve as a token of our regard: it is a modest re-creation of the most ravishing ceremony of retirement known to English literary history. It won't be as good as a George Johnston poem, but it seemed an appropriate tribute to a man who is a poet, a lover of music, and a much-appreciated supporter of drama at Carleton.

[*The lights die, and a chord sounds on the lute. The singers begin Peele's "His golden locks" (in John Dowland's setting, scored for two sopranos, contralto, tenor, and bass).*]

His golden locks Time hath to silver turned;
   O Time too swift, O swiftness never ceasing!
His youth 'gainst time and age hath ever spurned,
   But spurned in vain; youth waneth by increasing:
Beauty, strength, youth, are flowers but fading seen;
Duty, faith, love, are roots, and ever green.

[*As they sing, light comes up on the stage, which presents a framed tableau vivant:* QUEEN ELIZABETH I *standing before a taffeta pavilion. An elderly knight enters to her, kneels, and surrenders his armour and staff of office. She vests him with a hermit's gown and gives him book, beads, and maple dish. The whole thing will and should seem a little precious.*]

His helmet now shall make a hive for bees;
   And, lovers' sonnets turned to holy psalms,
A man-at-arms must now serve on his knees,
   And feed on prayers, which are Age his alms:
But though from court to cottage he depart ...

[*A massive voice is heard at the entrance to the hall.*]

Presbyter.   RUBBISH!

[*It is the voice of* PRESBYTER, *a ghost out of George's past, dressed in Geneva gown and tabs, looking for all the world like Lawren Harris's* Dr. Salem Bland. *He is striding to the tableau.*]

Presbyter.   Rubbish! Rubbish! Rubbish! Utter tripe and twaddle! Come to your senses, ladies and gentlemen! You do this man no good. Here he is, at the turning point of his life, and you mark it with this trivia, hiding him from the truth that any man forgets at the peril of his immortal soul. He is drawing near the end of his days. Yet here you are, twittering like thoughtless nightingales. Lift up your voice indeed, but put him in mind of his mortality.

[The pavilion collapses and the actors retire sheepishly. The choristers clear their throats, embarrassed, tune up, and launch vigorously into Walter Scott's Dies Irae, set to Vater Unser.]

That day of wrath, that dreadful day,
When heaven and earth shall pass away,
What power shall be the sinner's stay?
How shall he meet that dreadful day?
When, shrivelling like a parchèd scroll,
The flaming heavens together roll;
When, louder yet, and yet more dread,
Swells the high trump that wakes the dead —
O, on that day, that wrathful day,
When man to judgement wakes from clay,
Be Thou the trembling sinner's stay,
Though heaven and earth shall pass away.

[Meanwhile, PRESBYTER goes to the lectern that has appeared out of nowhere, complete with pulpit cloth and cushion. He meditates, then begins his speech, and the music fades to a hum and dies.]

Presbyter. [To George.]   Dearly beloved brother, you have spent your days as a teacher. Have you taught any wisdom as precious as this of David: "All our days are passed away in thy wrath; we spend our years as a tale that is told"?

A tale that is told is a tale that has an ending. The ending of a tale reveals the shape and truth of all that has gone before. So it is with the life of man. But listen further, O my beloved brother. At this very moment the tale of our life is told, for our tale ends in the moment we are living. This very moment tells our tale, shows the shape of our story and the truth of our past. Lo, therefore the tale of our life can change utterly with the winking of an eye. How many of these people around us will be living the same story when the sun rises tomorrow? The sun sets, their story, a high romance. But oh, an hour of feasting, an hour of drinking, an hour of sensual abandon, and at dawn — a shabby melodrama.

My beloved brother, as you withdraw from the life of action, what tale must be told of you? It is a tale of wrath. Was it once a saint's life? Was it once a portrait of the young artist? A saga of noble deeds? A brief epic of unspotted love? So it might have been. But what is your story now, the story that ends this minute, as you welter on your bench of ivory, scarce able to lift your goblet to your lips? The epicure's memorial? The annals of a fribbling voluptuary? The dreary adventures of a catch-penny reprobate, filled with insipid iniquity and feeble repentance! Turn, O my brother, turn, turn while yet you have time. Behold: the holy city lies yet before you. Press towards it! Beleaguer its walls! Take it by storm! Then at the moment of death will the tale of George Johnston be a mighty epic indeed.

[*Pause*]

Host.   Uh, I'll handle this, George. Excuse me, sir, would you like to join us for dessert?

Presbyter.   Caterpillar! Laodicean worm!

Host.   Look, if you're going to call names, well, all right, you asked for it. I'm not very impressed with what you've just done. You come in here uninvited, you interrupt our banquet, and on top of it all you say a number of nasty things about a man we all think very highly of. And not a single one of those things is true. If ever any man could stand up and lay claim to a life well lived, it's our George.

Presbyter.   No man can make that claim before the tribunal of the last day.

Host.   I don't know about the last day, but any court in the land would rule that George Johnston has lived a better life than could be expected of any man.

Presbyter.   Pelagian fool! Not if the judgement is grounded in true principles of morality.

Host.   We'll see about that.

[*He gestures toward the end of the hall. Zap! Some flashes, a cloud of smoke, a court fixture rolls forward. Another gesture. Zap! A flash at the entrance to the hall, and in come a set of barristers, wrangling.*]

Crown.   You should plead *nolo contendere* ...
Defence.   No, no, no ...
Crown.   And then if ...
Defence.   You get Regina versus Muffle thrown ...
Crown.   Get to Rex versus Sweeting first.
Defence.   It's got nothing to do with *nolo contendere* ...
Crown.   Rex versus Sweeting, Blackstone, Coke upon Littleton ...
Defence.   Ha! The principles of pleas ...
Crown.   He loves Coke upon Littleton. Better even than Rex versus Sweeting.

[*Another gesture. Zap! Smoke rises beside the bench, and through it enters a court clerk.*]

Clerk.   Oyez, oyez, oyez, court is in session. Rise for his lordship.

[*Assistants pull James Steele away from his table, vest him with a judge's robe and hood, and place him behind the bench.*]

Clerk.   Bring in the prisoner.

[*Assistants place a chair in front of the head table and seat George on it.* THE HOST *has them fetch the pulpit cushion and give it to George to sit on.*]

Host.   We're all behind you, George.
Clerk.   Who appears for the Crown?
Crown.   I appear for the Crown, my lord.
Clerk.   Who appears for the accused?
Defence.   I appear for the accused my lord.
Clerk.   Our sovereign lady the Queen against George Johnston. George Johnston stands charged that he from a time on or about the seventh day of October, 1913, to a time on or about the eighth day of June, 1979, did govern himself no better than the generality of the Queen's subjects do usually govern themselves, to wit, thoughtlessly. George Johnston, how say you to that charge, guilty or not guilty?
Defence.   Not guilty, my lord.
Judge.   Very well, proceed.
Defence.   My lord, I intend to argue that the accused, far from governing himself in the manner charged, has succeeded in two most exacting

professions and has likewise succeeded in two most exacting estates of human life. For the accused, my lord, has distinguished himself as a professor of humane letters, a poet, a husband, and a father, and so will I prove. If your lordship please, I will call my first witness.

Judge. Very well, proceed.

Defence. I call Doctor Universitas.

[*"Doctor Universitas" is echoed around the hall. The assistants spy William Beckel, President of the University, at the head table. They bring him forward, vest him in his official robes, and place him in the stand.*]

Defence. Doctor Universitas, is it true that this man has been for some thirty years a member in good standing of the faculty of your university?

Doctor Universitas. Yes.

Defence. Has he attended all his classes on time, graded all his papers, submitted his marks punctually, and done his duty in the councils and ceremonial of the university?

Doctor Universitas. Yes.

Defence. Has he advanced in a due and orderly fashion from lecturer to assistant professor, from assistant professor to associate professor, and from associate professor to professor?

Doctor Universitas. Yes.

Defence. Is it true that he leaves behind him a circle of grateful students and edified colleagues, the respect of the scholarly world, and the admiration of the community at large?

Doctor Universitas. Yes.

Defence. That is all.

Crown. Just one minute please. Doctor Universitas, is it true that when this man was promoted to associate professor he had published nothing but a few short poems and two stories?

Doctor Universitas. Yes.

Crown. Is it further true that these poems and stories had all been published in popular magazines?

Doctor Universitas. Yes.

Crown. Is it true that when he was promoted to professor he had published only one book and that a book of only seventy-two pages, a book of poems, most of which had been previously published in popular magazines?

Doctor Universitas. Yes.

Crown. Is it true that today, at the end of his academic career, the weight of all his publications taken together is only one pound three ounces, including the boards in which his various books are bound?

Doctor Universitas. Yes.

Crown. Thank you. If your lordship will hear me in this matter, I submit that bulk is substance. Where there is little bulk there is little substance, and where there is little substance there can be no academic or professorial merit.

Defence. My lord, I object most strenuously. There is a point here my lord which must be cleared up.

Judge. Very well, proceed.

Defence. Doctor Universitas, is it true that intelligence and intelligence alone can do credit to a university.

Doctor Universitas. Yes.

Defence. Now, is it true that this man is endowed with a lively imagination, a tenacious memory, a tough and insistent reasonableness, and an independent but balanced judgement?

Doctor Universitas. Yes.

Defence. And is it true that these qualities comprise intelligence and therefore have done great credit to your university?

Doctor Universitas. Yes.

Defence. That is all.

Crown. If your lordship will hear me, intelligence is represented on paper. Paper has weight. Therefore, intelligence is measured by the weight of paper. Nothing could be more simple.

Defence. What pestilence are we hearing, my lord? If the argument of my learned friend is true, there is no genius in Parmenides and no sense in Anselm. The argument, my lord, is ridiculous, it is utterly false, it is pernicious, noisome, leprous, and foul. My learned friend is propagating unmitigated philistinism unworthy of a learned court of law. Close your ears to it, my lord.

Crown. My lord, I crave indulgence for my learned friend. The man is a relic of time, a poor disconsolate dinosaur, but he is without malice, my lord, and deserves your lordship's indulgence. In any case, he has detained this witness long enough. Let the good doctor step down.

Defence. I don't like the look of this, George. My lord, I call Mr. Criticus Elegantissimus.

[*The name echoes around the hall as before. The assistants find and fetch Munro*

Beattie and vest him in a cape, broad-brimmed velvety felt hat, and gold-tipped walking stick.]

Defence. Mr. Criticus, is it true that this man's poetry tells us, in stanzas of exquisite wit and precision, that the certainties of childhood do not endure, that no man can wholly communicate with another, and that the quest for perfect happiness can never be fulfilled?

Criticus Elegantissimus. Yes, that is true.

Defence. His poems, therefore, are wise and witty?

Criticus Elegantissimus. Yes.

Defence. Is it true that by slight pushes of pause or accent they give their reader's ear a constant succession of delicious little shocks?

Criticus Elegantissimus. Why yes, that's rather well put.

Defence. Is it true, then, that they are small masterpieces, enchanting to read or hear, worthy of being memorized and recited to one's children?

Criticus Elegantissimus. Yes.

Defence. Thank you. That is all, my lord.

Crown Mr. Criticus, is it true that George Johnston's most pellucid lyrics have to be read as carefully as the most baffling paper chase of e.e. cummings?

Criticus Elegantissimus. Yes.

Crown. Does he use irregularity as a means of intensifying his parody of imitated forms and his mockery of the middle-class delusions that haunt his poems?

Criticus Elegantissimus. Yes.

Crown. Is it true that each of his poems expands the enchanting and gossipy world of his private mythology and that Protestant sense of the pains that necessarily must accompany joy?

Criticus Elegantissimus. Yes.

Crown. Thank you. If your lordship will hear me, I submit that, on the testimony I have presented, it is impossible to tell whether we are dealing with poetry or whether we are dealing with piddle.

Defence. A supplementary question, my lord.

Judge. Very well, proceed.

Defence. Mr. Criticus, is it true that this man's poetry is a poetry of limits and depths, of the profound ordinary, a moving celebration of the mingled pain and glory of man's lot?

Criticus Elegantissimus. Yes.

Defence. Thank you.

Crown. Mr. Criticus, does one sense in his poetry the spectral image of a downtrodden fellow, full of peeves, trudging the streets in damp shoes and an old mac?

Criticus Elegantissimus. Well, yes.

Crown. Thank you. Piddle, my lord? You may step down, Mr. Criticus.

Defence. George, I don't like this at all. My lord, I call Mr. Paterfamilias.

[*The name echoes around the hall. Assistants take James Downey, Vice-President of the University, from the head table and vest him in a ragged and threadbare overcoat, a dingy scarf tied at the neck, fingerless gloves, and a peaked tweed cap.*]

Defence. Mr. Paterfamilias, is it true that this man has been a devoted companion to his wife during a bittersweet wartime courtship, a romantic honeymoon on the train to Penatang, an idyllic *entre-temps* in the Tantramar marshes of New Brunswick, and a lengthy residence in the city of Ottawa?

Paterfamilias. Yes.

Defence. Is he the father of six children?

Paterfamilias. Yes.

Defence. Has he provided for the physical and spiritual needs of those children?

Paterfamilias. Yes.

Defence. Is it true that during their childhood, he took delight in their every action and gesture?

Paterfamilias. Yes.

Defence. Is it true that when they were between the ages of thirteen and twenty he was sometimes seen laughing with them?

Paterfamilias. Yes.

Defence. And is it true that some of his family's rarest pleasures occur when it gathers together with him near the village of Athelstan in the province of Quebec?

Paterfamilias. Yes.

Defence. My lord, that is all. This evidence speaks for itself.

Crown. Not quite, my lord. I have a question for this witness.

Judge. Very well, proceed.

Crown. Mr. Paterfamilias, I am going to read you something I have here, and when I have finished I am going to ask you a question about it. Would you listen carefully, please.

[*Pause*]

Always the same story,
   Too many bills to pay,
Telephone threatening disconnection
   And another baby on the way.

She lies like a bag of things
   On the bed
And schemes go round in circles
   Round and round in her head,
Many of them not good.

Some of the circling schemes
   In her head
Have to do with the propinquity of her husband,
   Whether him dead
Would be bad
Or just sad.

She thinks of some bright fields
   Where they might go
And she under the bright sky clobber him
   Lay him low,
Bury him,

And then set up a wailing,
   Make the ground wet
With the bitter tears she would be shedding
   Of regret,
Inconsolable
   Regret.

   Mr. Paterfamilias, did this man write that?

Paterfamilias. Yes. I'm afraid so, yes.

Defence. My lord, I resent the implications of this question. Welive in the
real world, my lord, everybody has a gray day from time to time, and
one gray day does not unmake a devoted husband and father. We have
come together to try realities, my lord, not fantasies such as apparently
exist in the mind of my learned friend.

Crown. If my learned friend is finished, my lord, I believe that was his last witness. If your lordship please, let us dismiss the witness and I will get on with my case.

Judge.   Very well, proceed.

[*Paterfamilias steps down.*]

Defence.   This looks very bad, George.

Crown.   My case, my lord, is simply this: by his fruits shall ye know him. I will bring in witnesses, my lord, whose testimony will be facts, not opinions and impressions and hearsay recollections, but facts, the actual products of this man's hands. They will provide you with conclusive evidence, my lord, that he is not the man my learned friend has tried to picture for you. Quite to the contrary, the facts prove that this George Johnston is, that he is, well, that he is no better than he ought to be. If your lordship please, I will bring in my witnesses.

Judge.   Very well, proceed.

[*The lights go out in an explosion of sound. It is a barrage of acid rock guitars. Then the air is filled with psychedelic illumination. Smoke billows in through one of the doors. Out of it come a group of hippies, moving ecstatically to the music. They take over the playing area and continue the dance, with appropriate groans, grunts, and cries of pleasure. They surround George and place a headband, granny glasses, and strings of beads on him. They pull away and leave one of their number standing apart. The music fades, but they continue their movements silently as he recites:*]

> Why I wear an ear ring:
>   Peg put it in;
> point in hand, unerring,
>   stabs through the skin;
> pre-prandial beering,
>   post-prandial fun,
> wit uninterfering
>   is how it gets done;
> now my whorl of hearing
>   holds a gold thin
> round to show I'm nearing
>   my gold time again.

[*The dancers give a scream of applause as the music comes up again, and they exit orgiastically. The acid rock fades into a bluesy jazz trio, and the hall darkens. The light comes up soft and sensuous, and a young woman enters, her hair down. She is wearing a loose silk negligee and nightgown. She circles George, strokes his beard as she passes by, slides the nightgown off, and places it around his shoulders. He lunges, she moves apart, and she recites:*]

> A touch of perfume upon her feet
> To give them comfort and make them sweet,
> Perfume also on either knee
> And where her bosom parts company
> Perfume and reconcilement there:
> Perfume atomized through her hair.
>
> Who was little and full of guile,
> Calculating to storm or smile,
> Whole in happiness, deep in woe
> Only a peace or two ago
> Is now a woman with musk in her hair;
> Power, and power's sweet sister, care,
> Drift in a scented casual breeze
> After her person, from her knees
> And from her intimate, hinted places
> Into the market world of faces.

[*As she exits into a world of faces, the lights dim, but not for long. Fiddles strikes up a lively country tune and in come a group of step dancers dressed for Saturday night. Punctuating their footwork with claps and shouts, they circle George and place a hillbilly straw hat on his head, a corncob pipe in his jaws, and a bandana around his neck. They pull away and leave one of their members apart. The music fades, they continue their movements silently, and he recites in a good west-Carleton accent:*]

> The green we see
>   from our kitchen:
> Fred's oatfield,
>   aging now, turning bronze.
>
> His old thrashing mill
>   gone to ground

hears of a sale;
 back home again with another old one.

All afternoon hammer the pulleys
 until they budge;
glum kind of an afternoon, cussed at,
 spoiling to rain.

Next fine day, coupled up,
 the jaws accept the proffered oat bundles
and thrash them, thrash, thrash, thrash,
 forked load after forked

load, what's left of summer.
 We lean against the truck, finger the grain
and drink Fred's apple wine
 for the truth in it.

[The fiddles pick up their tune, and the dancers give a shout, then exit with whistles and cries, everyone dancing every kind of step, with growing disorder and noise. There is a strident and repetitive squawk somewhere in the midst, and as the din subsides the squawk is discovered to be the CROWN's, *who is standing, like John Diefenbaker in full forensic fury, hurling his arm at the bench as he chants "My lord ... my lord ... my lord ... " until the dancers have gone. Then he rips grandly into his summation.]*

Crown.   My lord, where now is the saintly sage, where is the learning and
    the civility and the wit and the charm and the profundity, my lord, of
    which we have heard so much and seen so little? We will look in vain
    for these things, for what we have found in this Mr. George Johnston is
    a dabbler, a trifler, a man who should know better ...

[A tympani roll rises to a great climax just outside the door of the hall, and all the players run in with shrieks of terror, fleeing before something that is approaching. As they rush in, the hall becomes dark and silent, and then a beam of light emanates from the entrance. Enter in procession, to appropriate music and with torch-bearers, ANCIENT LIBERTY *(played by Albert Trueman) and his consorts,* PHILOSOPHY, POETRY, *and* FAMILIARITAS. *They are led by* NUNTIUS *and are accompanied by armed servants.* NUNTIUS *takes a commanding position in*

*the middle of the hall. The four abstractions take commanding positions in the
space behind him.]*

Nuntius.   Let there be light. This dark and murky hall
          Illumine with the fire that long ago was
          Plucked from the heav'ns by man's courageous hand.

[*The lights come up to reveal the whole company, barristers included, crouching
in burlesque terror about the bench.*]

          Come, clear away this scum! Rabble, begone!
          Flee, flee the wrath of this most mighty prince!

[*Servants drive the company out. The court fixture opens into a raised dais with
stairs leading to a throne.*]

          Be pleased, good prince, to ascend this chair of state.
          Good people all, be greeted by this prince
          By name called Ancient Liberty. For know ye,
          Whene'er the resplendent wings of fame bring word
          That some sage silver-headed soul must bend
          His way unto the life contemplative,
          Then swiftly comes my lord to hold his court.
          If it should be that that same silv'ry soul
          Be pleasing to these princely dames attendant,
          Then will my gracious lord confer on him
          The rights and privileges of his estate
          Of ancient liberty. O blest estate!
          Free from all base and mercenary toil!
          No time but what is free, time free for thought,
          Time free enough for living, time for joy,
          Time to create mighty works of the mind,
          Ancient Liberty's great monuments —
          The *Otello* of grand old Giuseppi Verdi,
          The Canterbury Tales of agèd Chaucer,
          The final *Dunciad* of wizened Pope,
          Gulliver's Travels, writ by doting Swift,
          Broken old Rembrandt's portraits of himself,

And slavering Beethoven's great Grand Fugue,
All mighty works of this my gracious lord.
Good people, say. Where is the man whose fame
Drew these right goodly princes to this hall?

[*A pause, as* NUNTIUS *is casts his eye over George, taking in the bandana, straw hat, corncob pipe, granny glasses, beads, and silky nightgown.*]

Is this the man?
                    Say ye the truth?
                                        Good sir,
Arise, approach. Gentle my servants, lift
This hateful clutter from his shoulders. Hurl it
Ten thousand fathoms down the hideous
Abysm of Hogsback fault. Infix it there
And let it lie till Arthur come again.

[*Assistants unmask George and place him in a chair of honour at the foot of the dais.*]

Nuntius.   Good lady of philosophy, what say?
Philosophy.   I've searched his works and find some words of merit. Listen!

The little blessed Earth that turns
Does so on its own concerns
As though it weren't my home at all;
It turns me winter, summer, fall
Without a thought of me.

I love the slightly flattened sphere,
Its restless, wrinkled crust's my here,
Its slightly wobbling spin's my now
But not my why and not my how:
My why and how are me.

I will confess that this does not displease me.
Nuntius.   And you, my lady Familiaritas?
Familiaritas.   Listen to this — it has a friendly ring.

The day that would never come comes, it is
not what was expected, not the dreamed of
gay trip to Montréal and the gay leave
taking on the dock for Europe for whose

conquest, making of many friends; she
no longer wants to go but she must;
nobody says so, but the last
thing she would do is turn back and I

think That's my Peggy, which makes this a love
poem. Is there another kind? but is there
something else to be told, of the tremor
of the ship, the day's departure, her wave?

    My lord, this pleases me right well.
Nuntius. And you, my lady Poetry, can you
    Among his works find ought to praise?
Poetry. Silence!

We smell it
coming back
    years on, late in the year
    and the day
    sea fog among the branches;
smell rock and tide,
the drowning that climbs and falls away.

Cove, open sea; the boat
clambers into the swell;
    we shout at one another
    groping out of the past:
    Harris dead, Percy crippled up,
    still out to the nets, though, him and young Paul.
Hull plunging;
our words against the exhaust.

Occulting light
narrows our void,

the foghorn corners the dark.
   We look for homelier rays:
   Purl's first, then Percy's, Isaac's, Charley's;
   the island adumbrates itself
   in their windows.

In hollow light the winch
tugs us up the lanch:
   fish gut, fish liver, fish in brine,
   we know them,
   stink of the salt muck
   among the stones,
   the quick of the shore.
We follow the dark path
to Percy's.

The door opens into warmth.
   What body do we take to judgement?
   whitehaired, weathered, arthritic?
   sturdy, still gentler than one remembers,
   Percy between his canes, Eva watchful.
The room judges:
don't stay away so long
we may not be here next time.

   This is a man in whom I am well pleased.
Ancient Liberty.   Well, young man, you've heard them: prepare yourself.

[*Holding a wreath of laurel over George's head.*]

   Poeta
   illustrissime
   callidissime
   pollitissime
   et dignissime
   divino spiritu
   inflatissime
   te laurea coronamus
   veluti laureatamus te.

Nuntius. Ite, Carletonnorum lux O radiosa, Carletonensem
Carmina nostra pium vestrum celebrate Catullum!
Dicimus, Johnstonis noster Adonis est;
Dicimus, Johnstonis noster Homerus est
Barbari cum Latio pariter iam currimus gente.

[*A general acclamation, the audience on their feet. Just as it climaxes, the company, who have returned to the playing area, hush it down. A voice can be heard singing. The singer is at the edge of the hall, up above the playing area, and the light very gradually focuses on her. She is singing an old ballad tune, a cappella, no words, just a hum or a* la *or a* loo.]

[*The second time round, the singer sings, still a* cappella, *these words:*]

> The call of the dufuflu bird
> For which I have an ear
> Falls like the uncreating word,
> But only some can hear.

[*The singer starts to swing the tune a bit when she gets into the next stanza. A piano and a set of traps join her, the swing builds, and soon the tune is bouncing ing the way it would if Maxine Sullivan and John Kirby were doing it. As the song proceeds, the members of the company take the audience by the hands and lead them into the playing area, joining everyone together into a snake dance, led by Ancient Liberty.*]

> And often at the droop of day
> When evening grumbles in
> The great dufuflu has his say
> Above the traffic's din
>
> All unattended save by me
> And by a special few

Who hear his awful summons; we
    Attend its meaning too.

We, maybe, when we're on a walk
    And maybe feeling low
Hear his apocalyptic squawk
    And think it's time to go.

Our hearts respond, our souls respond,
    The very we of us
Takes off, as one might say, beyond,
    But then comes back, alas!

We hardly fuss, perhaps we pray
    — The timid drop a tear —
And go our uncomplaining way
    Keeping a watchful ear

For when the great dufuflu bird
    May open up again
In such a voice as will be heard
    By us and all good men.

[*At the event itself, when the dance came to an end, George was left in the centre of the hall, with guests and company standing in a circle around him, demanding a speech. He had something much better to offer:*]

FAREWELL TO TEACHING

Knowing what I now know
would I have consented
to be born? Next question.
When it comes time to go
will I go forlorn or
contented? Ask again.
Anything in between
should be easier. O
K, what made up my mind
to come to Carleton? Work.

My kind of work was not
easy to come by, I
came by it at Carleton;
it was simple as that
and lucky, plain lucky.
I cannot account for luck
but I can be grateful.
What was my kind of work?
Presumably teaching,
whatever that may be.
Teaching is a kind of
learning, much like loving,
mutual goings-on,
both doing each to each;
mutual forbearance;
life itself, you might say.
Whatever teaching is
did I enjoy it? Yes.
Am I glad to leave it?
Even of life itself
enough is enough. Good-
bye Dow's Lake, good-bye Tower,
essays, papers, exams,
you I can bear to leave.
But how shall I improve
the swiftly-dimming hour?
I shall deteriorate
amid bucolic dreams
and gather in my fate;
there's lots worse ways than that.

Goodbye good friends. Alas,
some goodbyes are like death;
they bring the heart to earth
and teach it how to die.
Earth, here we come again,
we're going out to grass.
Think of us now and then,
we'll think of you. Goodbye.

[*The night the masque played was unforgettable, thanks to George Johnston's unexpected skill as an improv actor and thanks to the very bright work of the ensemble. Douglas Campbell directed, Faith Gildenhuys produced, Don Beecher directed the music, and Cedric Broten, Patricia Mark, and James Girling managed the lighting, the set, and the technical effects. The singers were Margaret McCoy, Barbara Garner, Alison Hall, Charmian Chapman, Ben Jones, and Steve Wilson. Faith Gildenhuys played* QUEEN ELIZABETH, *Don Beecher* THE OLD KNIGHT, *Douglas Campbell* PRESBYTER, *Parker Duchemin* CROWN, *Larry McDonald* DEFENCE, *Alan McLay* CLERK OF COURT, *Douglas Wurtele* NUNTIUS, *Albert Trueman* ANCIENT LIBERTY, *Maureen Gunn* PHILOSOPHY, *Claudia Persi-Haines* FAMILIARITAS, *and Alberta Aboud* POETRY. *Peter Sanders, Peggy Sample, and Bob Laird recited the poems of the anti-masque, and Peggy Vogan, Lynne Freeston, Andrew Morbey, and Jeff Hume played the assistants and the anti-masquers. Charmian Chapman sang "The Dufuflu Bird" with Alan Gillmor on piano and Alison Hall, our tympanist, on percussion. Enoch Padolsky coached the cast on West-Carleton English. Mary Huband, Laura Groening, and Pauline Hemming designed the costumes, and Andrew Morbey, Nancy McPherson, Hugh Gillis, and Devon Sliwka provided special assistance.*]

Contributors

GEORGE JOHNSTON was born in Hamilton Ontario on October 7, 1913. He graduated from the University of Toronto (Victoria College) in 1936 with a B.A. in Philosophy and English. He served for four and a half years with the Royal Canadian Air Force during the Second World War, as a general reconnaissance pilot in West Africa and as an instructor in the United Kingdom and Canada. He married Jeanne McRae in 1944. Their children are Robert, Peggy, Andrew, Cathleen, Nora, and Mark. In 1945, he graduated M.A. in English Language and Literature from the University of Toronto. He taught English and Old-Norse language and literature at Mount Allison University from 1947 to 1949 and then at Carleton University from 1950 to 1979. He remains Professor Emeritus at Carleton. He is the author of several books of poetry: *The Cruising Auk* (Toronto: Oxford UP, 1959), *Home Free* (Toronto: Oxford UP, 1966), *Happy Enough* (Toronto: Oxford UP, 1972), *Taking a Grip* (Ottawa: Golden Dog P, 1979), *Auk Redevivus: Selected Poems* (Ottawa: Golden Dog P, 1981), *Ask Again* (Moonbeam: Penumbra P, 1984), *Endeared by Dark: The Collected Poems* (Erin: Porcupine's Quill, 1990), and *What is to Come* (Toronto: St. Thomas Church, 1996). He is the author of *A Stratford Christmas of the Twenties* (Stratford: Peter à Brandis, 1998) and of a biography of Carl Schaefer, *Carl, Portrait of a Painter* (Moonbeam: Penumbra P, 1986). He has translated several Icelandic sagas: *The Saga of Gisli* (London: Dent, and Toronto: U of Toronto P, 1963), *The Faroe Islanders' Saga* (Ottawa: Oberon P, 1974), *The Greenlanders' Saga* (Ottawa, Oberon P, 1976), *Thrand of Gotu* (Erin: Porcupine's Quill, 1994), and he has translated, from modern Icelandic, Ólafur Jóhann Sigurdsson's *Pastor Bodvar's Letter* (Moonbeam: Penumbra P, 1985), and, from modern Danish, Jørgen-Frantz Jacobsen's *Barbara* (Norwich: Norvik P, 1993). He has translated various works of poetry: from Faroese, *Rocky Shores: An Anthology of Faroese Poetry* (Paisley: Wilfion P, 1981) and Christian Matras's *Seeing and Remembering* (Moonbeam: Penumbra P, 1987), and, from Norwegian, Knut Ødegård's *Wind over Romsdal* (Moonbeam: Penumbra P, 1982) and *Bee-Buzz, Salmon-Leap* (Moonbeam: Penumbra P, 1988). He edited George Whalley's *Collected Poems* (Kingston: Quarry P, 1986). He has published articles, stories, and poems in *The London Mercury, Fiction Parade, The Atlantic Monthly, The Avon Book of Modern Writing, Tamarack Review, Alphabet, Malahat Review, The Canadian Forum, University of Toronto Quarterly, Queen's Quarterly, The Saga Book of the Viking Society*, and *Bibliography of Old Norse-Icelandic Studies.* The March 1987 issue (no. 78) of *Malahat Review* was devoted to him and his work. Queen's University granted him the degree of LL.D. (*honoris causa*) in 1971 and Carleton University the degree of D.Litt. (*honoris causa*) in 1979.

ALBERTA ABOUD has had a distinguished career as an English teacher with the Carleton Secondary School Board. DON BEECHER, editor with Massimo Ciavolella of *Eros and Anteros: The Medical Traditions of Love in the Renaissance* (Dovehouse), translator and editor with Massimo Ciavolella of Jacques Ferrand's *A Treatise on Lovesickness* (Syracuse), and editor of Barnabe Riche's *Riche, his Farewell to the Military Profession* and Thomas Lodge's *Rosalynde* (both with the Barnabe Riche Society), is with the English Department at Carleton University. PATRICIA BETHEL, an Ottawa lawyer and consultant, has a doctorate in Old English and Old Saxon from the University of London. She has written on Old-English poetic metres. WILLIAM BLISSETT of University College, Toronto, is the author of *The Long Conversation: A Memoir of David Jones* (Oxford), to which George Johnston contributed the concluding pages. MARIANNE BLUGER, author of *Gusts: Selected Tanka* (Penumbra), *The Thumbless Man* (Three Trees), *On Nights Like This, Gathering Wild*, and *Summer Grass* (all with Brick Books), and *Tamarack and Clearcut* (Carleton), is an Ottawa poet. M.I. CAMERON, author with Michael Wendt of *For All Practical Purposes* (Broadview), is with the English Department of Carleton University. DOUGLAS CAMPBELL, editor and translator with Leonard Sbrocchi of Aretino's *The Marescalco* (Dovehouse) and Pirandello's *Questa Sera si Recita a Soggetto: Tonight We Improvise* (Canadian Society for Italian Studies), is coordinator of drama at Carleton University. RICHARD CARTER, who recently graduated B.A. and M.A. in English from Carleton University, is a winner of the George Johnston Poetry Prize. ROSALIND CONWAY, author of *Townswomen and Other Poems* (Mosaic), is an Ottawa lawyer and poet. THOMAS DILWORTH, author of *The Shape of Meaning in the Poetry of David Jones* (Toronto) and with Catharine M. Mastin and Robert Stacey of *The Talented Intruder: Wyndham Lewis in Canada, 1939–1945* (Art Gallery of Windsor), is with the English Department of the University of Windsor. JAMES DOWNEY is the author with Andrea Landry of *Schools for a New Century* and *To Live and to Learn: The Challenge of Education and Training* (Government of New Brunswick), editor with Ben Jones of *Fearful Joy* (McGill-Queen's), and author of *The Eighteenth-Century Pulpit* (Clarendon). CHRIS FAULKNER, author of *The Social Cinema of Jean Renoir* (Princeton) and *Jean Renoir: A Guide to References and Resources* (Hall), is with the Film Studies program of the School for Studies in Art and Culture at Carleton University. JOHN FLOOD, who has presided over Penumbra Press since its founding in 1979, is the author of two volumes of poetry, *The Land They Occupied* and *No Longer North*, and is the editor of scores of publications. He was the last Director of Carleton University Press, the founding editor and proprietor of *Northward Journal*, and a professor of

Contents

Kathryn Hunt

MACTAQUAC BEACH IN AUGUST
for my grandmother

I remember a spray of light.

Sky blue, dark blue, and green across the lake
and red and white buoys.

I remember water droplets in a fanning arc
catching the sunlight like a cut glass chandelier.

I remember the hands catching me,
and the feel of a smile on the face of a tiny woman
with eyes the same colour as the sky.
I remember ducking in cool-warm water
down over my waist — dangerous depth —
I couldn't swim. I was two.
The water could never close on me
though it rushed up around my body
her hands always caught me
and up I went again,
laughing.

I only remember this:
one swing up, one anticipated immersion in the water.
I am hovering in my memory at the top of the arc,
in a spray of light.

English for twenty-four years at Collège universitaire de Hearst. He is also a recipient of the George Wittenborn Award of Excellence for publishing in the visual arts, an honour bestowed by the Art Libraries Society of North America. FAITH GILDENHUYS, editor of *The Bachelor's Banquet* (Barnabe Riche Society), was until recently with the English Department of Carleton University. WAYNE GRADY, author of *The Quiet Limit of the World* and *Toronto the Wild* (both with Macfarlane, Walter and Ross), and editor of *The Penguin Book of Modern Canadian Short Stories* (Penguin), *Treasures of the Place: Three Centuries of Native Writing in Canada* (Douglas), and with Matt Cohen of *The Quebec Anthology, 1830-1990* (Ottawa), is a Kingston writer. NAOMI JACKSON GROVES, a specialist in German and northern languages (including Finnish), is a graduate of McGill University (B.A. '33, M.A. '35), Radcliffe College ('37), and Harvard University (Ph.D. '50). In addition to teaching German at McGill and Carleton Universities, she re-established and headed the Fine Arts Department at McMaster University (1951–57). She is the author of numerous books, many published by Penumbra Press, including translations from German and Finnish, major art history studies on German artist Ernst Barlach, as well as books on the work of her uncle, Group of Seven artist A.Y. Jackson. "A courageous little cuss" is how her uncle sized her up, after her wartime travel in waters infested by German submarines. MAUREEN GUNN was until recently with the English Department of Carleton University, where she taught everything from Middle-English language and literature to the modern British novel. BOB HOGG, author of *There Is No Falling* (ECW), *Heat Lightning* (Black Moss), and *Stand-ing Back* and *Of Light* (both with Coach House), is with the English Department of Carleton University. MARY HUBAND, who graduated B.A. and M.A. in English from Carleton University, was until recently with Carleton's Development Office. KATHRYN HUNT, twice winner of the George Johnston Poetry Prize at Carleton University, is a fourth-year Honours English student at Carleton. LORE JONAS of New Rochelle, New York, is at work on her memoirs, which will record her migration, with her husband, Hans Jonas, the historian of gnosticism, from Nazi Germany to Israel, Ottawa, and then New York. SEAN KANE, author of *Wisdom of the Mythtellers* (Broadview) and *Spenser's Moral Allegory* (Toronto) and editor of Alice Kane's *The Dreamer Awakes*, is with the Cultural Studies Program at Trent University. MARIUS KOCIEJOWSKI, author of *Coast* (Greville), which was awarded the Cheltenham Prize, and *Doctor Honoris Causa* and *Music's Bride* (both with Anvil), lives in London, England, and is currently working on *The Street Philosopher & the Holy Fool: Travels in Syria*. CHRISTOPHER LEVENSON, author of *Duplicities* (Mosaic), *Half Truths* (Wolsak & Wynn), *Arriving at Night*

(Mosaic), *Cairns* (Chatto & Windus), *Into the Open* (Golden Dog), *Stills* (Chatto & Windus), and *The Journey Back* (Sesame), is with the English Department of Carleton University. ROBERT MACNEIL, author of *Breaking News* and *Burden of Desire* (both with Doubleday), *Wordstruck* (Viking), *The Right Place at the Right Time* (Little Brown), and, with Robert McCrum, *The Story of English* (Faber), is a New York journalist and writer. JAY MACPHERSON of Victoria College, Toronto, is the author of *The Boatman* (Oxford), *Welcoming Disaster* and *Poems Twice Told* (both with Saanes), and *The Spirit of Solitude: Conventions and Continuities in Late Romance* (Yale). RICHARD OUTRAM, author of *Selected Poems 1960–1980* (Exile), *Man in Love* (PQ), *Turns and Other Poems* (Chatto & Windus), *Promise of Light* (Anson-Cartwright), and *Exsultate, Jubilate* (Macmillan), is a Toronto poet. EDITH PAHLKE, an Ottawa artist who has travelled extensively in Iceland, has had her work exhibited in Reykyavik as well as Ottawa and New York. She studied design and calligraphy at the Akademie der Bildenden Künste in Stuttgart and the Hochschule für Bildende Künste in Hamburg and has a special interest in books and book production. She is a member of the Ottawa Book Collectors and contributed to their *Miscellany 1: Papers on Books and Book Collecting*. IAN PRINGLE, author with Enoch Padolsky of *A Historical Source Book for the Ottawa Valley* (Linguistic Survey of the Ottawa Valley) and editor with Aviva Freedman of *Learning to Write: First Language / Second Language* (Longman), *Teaching, Writing, Learning* (Canadian Council of Teachers of English), and *Reinventing the Rhetorical Tradition* (L and S Books), is with the School of Applied Language Studies at Carleton University. CHILDE ROLAND, the pen name of Peter Noël Meilleur, a book art fabricator, concrete poet, and infamous one-word M.A. thesis graduate of Carleton University, was an editor and creative writer for the Canadian government before he moved to Wales in 1979. His "XYZ" marble torso is on display in the Carleton University libary. ISMAY WAND, formerly the Administrator of the English Department of Carleton University, is a Smiths Falls horsewoman. GURLI AAGAARD WOODS, editor of *Isak Dineson and Narrativity* (Carleton), is with the School of Languages, Literatures, and Comparative Literary Studies at Carleton University.

AGMV
MARQUIS
Québec, Canada
1999